THE AFRICANIZATION OF THE LABOR MARKET

REMI CLIGNET

THE AFRICANIZATION
OF THE LABOR MARKET

EDUCATIONAL AND OCCUPATIONAL SEGMENTATION
IN THE CAMEROUN

UNIVERSITY OF CALIFORNIA PRESS

BERKELEY · LOS ANGELES · LONDON

University of California Press
Berkeley and Los Angeles, California

University of California Press, Ltd.
London, England

ISBN 0-520-03019-2
Library of Congress Catalog Card Number 75-13145

CONTENTS

TABLES, FIGURE, AND MAP

Tables

Figure

Map

PREFACE

The major thrust of this book is to show that, far from being homogeneous, the labor markets of new countries are segmented and that the underlying patterns of differentiation reflect variations in the scalar characteristics of jobs and of enterprises. My demonstration is based on an analysis only of the Camerounian scene, and the reader may want assurance that the conclusions presented here are susceptible of generalization.

Like that of many other new nations, the population of the Cameroun is characterized by an extreme ethnic fragmentation. Local ethnic groups exhibit distinct traditional patterns of organization and culture. In addition they have had differential exposure to European and Western influences. Thus, they are liable to enter and function in the modern industrial labor force to a variable degree and in a somewhat different manner.

Further, like many other developing nations, the Cameroun is characterized by a high rate of population growth (approximately 2 percent per annum), but at the same time there has been little rise in the productivity of agriculture, in which some 75 percent of the population is still engaged.[1] This has led, as in many other African countries, to migration to urban areas and, concomitantly, to an expansion of that segment of the labor force involved in industrial activities. As in many other areas of Africa, the tertiary sector is even more sizable, due to the expansion of service and commercial jobs.[2] Thus, the Cameroun is undergoing very rapid change both from the point of view of the society in general (historical time) and in terms of the different positions that individuals occupy in their own life cycle (social time).

Finally, the Cameroun can be regarded as a "late developer" in industrial terms: local educational development tended to precede the growth of the modern industrial sector and the emergence of large-scale, bureaucratically organized enterprises.[3] Moreover, although the range of technologies available to modern enterprises enables them to vary capital and labor inputs, their growth has been paralleled by the emergence of

---

[1] There are in this sense similarities between African and South American countries. See J. Bàlan, *Men in Developing Societies* (Austin: University of Texas Press, 1973), chap. 1.

[2] Once more Cameroun presents similarities with South American countries or with India, whose labor forces have been carefully examined elsewhere.

[3] The expression "late development" has been coined and analyzed by R. Dore (personal communication).

powerful and sizable labor organizations that have had political and economic influence in both the pre- and postindependence periods.[4]

The Outline of the Study

The major theoretical issues concerning the development of a modern labor force in new countries are reviewed in the introduction (Chapter 1), and the second chapter summarizes the general political, social, economic, and educational characteristics of the Cameroun to see whether my general conclusions might be applicable to the modern labor forces of other developing countries. The subsequent analysis of the data follows the historical order in which labor market theories have been developed. Thus, in Chapters 3 and 4, I analyze contrasts in the background and occupational history of blue-collar and manual workers, holding type of employment constant.

The main purpose of Chapter 3 is to demonstrate that variations in the requirements attached to the performance of manual and non-manual tasks are associated with parallel contrasts in the educational background of the corresponding populations. The purpose of the chapter is also to demonstrate that because nonmanual tasks require more universalistic orientation, the educational level of white-collar workers is more independent of ethnic and residential factors. As Cameroun has experienced a high rate of educational development, the final purpose of Chapter 3 is to examine how both the differential educational background and the modes of entry in the labor market of the two categories of worker vary over time.

As indicated in the main part of the introduction, the determinants of occupational attainment are not necessarily alike for these two job families. My purpose in Chapter 4 is to show that both education and prior occupational experiences are more significant determinants of the skill level and the income of nonmanual than of manual workers. Insofar as formal schooling, seniority on the job, seniority in the firm, and prior occupational roles represent distinct signals, my purpose is not only to identify the general processes by which these signals may compensate for one another but also to determine whether such processes are alike for the two populations. To the extent that I am dealing with a new nation where pressures toward Africanization of middle-range positions are particularly strong, I also intend to demonstrate that patterns of access to higher occupational echelons and of mobility between skill levels are more achievement oriented and more universalistic in the case of non-manual populations.

Thus far, however, my analysis will have followed the human capital paradigm. Even though I will have shown that the patterns of access to the

---

[4] For a review of this theme, see E. Berg, "French West Africa," in W. Galenson, ed., *Labor and Economic Development* (New York: Wiley, 1959).

two markets as well as to the higher rungs of the corresponding hierarchies vary over time as a function of the relative development of Camerounian economic, educational, and political institutions, I will have assumed that employers do not differ from one another in their personnel policies. I reverse this approach in Chapter 5, which is devoted to an examination of Camerounian firms. The main purpose of the chapter is to demonstrate that contrasts in size, activity, legal status, age, and characteristics of the supervisory personnel of these organizations are associated with parallel contrasts in their hiring and promotion practices, in their modes of organization, and most important in their salary policies.

Chapters 3, 4, and 5 thus demonstrate the equal importance of variations in the characteristics of employers and employees, and the *interactive framework* necessary to examine the patterns of segmentation operating in the Camerounian labor market. Chapter 6 demonstrates how the differential pattens of access into manual and nonmanual occupations as well as the differential patterns of occupational attainment of the two populations vary across firms. Insofar as this segmentation results from strategies used by employers, I will also show that it is as important to identify the mechanisms that employers use to pay their workers a particular income as to evaluate the significance of interindividual differences in such earnings. Finally, I conclude the chapter by demonstrating that the determinants of occupational attainment are not alike when one considers the full population of manual and nonmanual workers and when one concentrates on the most modernized types of organization.

In the conclusion, I evaluate my findings within two major frameworks. First, I examine what the analysis tells us about the historical processes of industrialization. One line of investigation examines whether there is a uniform sequential order in the emergence of industrialized societies in terms of the successive development of primary, secondary, and tertiary sectors, and hence of the differential growth of manual and nonmanual occupations. Underlying this approach is the assumption that rises in the productivity of more basic forms of economic organization increase the number of workers available for participation in new and more complex activities.

But it is also possible in the context of this historical framework to speculate whether the emergence of distinct social strata is an inevitable corollary of economic development.[5] Specifically, it can be asked whether technological development is associated with an increased polarization of social classes.[6] This situation does not seem to have occurred in Europe,

---

[5] For a general review of this literature, see I. Horowitz, *The Three Worlds of Development* (New York: Oxford University Press, 1966), chap. 13.

[6] See J. Goldthorpe and others, *The Affluent Worker in the Class Structure* (Cambridge: Cambridge University Press, 1969), introduction.

where the most recent phases of industrialization have been associated with higher salaries, a greater participation of workers in decision-making, and a loosening up of the occupational hierarchy and differential life styles.[7] Rather than a polarization of social classes, there has been a decrease in the social and economic distance between different categories of worker and an increasing affluence that has not led to alienation in the Marxian sense.

Will development occur in the same way in some of the new nations? Perhaps one answer is that the only difference between industrial and less developed nations is one of timing; basically, all societies will undergo a generally similar process of industrial change, even though they may not do so at the same speed. However, an alternative view would argue that the unique situation of the contemporary European worker is the effect of the continuing exploitation of less developed nations: the Third World of today is no more than the successor of the Third Estate of yesterday![8] Yet this view essentially concerns itself with relations between nations and attempts to see stratification in an international perspective; it does not, however, address itself to processes of social differentiation occurring *within* the nations of the Third World. As these processes continue, is one to see the contemporary African farmer as the symbolic equivalent of the urban proletariat of the nineteenth-century European cities?[9] On the other hand, does one notice an increased polarization between a tiny nonmanual elite and the mass of the local population, with the former essentially taking over the status and roles of the former European colonizers?

Although little is known about processes of social differentiation, the fact that a country comes late or early to the industrial scene is likely to have a profound effect on the association between education, migration, occupation, and commitment.[10] Thus, late development leads the diffusion of formal schooling to be anterior to or relatively simultaneous with the demands of industry for trained manpower. Similarly, when countries come late to the industrial scene, there may be rapid changes in the control that government and employers exert over migration; in Africa, for example, the system of forced labor and migrations that occurred in the colonial era may have facilitated development, but the political changes

[7] Ibid., conclusion. See also S. Mallet, *La Nouvelle classe ouvriére* (Paris: Le Seuil, 1963).

[8] F. Fanon, in *Toward the African Revolution* (New York: Grove Press, 1967), is the main champion of this position. See also G. Arrighi, "International Corporations, Labor Aristocracies, and Economic Development in Africa," in R. Rhodes, ed., *Imperialism and Underdevelopment* (New York: Monthly Review Press, 1970), pp. 220-222.

[9] Such is the position of Fanon in *The Wretched of the Earth* (New York: Grove Press, 1965), which conflicts with the classic Marxist position. For a rebuttal of Fanon's view, see, for example, Nghe Nguyen, "Franz Fanon et les problèmes de l'indépendence," *La Pensée* 107(1953):23-25.

[10] For a discussion of the effects of historical factors on the process of industrialization, see A. Feldman and W. Moore, "Industrialization and Industrialism: Convergence and Differentiation," *Transactions of the Fifth Congress of Sociology* 2(1962):151-169.

associated with World War II have obliged entrepreneurs to innovate in their personnel policies. Thus, "late" development not only enlarges the range of technological choices available to employers, but it simultaneously may place closer constraints on the personnel policies they pursue. In other words, local concerns technically may have greater freedom in varying the combination of physical and human inputs they wish to employ, while the political forces at work in the new nations limit the extent of their control over workers. In this sense, the relation between education, migration, occupation, and commitment becomes indeterminate, and it is difficult to see what strategies will stimulate industrialization.

My second concern in the conclusion is, nevertheless, to focus on such strategies. Following Berg's description, it is apparent that some nations have attempted to pursue a gradualist strategy wherein increased industrialization and commercialization are achieved through the generation of a large number of relatively small-scale changes in the economy.[11] Although development is always market oriented and relies on the growth of activities out of the traditional sector, industrialization may still take second place to the expansion of an efficient export-oriented agriculture and the stimulation of initially small-scale enterprises. It can be argued that this pattern of development parallels that of Europe and North America, where such enterprises preceded the emergence of large-scale, highly bureaucratized concerns.

By contrast, a transformationist strategy implies that this kind of development sequence is unnecessary, for contemporary Western models can be borrowed where appropriate, to bring about revolutionary development in a relatively short time. Thus industrialization has a higher priority than the transformation of agriculture. Moreover, industrialization, far from proceeding from small beginnings, is believed to be best stimulated by the importation of large-scale organizations. In this perspective, scholars believe that the speed at which bureaucratic organizations develop conditions the emergence of a clerical labor force and hence the relative commitment of the entire local labor force.

Thus, the last part of the conclusion identifies more accurately the dilemmas African governments confront. First, what incompatibilities are inherent in a policy of Africanization? Second, in view of such incompatibilities, what kind of educational planning can best support the strategies adopted?

---

[11] See E. Berg, "Structural Transformation versus Gradualism" in P. Foster and A. Zolberg, eds., *Ghana and the Ivory Coast: Perspectives on Modernization* (Chicago: University of Chicago Press, 1971), pp. 187-230.

ACKNOWLEDGEMENTS

In 1951, when I entered the *Ecole nationale de la France d'outre mer,* my rank enabled me to choose between becoming a district commissioner and becoming a labor officer. Naively (I was young at the time) I chose to become a labor officer, because I thought that during that new decade the most significant events occurring in Africa would be economic and social rather than political, and therefore the labor scene would be the most spectacular and influential one. That was a double mistake: events did not turn out the way I expected.

To choose a career in the field of labor relations was to forego any power, including in the field of labor relations. Hence, I did not stay in the corps I had initially chosen, but I have never forgotten my earlier commitment to economic justice. This book is a modest way of paying back the "dues" I owed to the African workers I was supposed to help in their efforts to achieve greater independence.

But to write this book has been a sobering experience. Much too often, social scientists and economists are anxious to build models that are more ideologically than empirically justified. The game is to build abstractions that justify the existing social or ideological order, and this leads to the arbitrary exclusion or inclusion of independent variables. And yet to offer unwarranted recipes is both dangerous and unethical. In my efforts to avoid these pitfalls, I have been greatly helped by Martin Carnoy, John Simmons and Dolores Koenig. I hope the final product does not disappoint them. Of course, the whole enterprise would have been impossible without the generosity of Jean Chaumont, who helped me gain access to the data, explained them to me, and set up the initial framework of analysis. He would be at least the coauthor of this book if we had not been separated by many distances, including the ones created by lazy pens. I am also indebted to the National Institute of Mental Health, which supported the research through the grant NIMH 17359. As it is, I dedicate the book to my father, who will not necessarily like the ideas expressed here but will certainly enjoy the discussions I hope they provoke.

Chapter 1

INTRODUCTION

During the two decades following the end of the Second World War, the leaders of many underdeveloped areas, including those of European colonies in Africa, demanded the progressive or immediate independence of their homelands. They uniformly justified their demand by attacking the educational shortcomings of colonial regimes. For them, educational development was the panacea facilitating both political integration and economic growth, hence political and economic independence.

If the concept of independence is significantly related to the notion of "Africanization," such a notion presents conflicting facets. In political terms, Africanization refers to the substitution of African personnel for European administrative cadres and to the generalization to the local scene of so-called modernizing political structures, but it also reflects the concern for rehabilitating traditional institutions whose functions have been distorted by colonization. In education, Africanization refers to the desirable expansion of schools, curricula, and teaching forces, which should retain the profile of models provided by the industrialized countries; but it also refers to an adaptation of school systems to the needs and aspirations of local populations. Finally, in occupational terms, the concept of Africanization reflects the concern for achieving new patterns in the allocation of power and monetary rewards in favor of the local workers of the modern labor force; but it also corresponds to the desire for facilitating the growth of African-owned enterprises and, more generally, the so-called informal sector of the economy.

In brief, although Africanization suggests an uprooting of traditional political, educational, and economic structures and, paradoxically, their "Europeanization," it also suggests the importance of reconstructing such structures and of providing them with the capacity to resist pernicious exogenous influences.

To the extent that Africanization mirrors differing sets of goals, African governments are likely to adopt differing sets of strategies. For twenty years at least, political and economic planners have been anxious to assert the merits of strategies based on the proposition that the political and economic difficulties encountered by new nations result from a shortage of a local personnel properly trained to meet the requirements of political and economic modernization.

In this book, I am not concerned with a critical assessment of the influence exerted by schooling on political development and integration. Rather, I intend to explore some of the equivocations underlying the relationship between educational and economic developments. Even though planners have recommended heavy investment in the educational field under the assumption that the growth of educational institutions and notably of secondary schools stimulates the development of local economies, this assumption appears untenable on at least two counts. First, disparities in rates of economic and educational growth, as well as in their respective determinants, induce an increase in the number of jobless urban residents with a certain amount of education. In addition, the underlying theories often appear to have been based on faulty premises.

The most significant of these premises is that formal schooling profits evenly all segments of the labor market, and that the corresponding increase in productivity is equitably shared among all workers and all employers. My concern here will be to show that this is not necessarily the case, because of marked cleavages in the organization and the bargaining power of employers and wage earners. As a result, the impact of schooling on occupational attainment varies both by type of job and by type of employment.

To criticize the stance often taken by planners, I will rely on an examination of the functioning of the modern labor force in the Cameroun. In 1964, the government of the country undertook a systematic survey of the wage earners attached to the enterprises of the modern sector. As this survey facilitates distinctions between manual and nonmanual activities as well as between firms with varying organizational profiles, it is possible to ascertain the extent and origin of variations in the influence of educational attainment on occupational status as measured by skill level and income. Of course, a case study does not necessarily provide all the information needed to challenge existing theories, and it will be necessary to determine whether my findings can be generalized to other countries as well, both from a factual and theoretical viewpoint. Correspondingly, this strategy should enable us to identify the dilemmas that the governments of new nations must face in their policies on educational development and on Africanization of local labor markets.

Because the early theoretical literature on development stresses the notion of commitment, the first step of my analysis involves a critical evaluation of this term and of its theoretical substratum before suggesting alternative theoretical frameworks.

An Overview of Industrial Commitment

Although Clark Kerr writes that "men everywhere are transfering themselves fully and finally into an industrial way of life," it is not clear whether the resulting industrial commitment represents a societal or individual trait.[1] Kerr identifies four stages of commitment but assumes parallels and complementarities in the relevant societal and individual characteristics. At the lowest level of the continuum, patterns of interaction are dominated by ascription and particularism. Correspondingly, "uncommitted" societies are characterized by the significance of target migrations, and their tiny industrial labor force is largely comprised of migrants who move away from a traditional or ethnic environment for limited periods of time.[2] Thus, industrialism represents a temporary and small enclave in a sea of rurality.

During the stage of semicommitment, urban residents are encapsulated in specific neighborhoods and return periodically to their rural homestead in order to maintain their "rural" income.[3] Individuals cease to fully participate in all-encompassing familial structures and perform dual economic roles. Correspondingly, semicommitted societies are characterized by the rapid growth of large urban centers, whose populations are comprised primarily of male adults engaged evenly in modern and traditional types of activities.

In the third stage, individuals participate permanently in the modern labor market. Correspondingly, the cities of "committed societies" have more even sex ratios, and their growth ceases to be exclusively dependent on migrations. In addition, there is a significant increase in the participation of women in the labor force, particularly in the modern sectors.

Finally the last stage is reached with the total absorption of the labor force in the modern marketplace. Individual workers are committed to full-time employment not only within one firm but also within a single job category. As individuals become involved in one narrow and specific role, larger societal structures are influenced by the emergence of large-scale organizations regulating and conditioning the behavior of entrepreneurs as well as of wage earners.

This particular conception of stages of development raises a number of questions as to the interaction between individual and societal changes. Does industrial man precede industrial society, or vice versa? To what extent are there divergences in the changes affecting individual behavior and social processes?

---

[1] See C. Kerr, "Changing Social Structures" in W. Moore and A. Feldman, *Labor Commitment and Social Change in Developing Countries* (New York: Social Science Research Council, 1960), pp. 348-359.

[2] The migrations of Mossi workers to the modern plantations of Ivory Coast offer a case in point, as did the migrations of South African blacks to gold mines. For an examination of these target migrations, see A. Lux, *Le marché du travail en Afrique noire* (Louvain: Nauwelaerts, 1960).

[3] For a description of this encapsulation process, see P. Mayer's account of the contrasts between the "Reds" and the "Schools" in *Townsmen or Tribesmen* (Capetown: Oxford University Press, 1961).

Macrosocial approaches.

A macrosocial approach to development stresses the importance of societal processes and relies on aggregate data to identify the macrosocial correlates of industrialization.[4] For instance, some scholars have examined the conditions under which variations in technological complexity, in the size of a modern labor force or in the relative amount of division of labor are both interrelated and associated with parallel contrasts in the size of educational enrollment, the levels and rates of urbanization, and finally the volume of internal and external trade.[5] The ultimate goal of this approach is to ascertain whether varieties of societal change are accounted for by a single factor and thus whether the various facets of development are unidimensional.[6]

This particular approach however, assumes a marked interdependence between distributive and normative changes (that is, between the *allocation* of individuals in the social or physical space and *overall* social orientations) as well as between the evolution of societal structures and of individual psychological make-up.

Yet social institutions do not necessarily evolve at the same rate. In Africa, for instance, interaction within familial groups continues to be influenced by traditional factors long after political institutions begin to rely on universalist achievement-based sets of rules.[8] Likewise, to participate in the modern labor force may constitute an experience that individuals are able to isolate from other arenas of social interaction.[9] Like Janus, they may wear the masks of a modern man as long as they stay in the work environment but retain a more traditional behavior as soon as they return to their home.

---

[4] Many of these studies are inspired by the book of G. and M. Wilson, *Analysis of Social Change* (Cambridge: Cambridge University Press, 1945).

[5] See, for instance, J. Gibbs and W. Martin, "Urbanization Technology and the Division of Labor: International Patterns," *American Sociological Review* 27(1962), or J. Gibbs and H. Browning, "The Division of Labor Technology and the Organization of Production in Twelve Countries," *American Sociological Review* 31(1966), See also I. Adelman and C. Morris, "A Factor Analysis of the Interrelationship between Social and Political Variables and Per Capita Gross National Product," *Quarterly Journal of Economics* 79(1965): 555-578.

[6] For instance, D. McElrath, "Social Differentiation and Societal Scale" in S. Greer and others, eds., *The New Urbanization* (New York: St. Martin's Press, 1968), pp. 39-51.

[7] This assumption is a characteristic of the structural functionalist theories inspired by Parsons.

[8] For a discussion of the relevance of the Parsonian paradigm to the problems of industrialization, see B. Hoselitz, *Sociological Aspects of Economic Growth* (New York: Free Press, 1965).

[9] This problem is discussed by J. C. Mitchell in "Theoretical Orientations in African Urban Studies," M. Banton, ed., *The Social Anthropology of Complex Societies* (London: ASA Monographs 4, Tavistock Institute Publications, 1966).

Microsocial approaches.

Under such conditions, other sociologists and economists have defined commitment as an individual trait. They are mostly interested in identifying the processes by which individuals or cohorts of individuals join the labor market and, within that market, move in and across occupational categories or types of employment. This is the tradition I adhere to in this book. My examination of the Camerounian labor force is microsocial in its orientation.

Yet even if with this line of approach, I still have to ask how one develops reliable and valid measurements of industrial commitment. One obvious way is to concentrate on worker attitudes as well as behavior. To give only one example, Lambert asked his sample of factory workers in India a series of questions concerning their perceptions of their own occupational future and, perhaps more importantly, their aspirations for their own offspring.[10] A number of studies of this kind suggest that if one wants to understand what commitment is, the best way is to ask workers what they think about their jobs and their future.

This conception of industrial commitment tends to get linked in with the broader issue of what constitutes a "modern man," for industrial attitudes can be seen as an element within a broader syndrome of behavior that can be regarded as "modern."[11] Unfortunately, there is considerable disagreement as to what is meant by "modern" attitudes. Presumably, these attitudes predispose an individual to act in a manner consonant with the demands of modern society; without these orientations, the individual is unlikely to participate effectively in such a society. But these constructs may reveal an essentially ethnocentric bias and reflect those values deemed most characteristic of the Euro-American middle classes.[12]

In brief, to examine attitudes does not solve the questions concerning the meaning of "commitment" and "modernity".[13] This study takes another tack and eschews any attempt to examine industrial commitment as it is embodied in worker attitudes and values. To the degree that it is often

---

[10] See R. Lambert, *Workers, Factories, and Social Change in India* (Princeton: Princeton University Press, 1963).

[11] See A. Inkeles and M. Smith, "The OM Scale: A Comparative Socio-Psychological Measure of Individual Modernity," *Sociometry* 29(1966):353-377.

[12] Further, there seems to be some confusion about what to include and what to leave out of the "modernity syndrome." Some writers aver that specific attitudes toward family planning and religion are parts of this cluster of traits, whereas others suggest that such elements do not constitute a part of modern predispositions. For a discussion of the controversial results obtained by scales of modernity, see M. Peil, *The Ghanaian Factory Worker* (Cambridge: Cambridge University Press, 1972), chap. 8.

[13] See, for example, M. Armer and A. Schnaiberg, "Measuring Individual Modernity: A Near Myth," *American Sociological Review* 37(June 1972):301-316.

more meaningful to look at what people *do* rather than ask them how they feel, commitment is defined here in behavioral terms.

But in the context of this behavioral approach, what can be regarded as a valid measure of high or low industrial commitment? A significant body of research assumes that rates of worker absenteeism and turnover reflect levels of commitment to an industrial social order, and is primarily concerned with an examination of their incidence as well as their degree of intercorrelation, their antecedents, and their industrial consequences.[14] Alternatively, economists suggest that commitment should be measured in terms of productivity.

Methodological and theoretical fallacies
of the measurement of productivity.

There are some difficulties connected with this particular approach. First, one may posit that measurements of productivity are valid only when they concern individuals placed in similar job categories and sectors of employments.[15] In fact, occupational performances are comparable only insofar as they rely on comparable proportions of capital and labor. For this reason, estimates of productivity should be most valid in societies characterized by low levels of division of labor or, in the contemporary world, in the case of self-employed individuals who tend to control the type of technology they use and therefore occupy analogous positions in the labor market.

But in Cameroun as in many other new nations, the economic behavior of self-employed individuals is by no means totally governed by the principles influencing the modern, Western-type sector, and it is often difficult to establish any clear-cut boundaries between traditional and modern artisanal or commercial activities: self-employed traders and craftsmen frequently innovate in a modern manner when exposed to the forces of social change; but apparently "modern" occupations such as those of transport entrepreneur, photographer, or mechanic can be regarded as either traditional or modern not in terms of the nature of the work done but in relation to the social and cultural environment in which it is performed.[16]

---

[14] For Africa, see, for example, F. Wells and W. Warmington, *Studies in Industrialization, Nigeria and the Cameroons* (London: Oxford University Press, 1962). See also J. Guilbot, *Absentéisme et mobilité des travailleurs en Afrique equatoriale* (Paris: Ministère de la coopération, 1962). See also A. Hauser, *Les Ouvriers de Dakar: étude socio-psychologique* (Paris: ORSTOM, 1968), notably pp. 59-67. See also L. Biffod, *Facteurs d'intégration et de desintégration du travailleur gabonais à son entreprise* (Paris: ORSTOM, 1961).

[15] See M. Blaug, *Education and the Employment Problem in Developing Nations* (Geneva: ILO, 1973), pp. 27-39.

[16] See, for example, P. J. Jaeger, "The Kano Blacksmiths: A Study in Social Change" (paper presented to the Department of Sociology Seminar, Ahmadu Bello University, Zaria, Nigeria, April 1971). See also J. Harris, "Nigerian Enterprises in the Printing Industry," *New Journal of Economic and Social Studies* 10(July 1968).

Finally, some activities, such as petty trading in the West African urban environment, that are regarded as involving a nonrational and uneconomic duplication of effort, in fact perform modernizing functions for they involve a significant proportion of the population in a large-scale distributive system.[17]

There are, therefore, all kinds of equivocal meanings to be attached to the notion of self-employment, and for this reason the present study of Camerounian workers excludes self-employed individuals.

However, the study of workers employed by the government bureaucracy raises other problems. Evaluations of individual performances differ markedly between private and public modern sectors. Because the models underlying the recruitment and socialization of public employees differ from those in modern private enterprises, the commitments of the two types of wage earners follow distinctive patterns and are differentially rewarded. As public and private employment constitutes two distinctive labor markets, employees in public administration also are excluded from the present study.[18]

Explicitly, I am interested only in the behavior of full-time paid wage or salaried male African employees in the private modern industrial or commercial sector of the Cameroun economy. Although I restrict my analysis to the modern private labor market, I still assume that within one occupational category and one type of employment, employers still reward interindividual differences in commitment and productivity in terms of the skill levels they accord their personnel.

The second difficulty emerges, however, as soon as one adopts a more ambitious treatment of productivity and as one compares individual performances across occupational categories and sectors of employment. Is productivity an objective rational and universal term, or is it an a posteriori construct that reflects the relative bargaining power of different types of employees and employers? In the first perspective, one assumes implicitly that there is a stable consensus among workers and entrepreneurs as to the factors which affect the functioning of the labor market. One assumes therefore that differences in individual productivity and commitment are ultimately accompanied by various forms of inter- and intragenerational mobility. In the second perspective, one posits that the notions of commitment and productivity merely reflect unstable social cleavages and that such notions impede shifts in occupation or employer.

Before identifying the perspective chosen in the present study, I will

---

[17] For a discussion of this point, see B. Isaac, "Traders in Pendembu: A Case Study in Entrepreneurship" (Eugene: unpublished Ph.D. dissertation, Univeristy of Oregon, 1969).

[18] Although the colonial administration used to be the most important and most attractive employer, indirect evidence suggests that at least in French-speaking Africa private modern firms attract a growing number of highly educated individuals and are able to raid the public sector.

briefly review the changing models that economists and sociologists use to define productivity and to ascertain its implications on the functioning of the labor market.

Initially, all models rely on the premise that job seekers offer potential employers a set of characteristics (strength, dexterity, intelligence, docility, and so forth), and that the same employers seek the individuals who are able to increase the output of their enterprises by the largest amount. The problem remains, however, to ascertain whether interaction between the demand and the supply of labor follows a consistent pattern and more specifically to isolate the conditions under which this interaction reaches a certain equilibrium.[19]

Classical and neoclassical theorists assert that the "prices" attached to the characteristics of workers move to equilibrate the supply of and the demand for such characteristics. They assume, therefore, that it is possible to specify a set of *stable* and *universal* functional relationships between the characteristics of workers and the units of employers demand. Yet the validity of this postulate rests on two conditions. The units of demand and supply must be commensurable. In addition, all participants in the labor market must adopt a similar scale to rank order both jobs and the human traits relevant to their performance. Possibly, this is the case as long as there is a low division of labor and individual work represents a homogeneous commodity which remains stable over time. In such a context, the variety of jobs offered in the labor market is deemed to require a number of physical and social attributes which can be easily placed on a single preference scale.

However, as soon as technological and social arrangements exceed a critical level of complexity, new and more accentuated forms of social differentiation begin to emerge. As a result, there are increased contrasts both within and across various segments of the employer and employee populations. As these contrasts become themselves more salient, there is a parallel increased differentiation in the ideologies, models, and frameworks used by economists to explain the functioning of the labor market. Thus, whereas the original model used by classical theorists emphasizes the significance of variations in the scarcity of *individuals* available to the labor market as a whole, contemporary economists are more prone to stress the implications attached to variations in the scarcity of *skills* deemed necessary for delivering a fixed quantity of goods or services presenting required standards of excellence. The first definition of scarcity, which deals with pure numbers, is merely quantitive, but the second one involves qualitative elements.

---

[19] For a critical review of this position, see M. Carter and M. Carnoy, "Theories of Labor Market and Worker Productivity" (discussion paper 74, Portola Institute, Menlo Park, California, 1974).

The introduction of qualitative elements in the definition of scarcity, has progressively transformed the initial stance of classical economists. Three models are particularly pertinent to review here, for they deal with the problems posed by increased educational and occupational differentiation.

The first of these models retains the idea that both employers and employees rank occupations on a universalistic scale and that access to various jobs depends on the productivity of individual workers, deemed to be an objective and measurable attribute.[20] However, the model posits also that hiring decisions constitute specific forms of investment under conditions of uncertainty and that employers have to make educated guesses as to the effective productive abilities of individual job seekers. Provisional assessments of such abilities are based on two distinctive types of traits. The first type involves *indices* which, although most visible (as they pertain to the sex, age and ethnic origin of job seekers), are nevertheless particularistic and affected by irrational factors. The second type, labeled *signals,* pertains to the educational and prior occupational experiences of the candidates. It is universalistic and achievement based, as these experiences can be modified. Insofar as hiring decisions depend on *signals*, candidates for a particular position tend to acquire the level of signals which maximizes the differences between the earnings offered to them and the costs they had to incur to acquire the appropriate level of the given signal. Equilibrium is then reached when the expectations held about the productivity of job seekers who offer a certain amount of a particular *signal* are confirmed by their actual performance on the job. As these signals correspond to educational and occupational attainments, the model assumes that the currency attached to education and prior occupational status retains a rational universalistic and stable value for both employers and employees.

However, employers also base their conditional assessment of individual productivity on indices and, hence, on ascription-based characteristics. If for any reason employers expect certain categories of job seekers to have a lower productivity than the remainder of the population, they are likely to discriminate totally or partially against them. In this latter case, they will set educational or occupational requirements at a higher level, and this means that the equilibrium between "signals" and wage schedules varies in fact with the indices-oriented characteristics attached to various groups of workers. This is damaging to orthodox beliefs concerning the unity of the labor market, for ascription-based forms of discrimination may continue indefinitely.

Yet the model still attempts to establish bridges between ascription- and achievement-based components of the assessments of productivity. Even though the intervention of administrative regulations does not fit the

[20] See M. Spence, "Job Market Signalling," *Quarterly Journal of Economics* 87 (1973): 373.

original classical theory, this model asserts that the legal obligation to hire groups of workers with negatively valued indices educates employers and enables them to recognize the productivity of such groups. In short, the labor market may need some forms of tinkering at times but as basically all individuals, employers and employees alike, share similarly positive orientations toward achievement, the unity of the market is ultimately preserved and so is its rationality. In other words, history involves only small-scale and unidirectional changes.

The second model ceases to see productivity as an objective characteristic of individual workers.[21] Because this productivity is a variable attribute attached to distinctive occupational roles, the functioning of the labor market is less influenced by the scarcity of workers than by the scarcity of jobs. Insofar as competition for access to jobs supersedes competition over wages, the relevant analysis aims at identifying the factors accounting for the differential position that individuals occupy in the queue for being hired. This position is primarily determined by the costs that employers expect to pay for the training of candidates to a particular slot, and the functioning of the market remains therefore achievement oriented and universalistic.

Yet this model recognizes that competition among job seekers also involves particularistic components. First, employers base their assessment of the trainability of workers on the notion that the skills required to perform a particular role involve a mix of *general* traits that are transferable and of *specific* attributes that correspond to the particular social and technological arrangements of a particular firm. Insofar as the time necessary to train a particular individual already present in the firm to perform a job higher in the occupational hierarchy is often less than the time needed to hire and train an outsider, it is clear that the consequences resulting from an initial hiring may be cumulative, and hence that the model recognizes the development of particularistic internal labor markets. In contrast to the neoclassical scheme, there is a multiplicity of markets.

Second, the expectations that employers hold about the trainability of job seekers are not necessarily rational, and certain groups whose ascriptive traits are negatively valued by the remainder of the population may be deliberately placed at the end of the queue. But because marginal productivity is deemed to be an attribute of jobs rather than of job seekers, individuals with unfavorable positions in the queue are unlikely to be hired at lower wage rates than those at the beginning of the line.

In short, this particular model takes into account a number of imperfections in the labor market. To disassociate jobs from wages explains why discrimination may persist without disturbing this market; it also accounts for the lack of response of wage schedules to variations in the

---

[21] See L. Thurow and R. Lucas, "The American Distribution: A Structural Problem" Washington, D. C.: Government Printing Office, March 1972).

pool of available job seekers. Yet it does not address itself to the problems raised by the interaction between education and occupation. If the function of formal schooling is to reduce the training costs imposed on employers, it is indispensable to identify the conditions under which job seekers decide to stay longer at school in order to gain access to a rewarding job or alternatively to leave school immediately and enter the labor market in less favorable circumstances. Symmetrically, the existence of long lines of candidates anxious to enter rewarding jobs makes it necessary to specify the factors preventing employees with unfavorable positions from bidding down wage schedules or employers from exerting pressure in the same direction. Indeed, how is the absence of wage competition compatible with the maximization of profits sought by employers?

The third model rejects entirely the classical theory and relies on the assumption that the presence of several types of jobs and of several types of employers is associated with the emergence of distinct criteria for hiring and advancement, supervisory procedures, working conditions, and wage levels and that various jobs and various employers attract generally different groups to fill the relevant positions.[22]

Thus, jobs in the primary independent labor market demand a high creativity. The ability of reasoning deductively from abstract principles represents the chief prerequisite for productivity in this particular type of occupation. Its organization involves the use of formalized ladders, but also allows for a considerable amount of interfirm mobility. Wages, allocation, and training of personnel are more extensively controlled by economic variables (external market) than by administrative rules.[23]

Jobs in the primary routinized sector require a maximal dependability, stability, and acceptance of externally set goals. This stability is encouraged by a system of promotion which regulates individual advancement according to rules set up with the assistance of unions and facilitates the transfer of valuable know-how from experienced to novice wage earners.

Finally, the secondary labor market includes jobs requiring minimal skills and hence minimal training on the job. Occupational roles in this particular category are not governed by promotion ladders. They are not unionized, usually offer poor wages and working conditions. In fact, allocation of personnel and of earnings tends to vary with the whim of managers. In such a sector scarcity is defined in the most quantitative terms: candidates to such positions are highly interchangeable.

To establish this typology explains *how* employers entertain different

---

[22] The two major papers dealing with this question are M. Piore, "On the Technological Foundations of Economic Dualism" (MIT, Department of Economics Working Paper 110, May 1973), and D. Gordon, M. Reich, and R. Edwards, "A Theory of Labor Market Segmentation," *American Economic Review* 63(1973):361.

[23] See P. Doeringer and M. Piore, *Internal Labor Market and Manpower Training* (Lexington, Mass.: Heath Lexington Books, 1971).

sets of expectations toward a variety of jobs, but it does not explain *why* they do so. In fact, the segmentation of the labor market may reflect the intervention of two distinct forces. On the one hand, it may primarily result from a growing differentiation in the patterns of division of labor adopted by various types of enterprises. Indeed, changes in division of labor result from technological innovations and therefore require substantial financial investment. Entrepreneurs are prone to make such investments and to use capital-intensive modes of production whenever there is a massive and stable demand for the goods or services they are producing. Thus, insofar as such a demand affects the use of capital- or labor-intensive modes of production, patterns of division of labor and hence patterns of segmentation of the labor market tend to follow boundaries between branches of activity. But within one specific branch, only a few firms are likely to use large-scale capital-intensive methods of production to cater to the stable portion of the demand, whereas most marginal enterprises tend to rely on cheaper labor-intensive arrangements. However it is still necessary to identify the processes by which the differentiation of firms within a same branch takes place and to examine in this regard the influence of size, legal status, and age.

On the other hand, the segmentation of the expectations held by employers may also correspond to the evolutionary patterns of interaction between labor and management. Employers are as much interested in the perpetuation of the power they have already acquired (as in the maximization of their profits) and tend to adopt technological innovations only when this consolidates the control they exert on labor. As long as an emerging industrial system undermines skill craftwork and is associated with a decline in the initial power held by the labor aristocracy, there is no need for a segmented labor market. Mechanization of production facilitates the formation of an amorphous and homogeneous class of unskilled and semiskilled laborers. Yet with increases in the size of enterprises or in the realm of various economic markets, and with the emergence of residential segregation, this homogeneous class may become partially structured and threaten partially the power and authority accumulated by entrepreneurs. At this point employers will have recourse to strategies liable to segment the labor market. Such a segmentation cannot but prevent the coalescence of the most socially conscious segments of the working class into an active movement. Thus, in this context, the segmentation of labor markets is a managerial response to potential conflicts between social classes.

To sum up this brief review of contemporary economic models, the more conservative researchers minimize the range of variation in the behavior adopted by employers (who are deemed to be uniformly universalistic in their orientation) to maximize the importance of differences in the rationality of potential wage earners. In this perspective, individuals enter differing jobs because they do not have the same abilities or make the same choices with regard to formal schooling, but educational and hence occupational differences are independent of the policies adopted by governments and by public or private bureaucracies.[24] Alternatively, the more progressive economists or social scientists view employers' strategies and power-games as being more problematic. Accordingly, they emphasize the extent of cleavages *between* producers and their employees but eventually underplay the significance of the differentiation taking place *within* each one of these groups or classes.[25]

In the present study, I will give as much importance to inter- and intragroup differences in the behavior of employers and wage earners. This means that I will highlight contrasts in the composition and the attainment of white- and blue-collar workers but will also show that such contrasts vary with the profile of the enterprises to which they are attached. Of course, it remains necessary to explain why I distinguished jobs in terms of their manual or nonmanual traits rather than in terms of their primary or secondary characteristics.

Even though there is a certain overlap between the two systems of classification, the one I propose is more empirically oriented. First, the distinction between primary and secondary jobs stresses the significance of employer expectations toward the psychological and, more specifically, the emotional motivations of jobseekers, but it minimizes the differential cognitive requirements attached to various types of jobs. This is perhaps an acceptable view when one deals with a country characterized by a homogeneous level of education as well as by a homogeneous level of division of labor, but this is certainly problematic in countries where enterprises have markedly different organizational profiles. Second, the distinction between primary and secondary jobs eventually minimizes the problems of mobility across job families, whereas the contrast between manual and nonmanual activities leaves this question undetermined and hence open to empirical research. Last and most important, the distinction between manual and nonmanual jobs corresponds more closely to the perceptions of the actors present in the industrial scene. Not only do adults attach uniformly distinctive status to white- and blue-collar jobs but in

---

[24] For an illustration of this view, see R. Boudon, *Education, Opportunity, and Social Inequality* (New York: Wiley, 1974).

[25] "The view that a Marxian analysis requires a measurement of the consciousness arising from income differences *between* classes rather than *within* the class of industrial workers" is more ideological than scientific. Indeed, it minimizes the need of testing the empirical validity of the proposition. See P. Lubeck, "Early Industrialization and Social Class Formation among Factory Workers in Kano, Nigeria" (Evanston, Ill.: Ph.D. dissertation, Northwestern University, 1975). In more general terms it is noteworthy that polarized forms of conservative and radical views similarly minimize the interactive process present in the negotiations between demanders and suppliers. The position of "radical" social scientists is puzzling in this respect insofar as it treats the power held by workers as irrelevant or fixed.

addition, as is the case in the Cameroun, negotiations between employers and the two types of wage earners are governed by distinctive types of agreements and legislative regulations.[26]

Yet to assert that there are differences in the career profiles of manual and nonmanual workers and that, far from being constant, such differences vary across firms raises the question of determining whether the underlying differentiating principles are homogeneous or not. I suggest that because of its universality, the principle of scale may account for the cleavages with which we are concerned here.[27] However, whereas the notion of increase in societal scale implies increased differentiation, the relevant increase at the level of analysis retained here suggests the reverse: the higher the scale of a particular occupational category or of a particular type of firm, the fewer contrasts there are in the profile of the individual examples of the relevant gender.

Scale and the segmentation of the market.

Nonmanual work tends to involve a "higher" scale of activity than manual activities insofar as the scope of interaction it entails is greater in a spatial, temporal, and functional sense. In spatial terms, the distance between nonmanual workers and the product processed by the enterprise is greater, even though the differential distance between two types of wage earners and their individual outputs might be minimal. Additionally, nonmanual work tends to involve direct or indirect interaction with a larger number of individuals both within and without the enterprise.

Moreover, interactions developed in the context of nonmanual activities tend to have a broader temporal scale. For example, accounting and commercial transactions require relatively long-term memorization, longer term planning, and this leads to the division of time into rational and standardized units. By contrast, the temporal context in which manual operations are conducted tends to be more limited and, more important, less evenly distributed; even assembly-line production is marked by seasonal variations and thus by differences in the short-term deadlines with which workers are confronted

Finally, nonmanual work has a broader functional scope. Clerical jobs, for example, are largely coordinative in nature, and therefore employees tend to have a broader knowledge of the various departments and activities

---

[26] The distinction between manual and nonmanual work is particularly important in the context of countries where unionization has spread from the privileged segments of the white-collar workers employed by public services to the more marginal manual wage earners of plantations or primary concerns. In the Cameroun, as in other French-speaking African nations, white-collar jobs tend to be subject to the rules of the collective bargaining agreement passed by SCIMPEX (the association of commercial employees), whereas blue-collar activities are administered under the provisions of the agreement signed by UNISYNDI (association of industrial employees).

[27] See G. and M. Wilson, *Analysis of Social Change.*

of the enterprise for which they work. They are also more informed about other firms that their employer serves or that serve him. In contrast, manual work tends to have lower "scalar" properties, for the contacts of blue-collar employees tend to be more limited and are essentially related to the very particular phase of the production process in which they are involved.

To be sure, to highlight differences *between* manual and nonmanual jobs should not lead us to minimize the significance of the internal *variability* of these two classes of activity. For example, manual workers can be involved in maintenance as opposed to production activities, and this difference is necessarily associated with significant cleavages in the profile of their routines. Similarly, nonmanual employees may be primarily engaged in contacts with outside clients or in the internal workings of the enterprise.

In short, to stress the importance of the *mean* characteristics of manual and nonmanual tasks and of the relevant populations does not imply minimizing the significance of the *dispersion* of the corresponding distributions. At stake here is the difficulty raised by possible overlaps in these two distributions. To the extent that such an overlap exists, contrasts between manual and nonmanual jobs are likely to be invalid. This may be the case in industrialized contries where the growing specialization of nonmanual tasks leads to the formation of clerical "assembly lines" and mutes scalar differences between white- and blue-collar jobs. Although this specialization is not yet apparent in most developing countries, the validity of the distinctions in the relative scale of manual and nonmanual jobs is still dependent on the conventional criteria used to place specific jobs into either one of the two classes. The job of messenger is classified as nonmanual and certainly has lower scalar properties than that of telephone or television repair man; the question is to ascertain the numerical importance of such jobs in the distribution of white- and blue-collar occupations. In many developing nations, it is my observation that highly skilled manual jobs such as that of television repairman are too few to influence the contrasts I have just sketched.

But within the two occupational families, an effective socialization to the requirements of the job situation enables individual workers to ultimately move up in the hierarchy. Although the promotion of an individual depends on his earlier patterns of commitment, the activities associated with more skilled jobs subsequently enhance his sense of commitment. If a worker achieves a higher skill level or status, there is thus an increase in the scale of his activities. Whether manual or nonmanual, a skilled worker usually has more room for initiative and assumes a wider range of responsibilities; he usually interacts with a larger number of individuals within a broader physical range than do unskilled workers. Furthermore, these interactions develop within a broader temporal framework, for skilled workers must adjust the activities of their subordinates to the requirements of management. Finally, a more skilled position usually involves a broader range of contacts within and sometimes outside the enterprise.

The same broad scalar principles also affect the functioning of industrial or commercial organizations. In this case, we are concerned not only with the size of the enterprise but also with its organizational characteristics and degree of technological complexity. Firms vary greatly with respect to each of these three dimensions, and the resulting contrasts in patterns of administration often are associated with divergent personnel policies. Companies ranked high, for example, in terms of the scalar characteristics of size, organization, and complexity are most likely to pursue a more impersonal and formal style of interaction with workers; they tend to follow procedures concerning hiring, promotion, and payment that are directly borrowed from the more highly industrialized countries. Such "advanced" labor practices are not likely to be found in small-scale units, where relationships tend to be more personalized and where more "universalistic" criteria of worker promotion and reward are often less systematically adhered to.[28]

Several studies have drawn attention to the influence of labor policies on the commitment and mobility of workers in the developing areas. Thus, the placement, tenure, and earnings of Mexican workers depend on the size of enterprises located in the Monterey area. Similarly, in Peru, the characteristics and attitudes of workers vary with the size of textile enterprises, and the same holds true of India, where the composition and the income of the labor force seems to depend on the age, size, and pattern of division of labor of various enterprises.[29] Finally, in Africa it has been shown that the differential usage of physical capital and labor varies between locally and internationally based concerns and that the specific locale in which a firm operates affects rates of turnover and absenteeism among workers.[30]

Although these studies shed some light on the behavior of varying types of employers, it is possible to undertake a more systematic examination of the different scalar characteristics of private firms, and to see how these

---

[28] For an examination of the implications of these distinctions, see G. Ingham, *Size of Industrial Organization and Worker Behavior* (Cambridge: Cambridge University Press, 1970).

[29] See Bàlan, *Men in Developing Societies*, chap. 1, D. Chaplin, *The Peruvian Labor Force* (Princeton: Princeton University Press, 1967), and Lambert, *Workers, Factories, and Social Change in India*.

[30] On the first point, the ILO study, *Employment, Income, and Equality: A Strategy Increasing Employment in Kenya* (Geneva: ILO, 1972) suggests that foreign-owned firms have lower labor costs per employee and are more labor intensive than those which are locally owned, but are also more capital intensive in certain sectors of the market and have fewer difficulties in finding appropriate supervisory personnel (pp.437). On the second point, see Biffod, *Facteurs d'intégration et de desintégration*, or Guilbot, *Absentéisme et mobilité*.

affect personnel policies and hence exert some influence on level of worker commitment.

In summary, I posit that there are significant contrasts among types of jobs, skill levels, and firms which all can be subsumed in terms of their relative scalar properties. The use of the principle of scale enables us both to stress the broad *consensus* operating in the labor market, and to emphasize potential *discontinuities* in the respective characteristics of occupational families, skill levels, and types of enterprises. Further, this principle also makes it possible to assert that there are contrasts not only in the relative occupational attainment of individual workers, but also in the procedures which enable them to gain access to their current position in the occupational structure.

Determinants of Occupational Commitment

Thus far I have suggested that I shall adopt an essentially micro orientation in this study of industrial commitment and that my measures are behavioral rather than an attitudinal nature. Moreover, I have argued that the measures of commitment rest on the "assumed" differential productivity of workers employed by distinct types of employer and occupying different skill levels within the modern industrial private sector. As level of occupational commitment reflects prior educational, migratory, and occupational experiences, we should take a look at the operation of these latter variables in greater detail.

The significance of formal schooling.

Supposedly, formal education increases "rationality" because it leads to greater foresight and planning in the use of time and space and enhances workers' control over the allocation of their own resources.[31]

Initially, I assume that education broadens individual horizons and provides a greater knowledge of the occupational heirarchy and of new opportunities, even though these opportunities may be geographically distant.[32] Thus, educated individuals have not only less difficulty in obtaining employment, but they are also more willing to migrate than the unschooled: in relation to the number of job opportunities available in the area, the migratory movements of uneducated workers are far more limited than those undertaken by individuals possessing a few years of schooling.[33] In brief, education enables individuals to know where the action is.

---

[31] I take here the view developed by Goody in his analysis of the early stages of literacy. See J. Goody and I. Watts, "The Consequences of Literacy," in J. Goody, ed., *Literacy in Traditional Societies* (Cambridge: Cambridge University Press, 1968), pp.59-60.

[32] See D. Lerner, *The Passing of Tradtional Societies* (Glencoe: Free Press, 1958).

[33] See H. Rempel, "Labor Migration into Urban Centers and Urban Unemployment in Kenya" (Madison: Ph.D. dissertation, University of Wisconsin, 1970).

At the same time, education should have a more direct influence on occupational placement, mobility, and commitment. Earlier on, I noted that variations in productivity are most properly assessed within a single, particular occupational category. Even when one takes such a precaution, however,available evidence suggests that there is only a modest relationship between educational background and occupational attainment within the same occupational field.[34]

In comparing the relative productivity of various occupations, one may expect to find that the most qualified job seekers by educational standards enter those occupations requiring the highest skill level. Yet the importance that entrepreneurs attach to the training and education of workers varies greatly in terms of political as well as economic conditions. During the colonial period, for example, many employers were not particularly interested in obtaining a supply of educated manpower; schooling was often regarded as a consumption item having little to do with productivity.[35] As many of the less developed countries are, at present, *directly* importing some highly developed industrial technologies, the relationship between schooling and productivity should not only increase, but it should also be higher among newer than older branches of activity.[36]

Variations in the correlation between educational and occupational attainment also reflect contrasts in the effective functions of educational institutions. Although it is tempting to believe that there is a close correlation between the hierarchy of knowledge in school and the hierarchy of occupations in the world of business, this assumed correlation may have a variety of meanings. Does it reflect the pressures of employers or the power of organized groups of workers themselves?[37] Employers may view schools either as institutions that effectively *socialize* pupils to the demands of the industrial order or more simply as institutions that are useful in *selecting out* individuals, thereby reducing the costs attached to hiring and training. Yet the most organized segments of the working population also may regard academic credentials as offering some protection against the whims of local employers and as means of gaining some measure of control

---

[34] See C. Jenks and others, *Inequality: A Reassessment of the Effect of Family and Schooling in America* (New York: Basic Books, 1973), chaps. 6 and 7. See also C. Barberis, "L'influence de l'éducation sur le rendement de l'exploitation agricole dans une situation de changement," in R. Castel and J. C. Passeron, eds., *Education, développement, et démocratie* (Paris: Mouton, 1967), pp. 121-136. In this article, the author identifies the contingencies underlying the influence of education on agricultural activities.

[35] R. Clignet and P. Foster, *The Fortunate Few*, (Evanston: Northwestern University Press, 1966), chaps. 1 and 2. For a more economically oriented discussion, see Berg, "French West Africa," in Galenson, ed., *Labor and Economic Development.*

[36] For a general discussion, see W. Moore, *Industrialization and Labor* (Ithaca: Cornell University Press, 1951), or Moore and Feldman, *Labor. Commitment and Social Change in Developing Areas.* For a concrete example, see Belàn, *Men in Developing Societies.*

[37] Blaug, *Education and the Employment Problem,* pp. 27-39.

over the labor market.[38] The variety of cross-pressures exerted on schools by employers and workers obscure the relationship between the hierarchy of jobs and the curricular hierarchy of the school. Thus, it is not clear whether individuals enter jobs because of the differential socialization they have undergone during their stay in school or whether initial occupational choices lead individuals to stay longer in school. Quite simply, does an individual enter a particular job because he has stayed longer at school, or does he stay longer at school because he wants to enter a particular job?[39]

To the extent that individuals stay longer at school because they want to enter particular jobs, interindividual differences in productivity reflect less the socializing influences of educational than of familial environments. Whether inequalities in access to schooling reflect social, ethnic, religious, or regional factors, educational output tends only to confirm or replicate existing forms of social differentiation.[40]

Further, whereas the socializing influence of schools, and hence their impact on educational aspirations and orientations, probably increases with a *democratization* of their recruitment patterns, such an impact is more problematic whenever there is a marked *increase* in educational enrollments. Typically, the recent expansion of schooling in Africa has been conducive not only to a fall in the quality of the local teaching force but also to the perpetuation of existing curricula and teaching methods whose effectiveness declines as the student body keeps changing and becomes more diverse.[41]

But the influence of educational experience on occupation also varies with the relative status of schools in the hierarchy.[42] The occupational aspirations of the students enrolled in exclusive and prestigious educational institutions are only loosely related to their abilities and to their actual academic achievement. Although the aspirations of the student body initially may be uniformly high, academic competition obliges the less talented individuals to lower their educational and occupational aspirations. Conversely, in schools of lower status with a student clientele drawn from less affluent groups, continuously closer relationships between occupational aspiration and academic ability are more likely. The formidable nature of the initial hurdles that these less privileged students

---

[38] The more educated a labor force, the more it is able to impose closed shop in the recruitment of new workers. Printers offer a case in point.

[39] See Jenks, *Inequality,* chaps. 6 and 7.

[40] This is the theme developed by P. Bourdieu and J. C. Passeron in *La Reproduction* (Paris: Les Editions de minuit, 1970).

[41] Particularly at the post-primary level, a sharp increase in enrollments has necessitated a massive import of European teachers and hence the perpetuation of a metropole-oriented curriculum.

[42] This point is developed by Clignet and Foster in *The Fortunate Few,* chap. 4. It is more systemmatically treated by P. Blau and R. Duncan in *The American Occupational Structure* (New York: Wiley, 1967), p. 412.

must overcome actually increases their ability to cope with subsequent academic and occupational obstacles.

However, the socializing effects of schools depend also on their organizational profiles and on their relative centralization. First, the diversity of patterns of student selection into decentralized school systems makes more problematic the emergence of a unified occupational culture.[43] Further, the prestige of public and private teachers is different, and such contrasts should affect the extent of their socializing influence. Yet insofar as the differential prestige of these two types of teachers varies with the preeminence of the public and private sectors, contrasts in their socializing power should be culturally relative.[44] Third, the socialization processes used in the two types of schools also may differ in their emphasis. In public institutions, emphasis may well be on the development of commitment to nationwide networks of interaction, whereas socialization in private institutions may foster more intense commitment to local networks and groupings. Accordingly, conceptions of the labor market should be "cosmopolitan" the first case, but "local" in the second.[45]

The influence of schools on the occupational aspirations of students also tends to vary with the characteristics of local elites. In the early days of French colonization in Africa, for example, school graduates were primarily oriented toward the public sector of employment; and their position as elites was reinforced by the preeminent status of French administrators vis-a-vis private entrepreneurs or managerial personnel.

Finally, the relation between the educational experience and occupational expectations of students is modified by the rates of both educational and economic development. The coexistence of low rates of economic growth and high rates of educational expansion often entails disjunctions between student aspirations and actual occupational opportunities. Although students evaluate the rewards of education by reference to the actual experience of earlier cohorts, a rapidly increasing flow of school graduates onto the market will lead to a decline in the fit between expectations and reality.

This variety of contrasts in the structures of schools and in the place they occupy in the community at large explains in part why educational experiences are not treated similarly by the models dealing with the functioning of the labor market. Thus, the economists who use *human capital models* believe explicitly or implicitly that under modern

---

[43] See R. Clignet and P. Foster, "Convergence and Divergence in Educational Development in Ghana and the Ivory Coast," in Foster and Zolberg, *Ghana and the Ivory Coast*, pp. 255-291.

[44] See R. Clignet, "Teachers as Potential Agents of Modernization in the Cameroun" (forthcoming).

[45] This distinction was initially applied to various types of American educational administrators, but there is no reason to believe that its use cannot be extended to other countries and other occupations.

technological conditions, cognitive abilities and technical skills constitute the major components of individual productivity.[46] Schooling imparts cognitive skills and enhances abilities to learn, whereas both vocational institutions and job experiences enable job seekers to acquire the technical skills needed to perform a particular job. As differences in personality traits and values are assumed to be only secondary components of productivity, years of schooling and years of occupational experience are deemed to be adequate indicators of an individual's productive ability. As already noted, however, this assumption holds true only as long as there is a low level of differentiation in modes of production, patterns of division of labor, and patterns of interaction among various social groups.

Alternatively, the *signaling model* assumes that even though productivity is independent of education, educational costs incurred by the most productive individuals must be sufficiently low in order for schooling to act as a signal. In other words, the unit cost of signal acquisition must be negatively correlated with productivity. Should schooling have a productive component, the conditions of equilibrium require then an assessment of the distribution of signaling costs. If these unit costs are equal for everyone, everyone is likely to invest in the same amount of education, and the wages obtained by individual job seekers would cease to be differentiated. If costs of education are randomly distributed or positively correlated with productivity, individuals will, to be sure, invest in differential amounts of schooling, but employers will gradually observe that education is uncorrelated or negatively correlated with productivity, and will cease accordingly to offer premiums for formal schooling. Thus, in this model, schooling and productivity must be kept independent of each other, and the major function of educational institutions is to weed out the less productive individuals from the market.

In contrast, the *job competition model* stresses that education actually reduces the cost of training for both general and specific skills. But studies of the rates of return which are based on the model do not properly predict gaps between those individuals with different levels of schooling but similar ages, abilities, and socioeconomic classes and therefore do not measure correctly the gains that individuals or societies derive from education.

Finally, the *segmentation theories* suggest that the functions of formal schooling vary with the types of jobs under study. In the primary autonomous sector, individuals are not directly supervised; they must understand quickly the goals of their employers and be willing as well as able to take the relevant actions and to anticipate difficulties which may arise in the exercise of their roles. In the primary routinized sectors, individuals must come to work every day and be able to carry the task assigned to them within a standardized amount of time and without challenging the relevant sets of instructions. Last,

---

[46] See, for example, G. Becker, *Human Capital and the Personal Distribution of Income* (Ann Arbor: University of Michigan Press, 1967).

secondary workers are interchangeable and need a minimum of cognitive and technical skills. They must, however, feel they have no real alternative and believe that they are responsible for being trapped in their current job. Thus, the segmentation theories assume that employers are able to impose on educational institutions both screening techniques and a formal as well as informal curriculum tailor-made to their own needs.[47]

In the present study, I note the differential patterns of organization prevailing in Camerounian schools as well as the distinct curricula they offer to the student populations. However, the nature of the data does not enable us to test whether the distinctions between manual and nonmanual jobs, skill levels, and types of employers are associated with parallel contrasts in the specific nature of the educational experiences acquired by Camerounian workers. This shortcoming is not yet too serious: as long as a country is characterized by a relatively low level of educational development, there is probably a relatively low degree of differentiation in the noncognitive patterns of socialization exerted by schools with differing organizational patterns or with differential ranks in the academic ladder. I will, however, show that the occupational distinctions already sketched here are associated with contrasts in the overall educational profile of their respective populations.

Commitment and migration.

In Africa, as elsewhere, the development of a modern labor market leads to extensive migrations between rural and urban areas. Industrialization involves the constant reallocation of workers, both physically and occupationally, into more productive economic activities, which enhance individual social and economic rewards.[48] Yet the effects of migration on economic development are not entirely positive, for individuals are attracted toward urban centers already characterized by relatively high rates of unemployment.

The behavior of urban migrants remains nevertheless rational if one considers that during earlier stages of development the familial group rather than the individual remains the most significant unit of economic behavior. In fact, extensive migration into urban areas coexists with substantial urban unemployment only insofar as continuous and reciprocal exchanges continue between familial groups who remain in the hinterland and those who move to the city.[49] Because of this pattern of exchange, migration into urban centers

---

[47] This, it seems to me, reveals another weakness of radical economists. There is not reason to believe that bureaucracies and particularly educational bureaucracies do not enjoy a certain autonomy vis-à-vis employers. See R. Clignet, *Liberty and Equality in the Educational Process* (New York: Wiley, 1974), chaps. 4 and 5.

[48] Chaplin, *The Peruvian Labor Force* chap. 1.

[49] J. Gugler, "The Impact of Labor Migrations on Society and Economy in Subsaharan Africa," *African Social Research* 6 (1968):436–486.

varies as a positive function of *expected* urban/rural wage differences.[50]

Clearly such expectations vary among different groups in the rural population, largely as a result of the varying "push" and "pull" factors that lead to migration.[51] Push factors often are related to patterns of rural land utilization. But even in this context, the volume, social composition, and occupational destinations or expectations of migrating populations are likely to differ, depending on whether the push reflects increased or decreased agricultural productivity in rural areas.

Similarly, contrasts in traditional rules of inheritance may have a profound effect on selective migration patterns and hence on expectations concerning urban/rural income differentials. Thus Habbakuk shows that in Bohemia-Moravia, rural rules of primogeniture tended to force younger siblings into urban centers where employment was to be found and also stimulated a demand for education that enabled them to enter more lucrative forms of urban employment.[52] By contrast, in rural Slovakia, traditions of equal partition of land among siblings checked mobility into the towns, impeded the development of new agricultural techniques, and led to increasing rural pauperization. In Bohemia, migrants were usually younger siblings whose level of educational attainment facilitated their upward mobility in the urban setting, whereas in Slovakia a generally lower level of urban migration was not associated with sibling rank order nor with enhanced opportunities for occupational mobility.

However, migration patterns are not only influenced by rules of inheritance but also by types of descent systems and traditional patterns of residence. In Africa, matrilineal patterns of organization are less likely than patrilineal systems to lead to processes of segmentation. Accordingly, matrilineal peoples will have a lower propensity to migrate. If migrations do occur, they will involve larger groupings of individuals. As a result, matrilineal peoples will tend to arrive later on the industrial scene.[53]

---

[50] For an examination of various models analyzing the effects of a dual sector on migrations, see E. Berg, "Backward-Sloping Labor Supply Functions in Dual Economies, The African Case," *Quarterly Journal of Economics* 75(1961). As quoted by E. Wallerstein, ed., *Social Change: The Colonial Situation* (New York: Wiley, 1966), pp. 114-136. See also J. Harris and M. Todaro, "Migration Unemployment and Development: A Two-Sector Analysis," *American Economic Review* 60(1970):126-142.

[51] This point is argued at a general level by C. Kerr and others in *Industrialism and Industrial Man* (Cambridge, Mass.: Harvard University Press, 1960). From an African viewpoint, variations in migratory patterns are underlined by W. Hance in *Population, Migration, and Urbanization in Africa* (New York: Columbia University Press, 1970), pp. 161-191.

[52] See J. Habbakuk, "Family Structure and Economic Change in XIXth-Century Europe," *Journal of Economic History* 15(1955):1-12.

[53] For an empirical and theoretical review of this argument, see R. Clignet, "Environmental Change, Type of Descent, and Child-Rearing Practices," in H. Miner, ed., *The City in Modern Africa* (New York: Praeger, 1964). See also D. Scheider, "Introduction," in D. Scheider and K. Gough, eds., *Matrilineal Kinship* (Berkeley and Los Angeles: University of California Press, 1961), pp. 1-27.

Traditional rules of residence also may influence the propensity to migrate insofar as social groups have varying definitions of the range of persons with whom an individual can normally expect to interact. Thus, flexibility in traditional residence patterns that are not circumscribed by narrow definitions of kinship and family would constitute a type of "anticipatory socialization" that enables individuals from such groups to cope more effectively with the demands of the new urban and industrial society.[54]

Expectations concerning urban/rural wage differentials vary also, needless to say, with level of formal schooling. First, educational attainment affects modes of migration: it increases the willingness to migrate longer distances and gives a greater range of choices with regard to destination. The schooled individual has access to more numerous occupations, and he is less dependent on relatives already in the towns.[55] In addition, the expectations of the educated concerning urban/rural income differences also are often realistic, as income differentials are more marked in the urban than the rural setting. Formal schooling is more closely associated with higher incomes in the towns than in the rural hinterland.[56]

Clearly, contrasts in migratory experience affect individual patterns of access into the labor market. Because recent migrants tend to be concentrated in districts apart from those occupied by locally born or long-established residents, they are likely to use different information networks concerning availability of job opportunities. Whenever immigrant neighborhoods are situated at the extreme periphery of urban centers, job opportunities are reduced and so is individual adaptation to the requirements of the urban environment. These disadvantages are mitigated to some extent if immigrants are ultimately free to move and settle in more desirable neighborhoods, thereby enhancing their conditions of life and occupational opportunities.[57]

---

[54] See E. Segal, "Ethnicity as a Factor in American Urban Migrations," (paper presented at the 68th Annual Meeting of the American Anthropological Association, November 1969).

[55] See Rempel, "Labor Migrations into Urban Centers."

[56] In Uganda, J. B. Knight has shown that urban salaries have increased by 300 percent between 1957 and 1964, whereas rural incomes declines during the same period. See "The Determinants of Wages and Salaries in Uganda," *Bulletin of the Oxford University Institute of Economics and Statistics* 29(1967):233-264. In Ghana, D. Roy has shown that the average income of the poorest quartile of the rural population was 15.2 NC as opposed to 58.4 for the richest one. In contrast, the corresponding figures in urban areas were 16.9 and 67.8 NC, respectively. Finally, although there are hardly any differences in the monthly incomes of illiterate individuals and middle-school drop-outs in rural areas, these differences are greater in the urban context. See D. Roy. *The Eastern Region Household Budget Survey* (Institute of Statistical, Social, and Economic Research, University of Ghana Technical Publications 6, 1969).

[57] For a discussion of the impact of migration on ecological structures, see, for example, R. Clignet and F. Jordan, "Urbanization and Social Differentiation in West Africa: A Comparative Analysis of the Ecological Structures of Douala and Yaoundé," *Cahiers d'etudes africaines* 20(1971):261-297.

Yet the influence of migrating patterns on employment is also more direct. Migrants tend to gain a disproportionate share of new job opportunities whenever the ethnic groups historically associated with a particular town prefer to remain in traditional economic activities. Southern Ghana offers a case in point.[58] After all, to have deep roots in an urban environment facilitates the development and perpetuation of the social networks necessary for the survival of traditional economic activities.

Finally, different patterns of selective migration into towns are related to varying types of occupational placement. Thus, direct migrations from rural areas tend to be more frequent among unskilled than skilled manual workers.[59] Similarly, skilled white-collar wage earners are more likely to have grown up in the cities; if they are migrants, they have often migrated several times before they finally end up in town: further, for unskilled populations, the route to the city often involves a search for any kind of employment, whereas for their more skilled counterparts, migratory patterns normally involve continuing processes of upward mobility.

To summarize, migratory patterns involve complex and differentiated processes which have diverging consequences on the development of a modern labor force. But, as was the case for education, increasing complexity in migratory flows also leads economists and social scientists to take different stances in their analysis of the labor market. Even though empirical studies in this respect are scarce, many of the models which consider migrations take a view directly or indirectly inspired by the human capital perspective.[60] To the best of my knowledge, few scholars have examined migration from the firms' viewpoint and have accordingly focused their analysis on the institutional strategies used by employers to force or incite massive migrations toward places where labor is most needed.

In the present study, I am unable to examine how distinctions between blue- and white-collar work, skill levels, and types of employment are accompanied by parallel contrasts in the patterns and distance of migration of the corresponding wage-earning populations. The fact remains that it is certainly a crucial determinant of occupational placement and attainment in a country such as Cameroun.

Conclusions

My purpose in this chapter has been to sketch the theoretical framework within which I intend to develop the subsequent analysis of the labor force

---

[58] See Peil, *The Ghanaian Factory Worker*, p. 39.

[59] Ibid, pp. 143-144.

[60] There is the exception of P. Lubeck, whose dissertation "Early Industrialization and Social Class Formation" is concerned, inter alia, with an assessment of the influence of migration on class consciousness and participation in strikes.

employed by modern firms of the Camerounian economy. Even though the literature on industrialization and economic development stresses the notion of commitment, the relationship between such a term and the concept of productivity remains often obscure and undeterminate. A brief review of economic models dealing with this question suggests that they suffer from two complementary shortcomings. Because they are focused on the behavior of employers or, alternatively, of wage earners, they do not take sufficient account of the interactive nature of the labor market and of the dialectics between conflicts and consensus underlying the relations between employers and their labor forces.

In this chapter, I have proposed that the functioning of the modern labor market in a new country is determined by the principle of scale, and that increases in the scalar properties of jobs and of employers are associated with greater regularities in the profiles of the relevant populations. Although the data to which I had access do not enable me to test the influence of migration or of certain aspects of educational experience on the functioning of the various segments of the labor market, I still intend to examine the interaction between formal schooling and the scalar properties of various jobs and firms on the ongoing segmentation of the Camerounian labor market.

Chapter 2

THE SETTING OF THE STUDY

The Cameroun constitutes a particularly appropriate laboratory for assessing the commitment of workers and employers. Because of contrasts in the profile of Camerounian regions, local populations are not similarly involved in modernizing processes or in modern economic enterprises.

Accordingly, the first part of this chapter is devoted to an overview of the Camerounian geographic, ethnic, and historical scene in order to identify which parts of the country shelter modern activities and which segments of the population are absorbed by the modern sector of employment. In a second part, I examine the survey from which subsequent analyses are derived, and conclude with a comparison between the profiles of the workers sampled and of other major segments of the gainfully employed population.

The Cameroun: An Overview

The Cameroun is roughly triangular in shape, approximately 770 miles long, and has an area of slightly under 200,000 square miles.[1] The country is easily divided into five regions with differing economic oportunities. The coastal plain is largely covered with dense forests and is characterized by a hot and damp climate. Bordering this small area, there is a region of relatively high plateaus (with an altitude of 2,100 feet) equally characterized by dense vegetation, high temperature, and heavy rainfall. North of the Sanaga River, the Adamawa Mountains mark a transition between the forest-covered humid south and the northern savannahs. This particular region merges gradually into the flat Benue and Chad plains, which receive rain only during the five months of the summer and early fall and provide limited opportunities for agricultural enterprise. Finally, the fifth region comprises a chain of mountains which constitute the boundary between Cameroun and Nigeria. High in altitude and offering an invigorating climate, this area has volcanic soils and is hence suitable for intensive modes of land exploitation.

These regions are characterized by diversified modes of subsistence, and hence by various types of human organization. Peoples engaged in cattle-

---

[1] See V. LeVine, *The Cameroun from Mandate to Independence* (Berkeley and Los Angeles: University of California Press, 1964), chap. 1. See also V. LeVine, *The Cameroun Federal Republic* (Ithaca: Cornell University Press, 1971).

raising activities do not have the same territorial arrangements, the same kind of kin structures, or the same cultural outlook as their counterparts whose subsistence depends on agricultural activities.[2] Among farmers, the social structure of ethnic groups with itinerant modes of production differs from that prevailing among groups engaged in horticulture.

Because of initially distinctive modes of organization, these peoples are unevenly responsive to social change. The number and background of migrants derived from cattle-raising peoples differ from those of their counterparts originating from groups engaged in agriculture. Further, the original location of Camerounian peoples implies differing forms of contact with colonial authorities and a modernizing economy.

These regional contrasts are associated with differences in population density. In 1965, the Eastern State of Cameroun was divided into five large political units termed *inspections federales*.[3] The two most densely populated units were the *west* and *coastal* areas. In the *west*, density averaged 71 inhabitants per square kilometer but varied between 212 for the Mifi and only 24 for the Bamoun. Similarly, in the *coastal* region, the average density was 30.1 per square kilometer but reached 222.3 in the Wouri, where the economically dominant city of Douala is located.

The three other regions of the Cameroun were uniformly less populated, with the exception of the Mefou (which includes the capital city of Yaoundé), where the density was 60.7 per square kilometer. In short, the Camerounian population tended to be concentrated in three zones. In the western region, people were still engaged in intensive modes of agricultural exploitation. Overpopulated in terms of the opportunities offered by this particular form of agricultural activity, this region acted and still acts as a reservoir for the two most developed parts of the county, the departments of the Wouri and of the Mefou. Hence, massive migrations "push" individuals away from the least modernized but highly populated parts of the Cameroun toward the most economically developed regions surrounding the major cities of Douala and Yaoundé.

The influence of ethnicity on the labor market.

Like so many other African nations, the Cameroun is characterized by the diversity of its peoples, which may be grouped in five major clusters (Table 1).[4] The first cluster includes northern ethnic groups. Yet this cluster

[2] For example and illustration of this proposition, see W. Goldschmidt, "Variability and Adaptability of Cultures," *American Anthropologist* 7(1965):600-667. See also R. Edgerton, "Cultural vs. Ecological Factors in the Expression of Values, Attitudes, and Personality Characteristics," *American Anthropologist* 57(1965):442-445.

[3] See *Evaluations et projections démographiques en République fédérale du Cameroun* (Direction de la statistique et de la comptabilité nationale, May 1970), pp. 115-116.

[4] See LeVine, *Cameroun Federal Republic*, pg. 5, see also W. Johnson, *The Cameroun Federation* (Princeton: Princeton University Press, 1970), chap. 3.

TABLE 1

Ethnic Composition of the Cameroun Population

Groups	Number	Percentage
Northerners (including Hausa and Kirdi)	1,050,000	31.1
Highlanders (including Bamileke)	900,000	26.7
Equatorial Bantu (including Ewondo, Beti and Fang)	773,000	22.9
Northwestern and Coastal Bantu (including Bassa, Douala)	267,000	8.0
Other Camerounians	382,000	11.3
Total	3,372,000	100.00

Source: V. Le Vine, The Cameroun Federal Republic, p. 47.

is highly heterogeneous because its components (a) do not share the same religious orientations (Kirdi are animist, whereas Hausa Fulani are Moslem); (b) were not engaged initially in the same kind of economic activities (Kirdi were primarily agriculturalist, whereas Fulani were cattle raisers and herders); (c) do not have the same traditional systems of political organization (Fulani had a centralized system, but this was not the case among the Kirdi); and (d) do not live in the same kind of region (Kirdi tend to be concentrated in the hills).

The second cluster includes the highlanders. Although initially they shared the same cultural roots, they still differ in terms of their patterns of political centralization and of their vulnerability to Moslem influence. As an illustration, the Bamoun are not only more politically integrated than the Bamileke, but are also more often Islamicized.[5]

The third major cluster, the equatorial Bantus, are concentrated in the south-central part of the country. The various ethnic groups included in this particular cluster share similar linguistic patterns and social structures. Yet these various peoples did not migrate to the Cameroun at the same time. Settled in distinct regions, they have not enjoyed the same economic opportunities nor have been similarly exposed to other peoples. As a result, there are significant variations in their contemporary social and familial structures. Although the coastal Bantu share the same initial characteristics as the previous cluster, their original traits have been more deeply eroded as a result of their lengthy and intense contact with colonizers.

[5] See G. P. Murdock, Africa: Its People and Their Cultural History (New York: McGraw-Hill, 1959). See also I. Dugast, Inventaire éthnique du Sud Cameroun (Yaoundé: IFAN, 1940; Mémoires de l'IFAN Cameroun populations, no. 1).

Finally, the last cluster includes a variety of ethnic groups with disparate traditions, migratory patterns, and colonial experiences.

Ethnicity affects the functioning of the modern sector of the economy in a variety of ways. First, participation and success in the modern labor market depends on the relative congruence between the requirements of an industrial and a traditional social order. Yet this congruence is difficult to assess in the case of Camerounian peoples, for knowledge of their economic and familial structures remains quantitatively and qualitatively limited. Insofar as these peoples tend to follow patrilineal rules of descent which facilitate a segmentation of familial groups, there should be a uniform individualization of economic and social rights, and hence increased individual mobility. However, among the Douala, this segmentation of familial groups results from the challenges that successful individuals have exerted on the principle of seniority and, more specifically, from their refusal to be subjected to the authority of the elders of their own lineage.[6] In brief, this segmentation primarily reflects achievement. In contrast, among the Bamileke, familial segmentation results from the choices that a testator can make with regard to his heirs: an individual who is not chosen as an heir is entitled to move into a new territory, and to create a new lineage: in this case, ascription is more likely to interact with achievement in the ultimate fate of an individual.[7]

In addition, southern societies were initially characterized by a system of "age classes." This particular system of stratification emphasized solidarity among members of a same age group but could be still of importance in the modern context, for it might induce urban residents to share with newcomers both their shelter and their knowledge of the networks facilitating access to modern enterprise.

Initially, however, the organization of classes varied along ethnic lines. Among the Douala, the system was linear, with a corresponding flexibility in the system of rights and obligations between and within classes.[8] In fact, the age class system of the Douala mirrored the growing importance attached to achievement. Conversely, among the Bamileke the system of age classes was cyclical. Rights and obligations were defined by reference to alternate rather than adjacent age-cohorts, and this limited innovations in the relationships within and among age groups.[9] The cyclical nature of the Bamileke system made the members of a particular cohort subject to the power and authority of their grandparents' cohort rather than to that of their parents'. This particular pattern has probably contributed to maintaining the initial traits of the Bamileke social structure for a longer

---

[6] See Manga Bekombo Priso, "Les classes d'age chez les Dwala," in D. Paulme, ed., *Classes et associations d'age en Afrique de l'ouest* (Paris: Plon, 1970), pp. 286-307.

[7] Jean Hurault, "Les Classes d'age dans le systeme social des Bamileke," in D. Paulme, et., *Classes et associations d'age,* pp. 308-319.

[8] Bekombo Priso, "Les Classes d'age," p. 293.

[9] Hurault, "Les Classes d'age," p. 317.

period and to limiting the access of this people to modernizing processes.

As the Bamileke age class system was superseded by the existence of voluntary associations, whose membership was made dependent on individual wealth and hence success, this particular people has obviously experienced the conflicting pressures of ascription and achievement.[10] Modes of Bamileke participation in a modern economy should therefore differ markedly from that of other Camerounian ethnic groups, and notably of the Douala.

Islamized populations in the north also follow patrilineal rules of descent, but their system of social stratification is based on religious rather than economic factors and is accordingly more rigid.[11] Social distance between the various categories of the population is greater and avenues for upward mobility are more limited. The adaptation of such peoples to the requirements of an urban and modern economy should be more difficult. Migrants with such an origin should be few in number; they should be derived from marginal categories in their community of origin, and their upward mobility within a modern labor force should be problematic.

Ethnicity, however, does not only refer to distinctive initial patterns of social organization but also to differing modes of exposure to Western and colonial influences. Camerounian peoples have not been exposed to similar educational and occupational pressures, and their relative exposure to modernization follows a clear-cut pattern: maximal among coastal ethnic groups, modernization declines as one moves northward, eastward, and westward from the coast. As the Douala have been more durably and more intensely subject to modernizing influences, they are generally more educated than other groups. Indeed, this people settled in the Wouri area at the beginning of the seventeenth century at a time when the slave traffic was still flourishing, and by 1842 they played a significant role as middlemen in the trade of palm oil and ivory.[12] Clearly, the strategic position they occupied enabled them to perceive the benefits accruing to formal education more quickly than peoples in the hinterland.

Even today, there are significant contrasts in primary school enrollments in the areas where the distinctive ethnic clusters of the Cameroun tend to be concentrated. In 1970, school enrollments averaged 64 percent for the nation as a whole, reached maximal values of 94 percent for the center-south and 83 percent for the littoral area, to decline down to 80 percent in the west and 22 percent in the north.[13] Ethnic variations in the educational level of the adult population of Douala, the largest and most developed city of the country,

[10] Ibid., p. 310.

[11] For a description of Northern societies, see A Kirke-Greene, *Adamawa Past and Present* (New York: Oxford University Press, 1959). See also J. Barkow, "The Conqueror Assimilation Model: A Feedback Theory of Socio-Cultural Change among the Hausa of Nigeria" (mimeo, undated).

[12] See Le Vine, *From Mandate to Independence,* chap. 2.

[13] See *Evaluations et projections démographiques,* p. 101.

follow a similar pattern (Table 2). As expected, it is among the Douala that the percentage of illiterate males is minimal. But although the Bassa and the Beti Fang (originating from the Yaoundé area) fare almost as well as the Douala in this respect, one finds among northerners the smallest proportion of individuals who have completed a primary school education. As a result, there are marked ethnic differentials in the composition of the overall modern labor force and of its various components. The number and characteristics of wage earners coming from peoples with an overall high level of educational attainment (such as the Douala or the Beti) differ from those of workers originating from peoples whose involvement in formal education is both more recent and more limited (such as the Bamileke or, a fortiori, the northern populations).

The differential exposure of Camerounian peoples to social change also involves distinctive patterns of urban migration. In 1947 the Douala and the Bassa represented about 61 percent of the entire population of Douala. By 1956, the corresponding figure had dropped to 38 percent, and remained at that level at the time of the 1964 census. In contrast, the Bamileke represented only 16 percent of the total population of the city of Douala in 1947, against 26 percent in 1956 and 33 percent in 1964.[14]

To sum up, variations in the duration and intensity of the contacts established between Camerounian ethnic groups and European cultural models should affect individual modes of participation in the modern labor market. For example, migrations should be more socially selective among peoples entering relatively late into the processes of modernization than among their counterparts with a more lengthy and intensive experience. Although less modernized peoples should be underrepresented in the entire modern labor force, urban migrants with such a background should come from selected segments of the population and, as a result, should do at least as well as the members of more modernized ethnic groups once they have entered the modern labor market.

Finally, ethnicity implies variations in social visibility within the urban context.[15] Subpopulations with differing values and life styles are the object of discriminatory treatment. This treatment involves the emergence of norms governing the use of space; certain ethnic groups prefer to live close to certain peoples and as far as possible from others. For example, the Douala in Douala and Ewondo in Yaoundé tend to live in areas where the concentration of the Bamileke or of northerners is minimal.[16] This

---

[14] These figures are derived from Le Vine, *From Mandate to Independence*, p. 53; from W. and J. Hanna, *Urban Dynamics in Black Africa* (Chicago: Aldine, 1971), p. 127; and from my own analysis of the Douala census, 1964).

[15] For a theoretical elaboration of this particular point, see S. Greer, *The Emerging City* (New York: St. Martin's Press, 1965).

[16] For a verification of this point, see R. Clignet and F. Jordan, "Urbanization and Social Differentiation in West Africa: A Comparative Analysis of the Ecological Structures of Douala and Yaoundé, *Cahiers d'etudes africaines* 11 (1971):281-297.

TABLE 2

TABLE 2 Educational Level of Douala Adult Male Residents by Ethnic Origin (1964)
(percentage distribution)

Educational level	Ethnic Group							
	Douala	Bassa	Beti Fang	Bamileke	Northerners	Other Camerounb	West Cameroun	Foreigners
Illiterate	26.9	29.7	29.8	40.7	65.0	44.6	43.4	45.6
Some primary education	46.4	47.2	41.9	45.3	13.8	39.9	5.2	17.5
Primary education completed	21.8	19.9	23.5	12.3	1.0	12.9	2.1	7.9
Beyond primary education	4.3	2.7	4.2	1.5	0.0	1.8	0.5	0.9
Education in German or English	0.5	0.3	0.4	0.2	0.6	0.5	41.7	25.2
Unascertained or other educationa	0.1	0.2	0.1	0.0	18.6	0.2	1.1	2.8
Total	100.0	100.0	99.9	100.0	100.0	99.9	100.0	99.9
N	7,032	8,633	4,227	17,856	886	7,911	585	1,551

Source: R. Clignet and J. Sween, Analysis of the 1964 Census.

aIncludes Arab education.

bIncludes the Kaka, the Banagantou, the Bamoun, the Pol, the Baya, and the whole cluster of Mbam, Maka, Paleonegritic, and Pygmy populations.

treatment also involves the appearance of norms influencing hiring practices in the labor market. The ethnic groups represented in the urban scene do not enjoy equivalent access to the informal networks used to gain information about the various opportunities in the labor market. For example, the Bamileke are probably less informed than other peoples of changes occurring in the occupational structure of Douala or Yaoundé. Furthermore, the stereotypes attached to the Bamileke limit the hiring choices of firms; European employers may be reluctant to hire or promote Bamileke workers, whenever they suspect that the presence of such individuals is likely to lower the cohesiveness and hence the productivity of their entire labor force. Alternatively they may give preferential treatment to individuals with such a background whenever they think that a divisive strategy is convenient for the implementation of their personnel policies or whenever they accord special credit to the "working traits" attributed to this particular people.

To sum up, the three facets of ethnicity (distinctive value systems, variable exposure to modernization processes, and differential visibility) should affect not only the migration patterns of Camerounian peoples but also their particular modes of participation in the various sectors of the urban labor market.

Patterns of colonization.
The country was occupied by the Germans at the turn of the last century. Influenced by Bismarck's view on ideal patterns of administrative organization, German colonizers were accordingly anxious to impose a highly centralized bureaucratic structure on the new colony.[17] Yet the translation of these principles into action was hindered by two independent factors, which exerted convergent and negative effects on a policy of centralization. British travelers and traders had long operated in the region and had signed a number of treaties intended to improve commercial opportunities, but whose indirect effects legitimized the authority of local rulers. As a result, German colonial officials could not depart markedly from the practices of their predecessors and were obliged to attach more importance to the principles of indirect rule than they would have liked. In addition, German public opinion was not particularly favorable to colonial adventures, and the financial resources allocated to the colonies were limited. Hence, German officials were obliged to curtail their attempts to use patterns of centralized administration. For example, in the education field, they were obliged to delegate many of their responsibilities to religious missions, whose survival, in turn, was dependent on the good will

---

[17] For a review of the particular patterns of development of the various parts of Cameroun, see Le Vine, *From Mandate to Independence*, chap. 2, Johnson, *The Cameroun Federation*, chap. 4, and H. Vernon Jackson, *Language, Schools, and Government in Cameroun* (New York: Teachers College Press, 1967).

of local populations. In short, the mechanisms underlying the functioning of the German administration, far from eroding existing systems of social stratification, facilitated the development and perpetuation of a local social and ethnic elite.

After World War I, the Cameroun was divided into two parts, one of which was placed under French control while the other was subjected to British tutelage, with both colonial powers acting under the supervision of the League of Nations and, after World War II, of the United Nations. Within the limits imposed on them by this supervision, both powers still aimed at asserting their own administrative style on the local scene.

At the political level, marked contrasts between the traditional framework used by French colonial authorities in Africa and the constraints attached to their Camerounian mandate induced them to treat the Cameroun as an entity separate from the West African or the Equatorial Federation. Correspondingly, the French-administered part of Cameroun was able to compete directly with the two French African federations in order to get from the Metropole the direct financial assistance necessary for building roads, railways, airports, and ports. In consequence, the modern labor market offers a relatively large number of opportunities.

In addition, the educational and economic strategies used by French authorities in the Cameroun have been quite specific. These authorities have accorded favorable treatment to religious missions, and they have also made consistent efforts in the field of public education. As a result, increases in primary as well as postprimary enrollments have been substantial.[18] In the economic field, tensions between French colonial authorities and European-owned large-scale enterprises facilitated the development and perpetuation of both a numerous highy skilled public labor force and of a large number of small African-owned enterprises.[19] Even today, there is a significant small-scale labor market coexisting alongside that of the large modern enterprises. The Douala census of 1964 shows that no less than 41 percent of the African working adult population is self-employed, and the census of Yaoundé in 1962 reveals that the corresponding proportion in that city approximates 29 percent. In brief, the particular style adopted by French authorities in the Cameroun facilitated both a rapid growth of the economy and a relative differentiation of local elites.

In spite of the peculiar pattern of development of East Cameroun during the colonial era, the local political climate was still similar to that prevail-

---

[18] For example, primary enrollments per hundred population increased from 2 in 1930 to 37 by 1945. For a review of an historical account of educaitonal statistics in the Cameroun, see R. Mitchell and other, *Black Africa: A Handbook for Comparative Analysis* (New York: Free Press, 1970).

[19] In fact, Cameroun "exported" a relatively large number of highly qualified workers to other French-speaking African countries.

ing in other regions of French-speaking Africa. Everywhere, French colonial administration has been a major employer of labor, a key fixer of wage
rates, and the applier of all-encompassing labor laws.[20] The role played by
administrators in this regard has affected both the patterns of development
of local labor movements and the nature of the relations between private
employers and employees.

Labor unions have been particularly active in the public sector, notably
among teachers and railroad workers. As a result, these unions were most
anxious to obtain changes in the overall labor legislation and to obtain a
status comparable to that of their metropolitan counterparts.[21] Since the
actions of labor unions were as much political as economic, both labor and
managerial officials were anxious to establish close links with existing
political parties. In the Cameroun, as in other former French colonies,
cleavages among local labor unions paralleled metropolitan patterns, and
after 1947 one segment of the labor force joined the Socialist or the Christian-
dominated World Federations whereas the remainder remained attached to
the Communist-inspired *Confédération générale du travail.*

The politicization of labor unions had a number of consequences. As
already noted, bargaining strategies were rarely specific to a particular
place or branch of activity. In addition, participation in labor movements
was often a channel for a more direct political career, and there was close
interaction between political developments and labor agitation. Lastly, this
centralization has affected the role of unions after independence. President
Ahidjo decided in 1969 to oblige the existing unions to merge into a single
organization, the Union des travailleurs camerounais, closely controlled by
the party.[22] This merger is expected to facilitate the penetration of the
official ideology among differing segments of the labor force. It is also
expected to enable the government to give preeminence to *political* over
purely *economic* factors in its interventions in the economic field.

To conclude this section, three features of Camerounian political development have some bearing on this study of the modern labor force. First,
the political instability which has marked the past decade has slowed economic development and has exacerbated potential disparities between the
size of school outputs and the opportunities offered by the local labor

---

[20] For the first and third reasons, French colonial authorities resisted the adoption of laws
forbidding the practice of forced labor. Such laws were not passed until 1952. For a discus-
sion of the preindependence legal framework underlying the exercise of economic activities see
E. Berg "French West Africa" in Galenson, ed., *Labor and Economic Development.* Although
Berg's comments pertain to West Africa, many of his observations may be generalized to the
Camerounian scene.

[21] Thus, workers were interested in obtaining the same policies of family allowances as
those adopted in the Metropole. As a matter of fact, the adoption of such policies seem to
have facilitated the persistence of traditional patterns of familial behavior among the most
modernized segments of the African population.

[22] See LeVine, *Cameroun Federal Republic,* pp. 57-70.

market.[23] Second, this instability has given a new impetus to the traditional competition between certain ethnic groups. Finally, these centrifugal forces have strengthened the inclination of government to reinforce centralized patterns of administration. For example, the government exerts a tight control on labor policies or on the investment programs of foreigners, and it is able not only to limit the occurrence, frequency, and diffusion of strikes but also to select the entrepreneurs deemed to be desirable in the Cameroun. The notion of state socialism espoused by so many African nations today is particularly applicable to the Camerounian scene.[24]

Educational development

As already suggested, school enrollments vary markedly with the level of regional economic and social development and range from a minimum of 22 percent in the north up to 94 percent in the center-south.[25]

Three aspects of the Camerounian educational system are likely to affect the functioning of the local modern labor market. First, as in many other francophonic African countries, the postprimary system is divided into distinctive streams (academic and technical) and cycles (long and short).[26] Secondary students with differing academic experiences and occupational expectations should also have specific modes of adaptation to the labor market, notably in their job-seeking procedures and in their mobility within local occupational structures.[27]

Second, Camerounian schools are characterized by a high rate of attrition and wastage. As they enter the labor market, individuals differ not only in terms of their educational credentials but also in terms of the length of their educational career. Variations in the time needed to achieve a particular academic standard may influence orientations toward the modern labor market and more specifically, desires and abilities to enter a modern or a traditional occupation, to join a large- or small-scale enterprise, or to seek a manual or nonmanual job.[28]

---

[23] For an account of the most contemporary political development of the country, see Le Vine, *From Mandate to Independence,* chap. 7, and W. Johnson, *The Cameroun Federation,* chaps. 8, 11, and 14.

[24] For example, private firms are not allowed to individually search for the personnel they need. They are obliged to screen individuals from a pool of candidates presented to them by the Government Manpower Office.

[25] See *Evaluations et projetions démographiques,* p. 101.

[26] For a more elaborate description of this differentiation, see Clignet and Foster, *The Fortunate Few,* chap. 2.

[27] For an elaboration of variations in the occupational aspirations and expectations of individuals enrolled in different types of postprimary school, see ibid., chaps. 6 and 7.

[28] For a description of this wastage in the Cameroun, see "Camerounian Educational Planning Group," report drawn upon return of the first mission, March 10-May 20, 1962 (Paris: UNESCO, 1962), mimeo. See also H. M. Barga, *Problemes africains de l'éducation* (Paris: Hachette, 1962), p. 48.

Third, Camerounian educational institutions are characterized by diverse organizational patterns. As already noted, one of the legacies of the German heritage was the development of large religious missions. In the secondary sector, private enrollments have continuously increased in proportion to those in the public sector, and in 1970 students attending private institutions constituted two-thirds of the entire postprimary population.[29] The private sector is, in fact, divided unevenly into three types of schools differentially represented in the various regions of the country. Protestant schools, which absorb 9 percent of the private secondary population of the East Cameroun, are concentrated in the economically marginal eastern and northern regions; Catholic missions educate 44 percent of all private secondary pupils and are dispersed throughout various parts of the eastern state with the exception of the north. Finally, the largest segment of the private sector consists of privately owned institutions which are attended by no less than 47 percent of all private pupils and are concentrated in those parts of the country characterized by a high demand for schooling, that is, both in the large towns and in the Bamileke areas, for this people seems most anxious to compensate for their initial educational disadvantages.

The division of the Camerounian educational system into these various types of schools might be expected to exert conflicting influences on the labor market. First, employers and government do not necessarily accord the same value to credentials gained from different types of schooling. In addition, the relationships of public and private schools with businesses are different. The more centralized structure of public schools enables educational administrators to have more information about prevailing trends in the local labor market and to remain more independent of the pressures resulting from the rising aspirations of their student populations and their parents.[30] The networks used by the graduates of these various types of school in order to enter the modern economy are also probably different. Attendance in a private school often stimulates student solidarity and leads to the emergence of voluntary associations designed to cope with problems of employment.

Urbanization

The relative differentiation of local Camerounian elites and the limitations imposed on the traditional centralization policies pursued elsewhere by French colonial authorities have produced diffuse patterns of urbanization. The urban population is scattered among a variety of towns of varying

[29] See *Annuaire statistique 1970-1971* (Yaoundé, Ministere de l'éducation nationale services de la planification, de la documentation, et de l'orientation) part 1.

[30] This point is made by M. Blaug, who shows that in the Philippines, the large number of *private* institutions of higher learning is associated with a widening of variations in the quality of their teaching force, and hence with a lowering of the "fit" between school output and labor opportunities. See *Education and the Employment Problem,* p. 55.

[31] See *Evaluations et projections démographiques,* pp. 89-93.

size whose functions are highly distinctive. These major urban centers are Douala (250,000 inhabitants), Yaoundé (170,000), Nkongsamba (71,000), Baffoussam (55,000), and Foumbam (38,000).[31]

In this study, I am primarily concerned with four of these cities which were included within the survey from which the subsequent analyses are derived. They are Douala, Yaoundé, Nkongsamba, and Edea (23,000), and all have relatively high growth rates. Thus the population of Douala increased by 27 percent between 1965 and 1970. During the same period, the population of Yaoundé grew by 37 percent, that of Edea by 33 percent, and that of Nkongsamba by 55 percent. Because this growth is the result of migration, variations in the educational selectivity underlying such migration should affect the functioning of local labor markets. Among the adult residents of Douala, only 28 percent of the individuals who had arrived in town less than five years before the census of 1964 was taken were illiterate, as against 48 percent of the migrants with twenty or more years of urban residence.[32] More educated than their elders, younger waves of migrants should correspondingly exert greater pressure on the urban labor market. In addition, whereas 85 percent of the migrants who arrived in town before the age of fourteen and stayed there for a period of between five and ten years are at least able to read and write French, this is true of only two-thirds of their counterparts who arrived *after* their fourteenth birthday. In other words, early urban socialization is likely to raise occupational expectations.

However, the towns included in the survey differ from one another not only in terms of their size but also in their overall functions. Thus, Edea is primarily the locus of a hydroelectric dam and an aluminum-processing industry. Nkomgsamba is a trading center and railroad terminal.

It is, however, between Douala and Yaoundé that the most significant parellels and contrasts can be drawn. Yaoundé became the political capital of the Cameroun for two reasons. Europeans were convinced that the climate of the Yaoundé mountains was healthier than that of Douala. In addition, they were wary of the resistance that local Douala were able to muster against speculative deals involving the land necessary for the development of the city.[33] The local population of Yaoundé was apparently less aware of the implications of the policies that colonial authorities were eager to introduce, and its response was less effective than that of the Douala. The differential role played by local populations in the development of Douala and Yaoundé has had major consequences. Patterns of ecological differentiation are not the same in the two cities. The structure of Yaoundé is clearer and follows a pattern rather analogous to that found

---

[32] These data are derived from the analysis of the Douala 1964 census undertaken by R. Clignet and J. Sween.

[33] For a description of the political difficulties associated with land speculation, see D. Gardinier, "Political Behavior in the Community of Douala; Reactions of the Douala to the Loss of Hegemony" (Papers in International Studies, Ohio University, 1966), mimeo.

in the cities of industrialized nations.[34] In addition, whereas migrants tend to be concentrated in the central part of Yaoundé and are able to gain access to a large number of the most rewarding slots in the occupational structure, migrants to Douala are more frequently concentrated on the periphery of the city; they are also less likely to get their fair share of the opportunities offered by the labor market.[35]

Contrasts in the functions of the two cities are also associated with differences in the profile of their respective occupational structures. Thus, civil servants only represent 3 percent of the entire adult male and female population residing permanently in Douala, but 6 percent of the corresponding universe in Yaoundé. Alternatively, 20 percent of the permanent male residents of Douala are self-employed entrepreneurs (traders, artisans, farmers, and fishermen) as opposed to 13 percent of the males living permanently in Yaoundé. In addition, opportunities in the private modern sector have long been more numerous in Douala than in Yaoundé. The number and size of firms located in the former are greater than those of the capital city. Hence, the pressures exerted on the two local labor markets are not comparable. Yet insofar as "overurbanization" (that is, the relative disparity between the number of immigrants and the number of openings in the labor market) takes the same form in these two cities, local populations suffer from identical unemployment problems. About 13 percent of the adult male permanent population is classified as unemployed in Douala, but the corresponding figure is 20 percent in Yaoundé.[36]

To sum up this section, the differential size and complexity of the Camerounian cities should be associated with contrasts in the development of their respective labor markets and hence in the variety and number of job openings as well as in the opportunities for mobility. In addition, variations in the size and complexity of Camerounian cities should also be associated with corresponding differences in the work conditions and salaries of their labor forces.

A profile of the Camerounian economy

The Camerounian economy is still primarily oriented toward subsistence activities. By 1963, 84 percent of the local labor force was still engaged in agricultural activities, and this accounted partly for the low annual growth rate of the gross national product (1.1 percent as opposed to almost 5

---

[34] See Clignet and Jordan, "Urbanization and Social Differentiation."

[35] Hence I suggest here that variations in the spatial location of immigrating urban residents are associated with parallel contrasts in their modes of adjustment to an urban life style.

[36] For an overall perspective of the problems associated with urban development in the Cameroun, see B. Biyong, "La Croissance urbaine en Afrique noire et à Madagascar: L'Example du Cameroun," R. Nze Nguele, "Problemes démographiques de la croissance urbaine à Yaoundé " and A. Franqueville, "Les immigrés du quartier de la Briquetterie," in La Croissance urbaine en Afrique noire et a Madagascar (Paris: Editions du CNRS, Colloques internationaux du CNRS, 1972).

percent for the Ivory Coast). In U.S. dollars, the gross national product per capita inceased from 92 by 1958 to 142 by 1967.[37] Of course, the slow development of the Camerounian economy has also resulted from the political difficulties experienced by the country during the last two decades and from the ensuing inability of government to improve the basic economic infrastructure. By 1965, there were only 22 miles of improved roads per million square feet of surface area, as opposed to 65 in the Ivory Coast. Similarly, there were only 177 miles of railroad track per 100,000 square miles as opposed to 321 in the Ivory Coast.

As a result, the salaried population employed both by government and private modern concerns remains limited. In 1960, wage earners of the modern sector represented only 7 percent of all active adults between twenty and fifty-five years of age, and in 1970 the corresponding figure had increased to 21 percent. This modern labor force participates in many distinctive branches of activity, the characteristics of which are summarized in Table 3.

As in other developing nations, the Camerounian tertiary sector (insurance, banks, commercial import/export, transport, and services) is particularly important, for it absorbs 30 percent of the full-time salaried African population and pays no less than 43 percent of all wages and benefits distributed by modern enterprises. Of course, these figures reflect the important contribution of this sector to the Camerounian economy as a whole, for its financial turnover constitutes 57 percent of all the financial activities of modern enterprises in the country. As this type of activity develops, there is a parallel increase in the number of individual firms as well as an accentuated differentiation of their respective profiles.[38]

This sector is divided into four branches of activity with differing profiles. First, the twenty-seven banks and insurance companies (whose development in the Cameroun is relatively recent) employ 1,249 workers, 83 percent of whom are African. These particular concerns have adopted a high wage policy, and although their workers represent only 6 percent of the labor force used by the tertiary sector, they earn almost 10 percent of the salaries distributed.

Second, the sixty-six firms engaged in various forms of transportation (road, railroad, ships, handling, and so forth) absorb 7,500 workers (93 percent of whom are Africans) or 36 percent of the entire population present in tertiary activities. As the earnings of these workers represent 38 percent of the wages paid by the entire tertiary sector, the personnel policies of these enterprises do not seem to be as generous as those adopted by banks and insurance concerns. There are, however, significant differences

---

[37] These date are derived from Mitchell, *Black Africa.*

[38] All the following information is derived from *Recensement général des entreprises industrielles et commerciales de type moderne exerçant leur activité au Cameroun;* for primary and secondary sectors, the information pertains to the years 1967-1968 and for the tertiary sector to the years 1965-1966.

TABLE 3

Labor Force and Economic Profile of the Various Branches of Activity
in the Cameroun

	No. of firms	Avg. no. workers	Pctage. labor force	Avg. salary	Pctage. salaries	Pctage. Financial turnover
Agriculture	107	204	33.4	103	13.0	5.5
Mining	7	50	0.5	258	0.5	0.2
Food and chemicals	95	82	11.5	222	10.0	14.5
Mechanics and metallurgy	72	66	7.3	473	13.0	11.1
Public works and construction	74	149	16.9	200	12.8	7.5
Energy and water	4	257	1.8	342	2.3	2.4
Banks and insurance	27	46	2.0	647	5.0	2.2
Transport	66	114	11.4	420	18.0	7.8
Service	106	18	3.0	275	3.1	3.6
Commerce import/export	493	17	12.2	485	22.3	45.4
N or total value	1,049	62	100.0	265[a]	100.0[b]	100.0[b]

Source: Recensement général des entreprises industrielles et commerciales de type moderne exerçant leur activité au Cameroun; secteur tertiaire exercice, 1965-1966. (Yaoundé: Direction de la statistique, Table 15).

[a]Expressed in thousands CFA.

[b]Expressed in millions CFA.

between the practices of the state-owned railroad company (which is the largest employer of this branch) and those used by other enterprises.

Third, the "services" branch includes (a) teaching or research institutions, (b) advertising and public relations concerns, and (c) recreational enterprises. In addition, this sector also comprises art studios, restaurants, and hotels as well as barbershops, dry cleaning operations, and so forth. The 106 distinct businesses entered in this particular branch are usually small and absorb almost 2,000 workers, of whom almost 99 percent are African.

Finally, the 493 commercial firms specialize in the internal and external trade of the Cameroun and are highly differentiated. The traditional large-scale import/export companies such as Société commerciale de l'Ouest africain (SCOA) or Compagnie francaise de l'Afrique occidentale (CFAO), which absorb almost 14 percent of the 8,000 workers employed in this branch, pay lower salaries than oil importers. Thus, the average salary paid by the entire commercial branch approximates to 500,000 CFA a year, as compared with 843,000 CFA a year in the case of oil importers.

At the other end of the continuum, the primary sector represents 107 firms engaged in agriculture, cattle raising, fisheries, and timber. There are four major activities in the field of agriculture per se. By 1964, there were 35 distinct *coffee* plantations, employing over 3,000 wage earners and reaching an overall yearly output of 38,000 tons. This particular subgroup was and is still characterized by marked variations in the organization and the productivity of individual firms. The large-scale plantations created before World War II are to be contrasted with smaller enterprises run by individual Africans or experimental state-controlled units. By 1964, there were also sixteen *banana* plantations employing a little under 5,000 individuals and reaching an overall output of 52,000 tons. The largest of these plantations is located in the littoral area and is included in the survey from which my subsequent analyses are derived. In short, this particular branch is technically and financially more concentrated than the coffee plantations. The same features characterize the *rubber* plantations, recently developed in the country: the two companies engaged in this particular field employ about 5,000 wage earners and have reached an overall annual output of 4,200 tons of rubber. The last major product of plantations, *cocoa,* is grown almost exclusively by small-scale African farmers, who do not have a formal organization which enables us to classify them as "modern."

The presence of mountainous areas in the Cameroun has led to the development of cattle ranching. There are five firms involved in this activity, the most important of which is La Pastorale, which is characterized by a broad range of activities as it is engaged in both raising of cattle and meat processing.

On the coast, there are three fishing companies employing less than 2,000 African workers and aiming at a more systematic commercialization of ocean products. One of these is shrimp, which the Cameroun exports for canning purposes.

Finally, the timber industry remains one of the major sources of wealth. Indeed, forests cover over 60 percent of the Cameroun, and the major areas of exploitation are concentrated in the southern regions of the nation, with an annual output of 360,000 cubic meters. As in the case of coffee plantations, the organization and the productivity of these firms are quite diverse. Some of them are small-scale enterprises exhibiting a low level of technological development, but others have experienced a certain amount of vertical integration, as they are engaged in both timber cutting and in the subsequent manufacturing operations including the production of furniture.

To summarize, although 86 percent of the workers employed in primary branches of activity are Africans, these individuals receive only half of the salaries paid by the entire sector. This reflects marked disparities between the skill levels of expatriate and local workers who tend to be concentrated at the bottom of the occupational hierarchy.

Finally, the secondary sector of the economy has been long enough underdeveloped. The philosophy of the "Colonial Pact" stressed the importance of enhancing the profits of metropolitan industries by maximizing the exports of raw products from the colonies and increasing their imports of finished products from the Metropole. It was only in the early fifties that significant changes took place. First, European settlers had accumulated enough capital to organize activities able to compete with metropolitan firms in the exploitation of the African market. In addition, metropolitan governments began to perceive that their colonial policies constituted greater liabilities than assets.[39] Currently, the secondary sector in the Cameroun includes 309 firms whose activities are directed toward both internal and external markets.

A first group of secondary industries is involved in the development of the economic infrastructure, and is thus largely engaged in construction activities. It includes eighty-six concerns, with very heterogeneous profiles. At one end of the continuum, the large-scale public works enterprises are characterized by a high degree of technological development and financial concentration. Firms of this sort operating in the Cameroun are few in number and use a small, usually unskilled, African labor force. At the other end of the continuum, many construction firms take advantage of the ever-increasing demand for urban housing, retain a diversified organizational profile, and rely on a relatively numerous African labor force spread out among the various rungs of the hierarchy. Altogether, this group of industries employs 14,000 wage earners. This first group does not follow high wage policies. Although local workers represent no less than 94 percent of the entire labor force of this group, they receive only one-half of the salaries and benefits paid by this branch.

A second group of industries, engaged in mechanical and metallurgical work, includes firms specializing in the maintenance and repair of transport vehicles (there are 400 commercial vehicles per 100,000 inhabitants in the Cameroun) and of electrical hardware. They absorb 27 percent of the labor force in this particular branch. But this group also consists of heavy industries involved in the processing of aluminum and the construction of railroads, river barges, and seagoing vessels, which absorb almost three-quarters of the labor force used by this sector. No less than 93 percent of the 8,338 workers employed by the eighty-two firms in this second group are Africans who receive about 65 percent of the salaries and wages paid by this class of industry. As differences between the proportion of African workers in the overall labor force and the proportion of salaries these workers receive are relatively limited in magnitude, one can infer that this local labor force occupies relatively skilled positions and is rewarded proportionately.

---

[39] Changes in such views were also induced by the protests of African political leaders and notably Leopold Sedhar Senghor, who was obliged to use pressure to enable the construction of a flour mill in Senegal, a move to which metropolitan industrialists were bitterly opposed.

The last group of industries in the secondary sctor is involved in the processing of the raw materials produced by local agriculture (coffee, cocoa, tobacco, timber, cotton) or of finished products needed in the local market (bakeries, for example). The 141 concerns in this particular subsector have varying size and complexity. As could be expected, the largest segment of the labor force employed by these firms is concentrated in the textile, garment, and leather industries, which absorb no less than 34 percent of the workers in this particular group. Although 93 percent of wage earners in these processing activities are African, they receive less than 50 percent of the salaries distributed by this particular branch. The low status of these African workers seems to be akin to that of their counterparts in construction and public works.

In short, there are marked cleavages in the organizational profiles and hence in the wage policies of Camerounian enterprises, both *among* and *within* branches of activity. This is in part because firms do not establish the same type of relations with industrialized countries. Some branches of activity are still dominated by the philosophy of the colonial pact and are involved in the export of raw materials, the import of finished products, or in both; as they only need unskilled laborers, their behavior in the labor market is conditioned by the overall scarcity of workers available.

Conversely, other branches of activity are influenced by the "pacte metropolitain,"[40] and although their activities are correspondingly shielded from outside competition in the local or in the French metropolitan markets, their profits are still more dependent on the skill level of their labor force. Accordingly, their behavior in the labor market is affected by the scarcity of skilled job seekers. Their personnel policies are more differentiated, for they have a wider range of choices in the relationship between labor and capital. Some enterprises prefer to use labor-extensive technologies, but others are more likely to import from highly industrialized countries capital-intensive machinery and equipment.[41]

In more general terms, the profile of the emerging Camerounian labor market presents the same traits as those characterizing other new nations. First, an early diffusion of formal schooling erodes progressively the differential growth patterns of white- and blue-collar labor forces.[42] Second, particular political and economic factors have influenced the patterns of differentiation prevailing in the dominant sectors of activity. In the Cameroun as in other new nations, the growth of a tertiary sector is simultaneous and not consecutive to the development of primary and secondary activities. Third, local economic development and migrations do

---

[40] See Berg, "French West Africa."

[41] As indicated in the introduction, there is no reason to doubt that Cameroun is confronted with the same problem along these lines as a country like Kenya. See ILO, *Employment, Equality, and Income.*

[42] R. Dore sees these traits as characteristic of a "late development" effect; they tend indeed to prevail not only in Africa but also in South America (personal communication).

not result from a uniform increase in agricultural productivity. In fact, although the profits derived from agriculture result from the cultivation of new crops, the yields and returns from traditional plantations have not substantially increased.[43] Finally, variations in the dates at which firms have begun their operations in the Cameroun are associated with differences in the technology they use and in the personnel policies they practice. Older firms were created during the era of forced labor and have not been necessarily anxious, at least initially, to use a complex technology. The choices open to their counterparts who arrived after independence are much wider, and variations in the use of capital-intensive techniques should be associated with parallel contrasts in the relative commitment of workers as well as in the rewards they are able to gain from their employers.

The Sample

Like other new African governments, the Camerounian authorities have been concerned with the consequences of educational development and more specifically with the growing disparities between the volume of educational output and the current demands of the labor market. Because of this concern, in 1964 the government attempted an evaluation of the manpower needs of industry. This evaluation involved an assessment of the educational and occupational profile of wage earners currently employed by modern firms. In this section, I examine and summarize the sampling interviewing, and coding procedures developed in the design of the original survey. I also indicate how the data were organized for the purposes of the present study.

Sampling procedures.

First, the Camerounian authorities decided to limit the geographic scope of their study to the labor force of enterprises located in the littoral area or in the city of Yaoundé (see Map 1). It is in these parts of the country that the most significant components of the modern sector of the economy are concentrated. To give an example, in 1965, two-thirds of the 18,613 workers employed by modern enterprises in the tertiary sector lived in Douala and 17 percent of them resided in Yaoundé.[44] In addition, 73 percent of the salaries distributed by such enterprises was earned in Douala, and an additional 15 percent was earned in the capital city. Finally, no less than 55 percent of the gross income generated by such concerns was earned in Douala, while the

---

[43] Hoselitz, in *Sociological Aspects of Economic Growth,* underlines the significance of contrasts in the trajectories of development followed by countries whose growth results from an expansion of existing activities and those whose growh is the result of the development of new crops or new ores.

[44] See *Recensement général des entreprises de type moderne: Secteur tertiaire exercice, 1965-1966,* pp. 23-24.

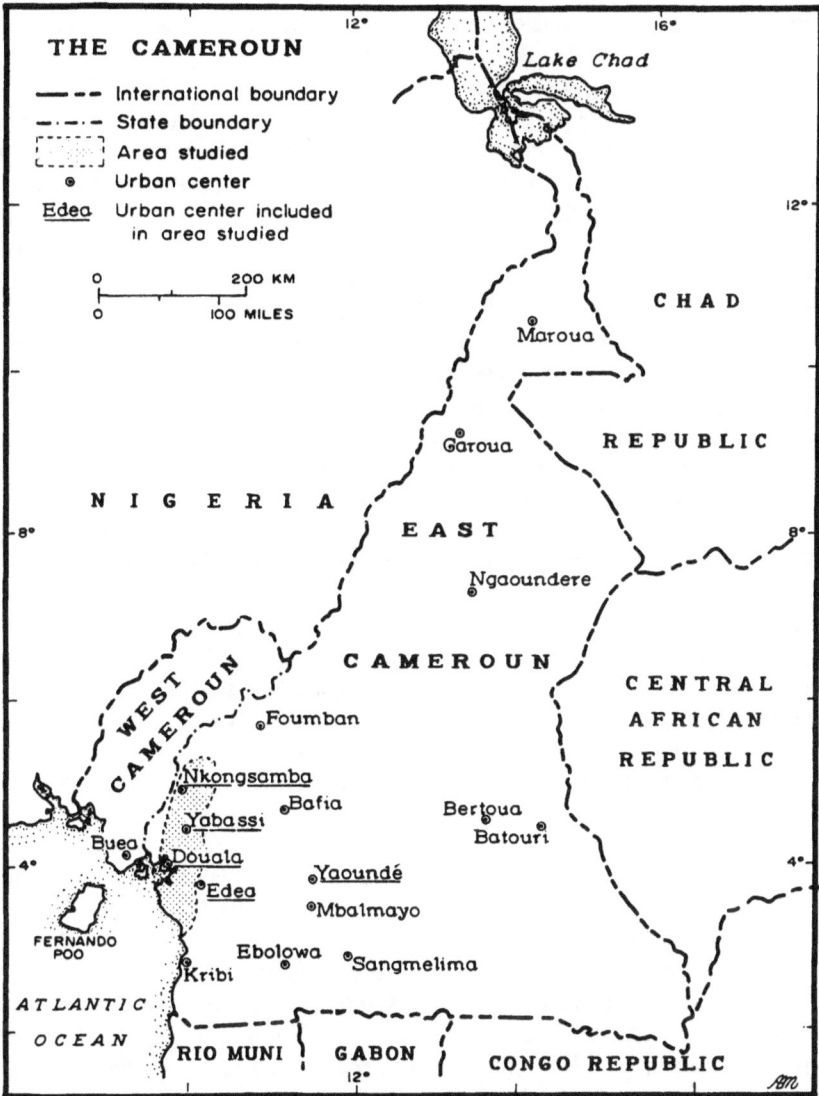

THE CAMEROUN

- – – International boundary
- – · – State boundary
- Area studied
- ⊙ Urban center
- Edea Urban center included
  in area studied

0   200 KM
0   100 MILES

Lake Chad

CHAD

Maroua

Garoua

REPUBLIC

NIGERIA

EAST

Ngaoundere

CAMEROUN

CENTRAL
AFRICAN
REPUBLIC

WEST CAMEROUN

Foumban

Nkongsamba

Bafia

Bertoua
Batouri

Yabassi

Buea

Douala

Yaoundé

Edea

Mbalmayo

FERNANDO
POO

Ebolowa   Sangmelima

Kribi

ATLANTIC

OCEAN

RIO MUNI   GABON   CONGO REPUBLIC

corresponding share for Yaoundé was one-fourth. In brief, an evaluation of those economic activities in the most developed parts of Eastern Cameroun should provide a reasonable image of the problems encountered by the modern firms in the country as a whole.

Second, the scope of the study was restricted, and thus all private concerns belonging to the service branch (that is, restaurants and hotels, private clinics, art studios, cinemas, management consultant firms, and advertising or public relations firms) were eliminated from it. For the same reasons all road transport enterprises were eliminated from the sample.

Finally, the government did not include in its sample the various services in public administration (ministries and regional offices).

Third, sampling procedures involved a selection of both firms and individual workers. The universe of the firms included in the study was derived from a listing prepared by the government after a census of industrial activites was undertaken in 1964. This listing included all firms that systematically followed the accounting procedures developed by the French *plan comptable*. Those procedures were designed to harmonize the systems of public and private accounting and thus to facilitate an accurate estimate of the economic profile of the society as a whole. Firms were then divided into two groups: all concerns with ten workers or more were included in the study; concerns with fewer than ten workers were selected according to a system of floating sampling ratios. Thus the chances of an enterprise being included in the study varied both as a function of its size (chances would be greater for concerns with nine workers than for those with two wage earners) and as a function of the size of the firms already chosen. The sampling ratios each differed for enterprises located in Douala, Yaoundé, Edea, and finally in the Mungo, the Ntam, and the Wouri.

It was decided that the labor survey interviewers should correct the listing initially established by the government, adding firms not included in the original document and subtracting those that had ceased to exist in the meantime. However, the final sample included certain organizations (particularly in the primary and tertiary sectors of the economy) which did not necessarily meet the criteria of "modernity" as defined by the authorities.

The sampling of individual workers followed simpler rules. It was decided to interview *all* wage earners with at least some minimal qualifications. Among their unskilled counterparts, the ratios varied between one-tenth of those in agricultural enterprises and one-fifth of those employed by construction and public work concerns.[45]

The exact representativeness of the sample of wage earners studied here remains difficult to ascertain with accuracy. This reflects the uncertainties surrounding the definition of both modern firms and of permanent wage earners.[46] It also reflects short-term changes in the sheer enumeration of both individual enterprises and their labor forces. In fact, the study led to the identification of 44,760 individuals associated in one capacity or the other with the concerns studied here. If one considers as adequate the definition of the full universe as given in one particular government document of 1965 which indicates a total of 53,358 workers in East

[45] All the preceding information is derived both from the written instructions to interviewers and supervisors and from verbal communications between R. Clignet and J. Chaumont.

[46] For an illustration of the difficulties encountered in defining a permanent male salaried worker, see the section "Ethnic Selectivity" later in this chapter for the categories of workers eliminated from my subsequent analysis.

Cameroun, one can infer that the survey involves 70 percent of the relevant population for the East Cameroun *in toto* and 90 percent of that in the particular region considered in the study.[47] However, if one takes the figures provided in another source (121,400), the population interviewed represents only 36 percent of the relevant universe for East Cameroun and 46 percent for the subregions chosen.[48] In other words, the conditions under which the results are generalizable remain difficult to assess with any certainty.

Interviewing procedures.

The administration of the survey was effected by the Direction de la statistique et des études économiques du gouvernement camerounais. The design of the procedures and of the questionnaire was the responsibility of Jean Chaumont, technical adviser attached to the bureau, and the fieldwork itself was controlled by Pierre Le Boulanger, a graduate student in economics at the University of Yaoundé. He was assisted by a number of supervisors, whose job was to exert direct control over the work performed by the Camerounian interviewers who were regular employees of the Direction de la statistique, and who had received special training before the survey in order to increase the reliability of the information collected. In addition, interviewers were provided with a set of instructions defining the sequential order of the operations to be performed in the context of the study.

The data to be collected were divided into two parts. The first pertained to a definition of each production unit examined and was gathered by supervisors. The responsibility of supervisors was (a) to ascertain whether the concern located could be legitimately included in the scope of the study, (b) to define the number and characteristics of the workers to be interviewed, (c) to identify the legal, financial, and technical nature of the concern itself, and finally (d) to collect information concerning the principles governing payment of wages and salaries in the period of employment preceding the survey.[49]

The second type of data was collected from individual workers themselves and pertained to their social background (age and ethnic origin), educational experience (amount of formal schooling, type of formal and informal vocational training undergone, and so forth), and their occupational life history (first and second job learned, occupation performed prior to present employment, time spent on the job and in the firm, charateristics of the task currently performed, and so forth).

[47] See *Recensement général des entreprises de type moderne: Secteur tertiaire exercice 1965-1966,* table 19.

[48] See *Développement industriel du Cameroun, rapport préliminaire 1964-1965,* part 1 (Paris: SEDES, undated), p. 12.

[49] This is because of the complexity of the principles used in the computation of individual paychecks. See chap. 6, this study.

The survey took place between the months of April 1964 and March 1965. Variations in the dates at which the survey took place are of significance insofar as they could introduce uncontrolled differences in the relative level of activity of the firms studies and, more specifically, in the amount of overtime hours performed by individuals as well as in their pay. Indeed, the dependence of the Camerounian economy on agriculture makes it subject to seasonal variations, with the overall level of activity being maximal in the period following the cropping of export products such as coffee and cocoa.

The Coding procedures.

The initial coding was undertaken in Yaoundé by the Direction de la statistique. This involved an elimination of coding errors as well as of inconsistencies in the data. For example, all the records which indicated a high level of qualification in the operations performed by the respondent and yet a low skill level were neutralized, that is, they were transformed into "no answer" or "indeterminate" on these two items.

The second step was performed in Evanston at the Computing Center of Northwestern University. It involved the following operations:

1. Elimination from the sample of European workers (N = 2,301), African female wage earners (N = 1,348), African seasonal and occasional workers (N = 1,092), Africans paid on terms other than wages or salaries (N = 221), and finally African wage earners whose ages were not ascertained (N = 3,748). To keep in the sample heterogeneous populations would have reduced the validity of the analysis. A final number of 36,281 persons was ultimately retained

2. Transcription on the records of firms' aggregate information regarding the characteristics of their labor force.[50] The model assumes that individual behavior is not independent of the organizational context in which it takes place.

3. Transformation of existing data. In the initial coding, the Camerounian authorities had been anxious to retain the 900 job positions as defined by the International Labor Organization. I decided to reduce such positions to 26 categories and to reduce the classification of branches of activity from over 400 to 12 distinct subcategories. Similarly, I translated data regarding salaries by reference to a standardized hourly rate, and this translation required some adjustment, for the relationship between number of hours performed and the number of hours remunerated differs among categories of personnel.

---

[50] As the minimal aggregation unit was the production unit (that is, each workshop, bureau, office, store, warehouse, and so forth with a distinct location), I was obliged to regroup these production units to obtain the overall profile of a firm. When these production units were engaged in distinct operations, I was confronted with the problem of determining the dominant activity of the entire firm. I decided to define the dominant activity as that type of work performed by the production unit with the largest number of workers.

4. Creation of new data. I took advantage of information existing about first and second jobs learned on the one hand and present job on the other to devise an index of occupational mobility. Similarly, I tried to translate the variety of educational and vocational experiences undergone by workers into an ordinal scale—an operation necessary for undertaking any form of multiple regression analysis.

5. A new transformation of the data so obtained in view of their treatment by multiple regression analysis. This entailed both the elimination of the "no-answer" records on variables deemed crucial and the transformation of the ethnic nominal scales, for example, into dummy variables.

Overall Characteristics of the Sampled Population

In examining the profile of the workers included in the sample, my major purpose is to assess the selectivity underlying patterns of recruitment into the modern sector of the economy considered as a whole.

The number of manual wage earners sampled is much larger than that of white-collar workers, and reflects the absorption of a large number of unskilled laborers by agricultural and other primary concerns (Table 4). Further, there are also marked cleavages in the hierarchical profile of these two sectors of employment. Only a trickle of African individuals is engaged in managerial and executive roles, and very few of them enter the labor market as highly skilled technicians. In other words, the differential nature of manual and nonmanual work implies parallel contrasts in the hierarchical profile of the two categories of workers. Although access to the very top of the nonmanual hierarchy is probably restricted, the majority of blue-collar workers are unskilled. Hence, there should also be differences between the *determinants* of upward mobility within blue- and white-collar jobs as well as in the *rewards* attached to such experiences.

Further, the distribution of individual workers among the various branches of activity surveyed is the same both in the sample and in the population at large (Table 5). This comparison enhances the confidence one may have in the reliability of the results of the study as well as confirms the skewed character of the distribution of workers across sectors of the economy. For the time being, the primary sector is the major employer in the modern Camerounian economy.

As the task is to identify the mechanisms underlying the functioning of the local labor market, the first step of the analysis involves a comparison of the patterns of access into the various parts of the entire labor force. Although we are mostly interested in the process of internal differentiation of the private modern labor market, it remains necessary to examine how wage earners employed by private and semipublic concerns differ from self-employed entrepreneurs or from individuals participating in government agencies. Contrasts between public, private, and "murky" sectors may be *ascriptive,*

TABLE 4
Summary of Modern Occupations in the Sample
(percentage distribution)

Nonmanual	N	Percent
1. Managerial and executive (engineers, administrators)	239	0.7
2. Technical specialists (lab technicians, draftsmen, specialized accountants)	428	1.2
3. Clerical workers (typists, bookkeepers, salesmen, storekeepers)	4,750	13.1
4. Unskilled nonmanual workers	381	1.1
	5,798	16.1

Manual	N	Percent
5. Skilled manual (woodworkers, construction mechanics, metalworkers, butchers, bakers, tailors, mobile machine operators)	8,978	24.7
6. Semiskilled (machine operators, seamen and fishermen, forestry and agricultural specialists, other)	8,340	23.0
7. Unskilled laborers	12,420	34.2
8. Other	7	--
9. No answer	738	2.0
	30,483	83.9
Total	36,281	100.0

and I will examine the representation of distinctive ethnic or age groups in these three sectors within the cities or regions where the firms are located. These contrasts might be also *achievement* based, and accordingly I will examine whether populations participating in the modern private labor force have a level of formal schooling or a set of migratory experiences different from the corresponding characteristics of other occupational groups in the society at large.

1. Ethnic selectivity. In preceding pages, I have asserted that contrasts in the initial cultural patterns of Camerounian peoples and in their relative involvement in modernizing processes should be associated with parallel differences in their modes of participation in economic activities. Table 6 suggests that the majority of workers employed by modern firms come from a Bamileke, Bassa and Beti ethnic origin. In view of the geographic dispersion of the firms surveyed, it is quite difficult to determine whether

TABLE 5
Broad Industrial Categories in Both Sampled Firms and in the Whole of the Modern Sector (percentage distribution)

	Sample		Universe[a]	
	N	Percent	N	Percent
1. Agriculture, forestry, fishing, mining	11,598	32.0	21,775	35.5
2. General manufacturing	8,360	23.0	12,478	20.5
3. Construction and public works	8,180	2.5	10,521	17.3
4. Transport and utilities	3,444	9.5	8,088	13.3
5. Banks and commerce	4,626	12.8	7.856	13.4
6. Undetermined	73	0.2	--	--
	36,281	100.0	60,718	100.0

[a]Source: Recensement général des enterprises, Table 15.

these groups are overrepresented and obtain a larger share of the jobs offered by the private modern labor market than what one could infer from their proportion in the population at large. Nor is it possible to determine whether these groups have had similar migratory experiences.

For these reasons, it is relevant to compare the ethnic profile of the wage earners employed in Douala and Yaoundé by public and private concerns and of self-employed individuals in the so-called murky sector of these two cities.[51] As Douala is an older city which serves a larger number of functions, its population is ethnically more diverse than that of Yaoundé. Further, in Yaoundé, the Beti (the peoples originating from the adjacent hinterland) participate evenly in the three major sectors of activity, and they represent a little less than one-half of the three corresponding populations. In contrast, in Douala, the local people, the Douala, are proportionately more numerous in the public and the murky sector than in the private sector.

Thus, in the Cameroun as in other developing nations, individuals who originate from the focal points of modernization and hence from the places where patterns of economic development and differentiation are most clearly established, are not necessarily overrepresented in the private modern sector of the economy. Although the populations of developing countries often tend to prefer self-employment or participation in the public sector to the status of wage earner in a modern firm, they do not actually enjoy similar occupational choices. Indeed, the persistence of particularistic orientations in local political structures enables individuals born in urban areas to have privileged access to

---

[51] In the following tables, I give data about household heads. I am aware of the biases so introduced in my evaluation of the three sectors of employment. In fact, the gainfully employed population of household heads represents about 87 percent of the overall gainfully employed population of the two cities.

TABLE 6
Ethnic Composition of the Sampled Labor Force and the Male Population of Yaoundé, Douala, and the Littoral Region
(percentage distribution)

	Sampled labor force	Yaoundé[a] Sectors of Activity			Douala[a] Sectors of Activity			Centre-Sud[b]
		Public	Private	Traditional	Public	Private	Traditional	
Beti-Fang	18.9	46.3	48.1	44.0	25.2	8.8	7.9	56.2
Bamileke	32.8	13.7	20.3	29.4	15.7	39.4	39.4	51.5
Mbam	8.3	7.8	7.2	5.8	6.9	7.8	4.9	29.2
Bassa	22.5	8.5	7.9	4.7	16.2	17.1	14.9	10.4
Douala	8.6	4.1	2.6	1.4	22.6	13.3	19.8	1.1
Northerners	1.6	13.1	7.9	10.9	8.6	6.4	7.4	0.0
Other East Camerounian	1.4	2.8	2.5	1.2	2.4	1.1	0.3	1.2
Foreigners (including West Camerounians)	5.0	2.8	2.3	1.5	2.1	4.3	5.2	0.4
Unknown	0.9	0.9	1.2	1.0	0.3	1.8	1.2	0.0
Total	100.0	100.0	100.0	100.0	100.0	100.0	100.0	100.0

[a]Raw census materials. Analysis of the male household heads permanent residents by R. Clignet and J. Sween.

[b]*Enquête démographique au Cameroun: Résultats définitifs pour la région sud-est, 1962-1964*, p. 21.

the civil service. In addition, these individuals have also a privileged access to the social and economic networks necessary for the perpetuation of self-employed activities.

Although one could infer from this observation that urban migrants are most frequently employed as wage earners in the public or private sectors of the economy, the effects of migration on employment vary along ethnic lines. Migrants from the most modernized groups (the Douala and the Beti-Fang), tend to be more often employed in the public sector of the economy. Conversely, among peoples with a marginal involvement in modernizing structures, such as the Bamileke, migrants are most often self-employed but least likely to participate in government services.

The relationship between migration and employment is also changing *within* particular ethnic groups. For example, time lags in the relative growth of the two major Camerounian cities are associated with contrasts in the occupational destination of those Bamileke who have migrated to Douala and those who have moved to Yaoundé. The Bamileke migrants attracted to Douala are proportionately more numerous in the private modern sector of the economy than their counterparts living in Yaoundé.

To sum up, the occupation of active adults is first influenced by whether or not they have migrated. Among migrants themselves, occupation is influenced by the overall volume of individuals of the same ethnic origin, by the distance between their places of origin and of destination, by the length of time during which the place of origin has acted as a feeder of the place of destination, and finally by the relative degree of modernization of the area from which these individuals come.

2. Age selectivity. The age characteristics of the modern labor force should be influenced both by the mechanisms underlying migration patterns and by the relative growth rate of the local economy. Two competing hypotheses may account for differences in the age profile of the labor force engaged in the three major sectors of the economy. Because economic development is both recent and localized in the largest cities modern public and private activities should attract younger urban migrants than the remaining sector of the economy. Alternatively disparities between the growth of the modern labor market and of migration may enable older individuals with more urban experience to preempt the opportunities offered by modern public and private enterprises. In fact, the age distributions of sampled workers and of urban household heads employed by private firms are alike (Table 7). In addition, individuals employed by public bureaucracies tend to be older, and this reflects the particular forms of geographic and occupational mobility operating in the civil service. Because of the centralized nature of Camerounian administrative structures, the most rewarding slots of the hierarchy, which are located in the largest cities, tend to be preempted by older individuals, who have a maximal seniority. In this sense, the data support the second assumption. However, self-employed individuals are more often concentrated at the lower and upper ends of the age continuum than their counterparts

TABLE 7
Age Composition of the Labor Force and the Male Population of
Yaoundé, Douala, and the Littoral Region
(percentages)

| Age Group | Sampled labor force | Urban sectors of employment | | | Littoral[a] |
		Public	Private	Self-employment	
15-25	17.8	8.1	12.9	15.6	28.2
26-34	43.3	42.3	45.5	28.7	28.8
35 and above	38.9	49.6	41.6	55.7	43.0
Total	100.0	100.0	100.0	100.0	100.0
N	36,281	3,702	25,936	17,551	(not available)

[a]*Source: Evaluations et projections démographiques en République Fédérale du Cameroun (May, 1970), p. 76.*

employed by private firms. The proportion of younger individuals is lower among private wage earners than artisans, farmers, or traders because of disparities in the growth rates of urban populations and of the local economy. The ever-increasing pressures exerted on the private sector lead a growing number of young urban migrants to accept employment in the murky sector. At the other end of the age continuum, older self-employed individuals are also proportionately more numerous than wage earners because Camerounian migrants continue to view modern employment as a "target" and hence as a temporary experience. After having been initially employed in modern concerns, many of these migrants probably shift back to more traditional forms of economic activity.[52]

In the Cameroun as in many new nations, variations in the relationship between occupational status and age seem to reflect both changes in the characteristics of the society at large and contrasts in the positions that individuals occupy in their own life cycles. High rates of educational and urban development blur the effects of aging on the occupational trajectory of individual migrants.

3. Educational selectivity. The differential requirements and attractiveness of the tasks characteristic of the three sectors of employment are associated with significant contrasts in the educational attainment of their

[52] For a discussion of the shifts back and forth between murky and wage-earner sectors of employment, see A. Lux, "The Network of Visits between Yombe Rural Wage Earners and Their Kinsfolk in Western Congo," *Africa* 61(1971):106-128. The author shows that 13 percent of individuals interviewed begin their lives as farmers, shift to wage-earning activities, to return ultimately to their initial farming role. Although 19 percent begin their active life as wage earners and become agriculturalists later on, 24 percent follow the opposite path. Over 30 percent have spent their entire life in the wage-earning sector, and 15 percent participate simultaneously in the two types of activity.

respective populations. Both the relatively high rank of individuals employed by urban public bureaucracies and the rigidity of the educational prerequisites for gaining access to civil service account for the high proportion of the individuals employed in the urban public sector who have at least completed their primary schooling. Indeed male adults with this level of attainment are almost three times as numerous in this sector as they are in the two other types of economic activity (Table 8).

Furthermore, populations employed in the modern private sector have less diverse levels of education than their counterparts in the murky sector. To be sure, participation in modern private firms requires individuals to have the ability of communicating in French, a condition which is of less importance in the case of traders and artisans. Thus, the proportion of individuals unable to speak French is twice as high in the murky than in the private sector. At the same time, however, the particular patterns of educational and political development prevailing in the Cameroun have also facilitated the emergence of a class of modern entrepreneurs, who tend to have a higher level of schooling than wage earners in modern private firms.

Finally, although the percentage of individuals who have at least completed primary schooling is alike in the sample and in the urban private labor force, differences do emerge at the lower end of the educational continuum. The sample includes a large number of unskilled laborers employed by agricultural and mining concerns operating in the hinterland, but such branches of activity are absent in urban areas. As a result, the proportion of individuals unable to speak French is twice as high in the sample as in the census of Douala and Yaoundé.

To sum up, these data reveal the differential value that educated African adults attach to distinctive types of employment. The importance they accord to occupational security leads them to rank participation in public services above all other possible occupational outlets.[53] Further, the importance they attach to autonomy induces a number of these educated individuals to prefer the ownership of an economic enterprise to the status of highly skilled cadre in a private foreign-owned company. Yet as educational development proceeds and as the pressures exerted on the various sectors of employment grow in proportion, there are changes in the relative attraction exerted by these differing types of activity and hence in the educational profile of their respective populations.[54]

---

[53] For a discussion of the occupational aspirations of students, see Clignet and Foster, *The Fortunate Few*, chap. 7.

[54] An analysis of the educational attainment of urban teachers in the Cameroun offers a case in point. In the early 1960's only one-third of the Yaoundé and Douala teaching force under thirty-five years of age had a postprimary training. For their counterparts forty-five years and older, the corresponding percentage increased to 43 percent. See Clignet "Teachers as Potential Agents of Modernization," (forthcoming).

TABLE 8

Educational Background of the Labor Force and the Male
Population of Yaoundé, Douala, and the Littoral Region
(percentages)

Educational Background	Sampled labor force	Urban sectors of employment			Centre-sud[a]
		Public	Private	Self-employment	
Does not speak French	24.7	2.2	11.5	23.9	51.0
Speaks French	17.5	10.1	26.5	25.1	12.6
Reads and writes French	35.1	36.2	45.4	31.5	27.5
Completed primary	17.7	32.2	14.4	14.7	8.5
Postprimary	1.6	16.8	1.6	4.5	0.4
Other (English German, Arabic)	1.7	2.5	0.6	0.3	0.4
Undetermined	1.7	0.0	--	--	--
Total	100.0	100.0	100.0	100.0	100.0

[a]Source: *Enquête démographique au Cameroun: Resultats définitifs pour la region sud -est; 1962-1964*, p. 49. Unfortunately, such data do not correspond exactly to the geographic scope of the present study.

4. Migratory selectivity. Although the data included in the labor survey do not include any information concerning migratory experiences, it is still important to compare in this respect the urban populations employed in public, private, and self-employed sectors.

This comparison confirms the conclusions derived from an analysis of the ethnic composition of the three populations employed in major sectors of the economy. No less than 16 percent of self-employed is locally born, as opposed to 9 percent of individuals participating in other activities. Because of their relatively higher educational level, wage earners employed by public bureaucracies are more frequently migrants, but they also originate more often from an urban environment than other components of the population of Douala and Yaoundé. No less than 37 percent of the civil servants currently working in the two major Camerounian cities have migrated from other urban areas, against 27 percent of the wage earners employed by private concerns and only 20 percent of self-employed entrepreneurs. Similarly, the hierarchy of jobs in the public service increases the overall mobility of civil servants.[55] Whereas 37 percent of these civil servants have had at least one intermediary stop over between

[55] In the context of a centralized public bureaucracies, the personnel is often transferred from one locale to another either because of the needs of the bureaucracy or because such transfers are associated with occupational reward or punishment.

their birthplace and their current residence, this characterizes 22 percent of wage earners in the private sector and 19 percent of self-employed individuals.

To sum up, participation in differing sectors of activity is associated with varying sets of migratory experiences. As expected, work in the governmental offices requires individuals to be more "cosmopolitan" and hence to be more mobile as well as to have more urban experience. In contrast, there are few differences in this regard between the workers of the private sector and the self-employed present in the murky sector.

Conclusions

In the present chapter, I have summarized the current profile of the Camerounian society and the influence it might exert on the functioning of the private labor market. First, differences in the climatic and soil conditions of the Camerounian regions contribute to the differential location of modern enterprises. Similar in effect is the differential exposure of these regions to modernizing influences; this exposure determines not only the quality of the public support and services needed for the functioning of modern enterprises but also both the quality and quantity of the manpower available to them.

Second, Camerounian history influences the functioning of local private enterprises in a variety of ways. This history involves alternating cycles of centralized and decentralized patterns, the conjunction of which has stimulated the growth of educational facilities, the emergence of a multifaceted local elite, the development of locally owned modern enterprises, and the segmentation of the modern sector of the economy into a number of geographically and functionally distinct labor markets. Yet the centrifugal forces that accompany decentralized patterns of development have also impeded the development of the economy by facilitating serious widespread political violence at the time of independence; subsequent centralization has enabled the government to impose a rigid bureaucratic framework on economic activities.

Finally, the labor forces employed by the three major sectors of the Camerounian economy have contrasted profiles. The bureaucratic nature of the public services implies a high concentration of educated and "cosmopolitan" individuals with marked seniority in the major urban centers of the country. Yet while the murky sector involves the mixed presence of tradition-oriented and "modern" entrepreneurs, the population employed by private concerns is more homogeneous. Finally, disparities in the growth rates of urban and educated populations and of economic opportunities lead to an increase in the number of crossovers between self-employed and private modern labor markets.

Chapter 3

MANUAL AND NONMANUAL WORKERS: AN OVERVIEW

To identify contrasts in the educational and migratory experiences or in the ethnic background of populations employed in public, private, and murky sectors of activity is yet insufficient. As the ultimate goal is to isolate the processes of segmentation operating in the Camerounian modern labor market, the thrust of the present chapter is to contrast the profile of white- and blue-collar populations. More specifically, I intend to show that the former have a higher and more homogeneous level of educational attainment. I also will show that such differences are accompanied by distinct modes of entry into the labor force.

But where do these differences come from? In the present chapter as in the next one, I assume that employers adopt uniform sets of universalistic and rational behavior toward all workers and, hence, that they do not differ from one another in their personnel policies. As in this context, I still assume that formal schooling conditions access to modern occupational roles, I may then posit that educational contrasts between manual and nonmanual workers reflect the interplay of two complementary forces. These contrasts result both from the differential requirements of the two types of activity, and from the varying orientations and aspirations prevailing among job seekers.

In a first general perspective, I assume that there are sharp and universally recognized differences in the contribution of different jobs to the overall productivity of a particular economic system. Correspondingly, nonmanual work is deemed to have higher scalar characteristics than manual activities. To the extent that there is a marked interdependence between the worlds of businessmen and educators, these imputed differences in the "scale" and in the productivity of distinct occupational families are associated with parallel contrasts in the educational standing of the corresponding populations. Because the performance of white-collar activities is deemed to require higher cognitive skills, educated job seekers tend to be more numerous in the more productive white-collar sector.

At the same time, it is also possible to posit that differences in the productivity of various types of jobs are also universally recognized by the job-seeking population. These differences are supposedly associated with parallel contrasts in the monetary and nonmonetary rewards they yield.

Indeed, a number of cross-cultural studies suggest that nonmanual jobs are perceived to be more prestigious than manual activities and that the differences attributed to these types of work are independent of the levels of economic development of the countries studied.[1] More sensitive to the differential values attached to occupational roles, secondary school leavers and university students are naturally more prone to preempt the most attractive jobs available in local labor markets. But is this preference for nonmanual work universal, or does it vary with specific cultural orientation? Some anthropologists have asserted that manual work is negatively valued in a number of African cultures.[2] Should their assertion be valid, one might suspect that formal schooling is used to satisfy specific occupational orientations, which vary along ethnic lines. Nevertheless, insofar as educational experiences lead to the formation of a universal culture, nonmanual workers should have a higher and less variable level of educational attainment than their manual counterparts. As the definition of clerical jobs is closely influenced by universalistic-oriented models originating from European bureaucracies, the educational prerequisites underlying access to such roles should be relatively independent of the ethnic background, place of residence, or the age of job seekers.

Even though this type of analysis highlights the differential principles underlying the patterns of access into the two occupational families, it does not focus on the stability of their boundaries. With the passage of time and further educational development, employers should be able to uniformly raise the educational credentials they ask of candidates to positions in the modern sector of the economy. Thus, the boundaries between the educational attainments of white- and blue-collar populations should be less evident wherever and whenever there is a sizable pool of job seekers and, hence, among younger age groups, among the most Westernized ethnic groups, and among urban residents. Alternatively, the differential modernization of the Camerounian adult population may also be accompanied by parallel contrasts in the crystallization of the stereotypes attached to various occupational roles. Should this be the case, the

---

[1] For a full discussion of this point, see D. Treiman, R. Hodge, and P. Rossi, "A Comparative Study of Occupational Prestige," in R. Bendix and S. Lipset, eds., *Class, Status, and Power* (New York: Free Press, 1965), pp. 309-321. The authors demonstrate that there is no relationship between gross national product per capita and the ranking accorded a number of selected occupations.

[2] European employers operating in Africa have been vocal about the traditional distaste of African job seekers for manual occupations. Further, many anthropologists suggest that the negative stereotype attached to manual work is more evident in societies with social stratification. Among the Agni of the Ivory Coast, to owe one's own income to manual work rather than to the renting of capital is too much a reminder of the status of a slave. See M. Dupire, "Planteurs autochtones et étrangers en Côte d'ivoire orientale," *Etudes éburnéennes*, 6(1960). However, many sociologists have criticized the "endogenous" cultural hypothesis. See, for example, R. Bastide, *Religions africaines au Brésil* (Paris: Presses universitaires de France, 1960), pp. 94-95, 528-545.

influence of education on occupational placement should be most evident among the populations most intensely exposed to the norms of an industrial order, and, hence, among the most Westernized ethnic groups, individuals living in large cities, and among the youngest cohorts of job seekers.

Thus far I have stressed the extent of potential differences in the educational profile of the individuals *currently* performing white- or blue-collar activities. Yet contrasts in the requirements of the two types of jobs are certainly associated with differing modes of entry into the labor market. Because there are deemed to be convergences in the determinants of educational and white-collar attainment, nonmanual workers are more likely to enter the modern sector of the economy directly from their schools. Alternatively, insofar as differences in the nature of the manual work performed in the context of modern and "murky" enterprises are deemed to be relatively inconsequential, blue-collar workers tend more frequently to begin their occupational life by working with a relative or friend. Yet such contrasts do not necessarily remain stable, and they depend on disparities between the growth rate of educational and occupational opportunities.

Educational Qualifications: Definition and Operationalization

The complexity of the organizational structure of Camerounian educational enterprises makes it difficult to evaluate the impact of schooling on occupational placement. Because the Cameroun follows the same educational pattern as the majority of former French colonies (with a system of postprimary education characterized by distinctive streams and cycles), students who have followed four years of postprimary schooling within a long cycle of academic studies or of a short cycle of technical or agricultural education have not been similarly exposed to a modern occupational hierarchy. Hence, they may entertain different aspirations and be differentially attracted by the blue- or white-collar labor market.[3] Further, employers do not necessarily feel that various types of formal training contribute evenly to enhance individual productivity and commitment.[4]

---

[3] For a discussion of the association between occupational aspirations, expectations, and placement, on the one hand, and type of studies undertaken on the other, see Clignet and Foster, *The Fortunate Few*, chaps. 6 and 8. The occupational commitment of students enrolled in vocational institutions is not necessarily higher than that of their fellow students engaged in a more general course of studies. For another, albeit indirect, discussion of the association between education and occupational adaptation, see A. Jensen, "How Much Can We Boost IQ and Scholastic Achievement," *Environment, Heredity, and Intelligence* (Harvard Educational Review Reprint Series 2, 1969), pp. 13-16.

[4] Employers in Africa often take a negative stance toward vocational training offered by technical schools. They feel that such schools prepare their students for a technology at variance with that used in local enterprises, and that the students graduating from such institutions often have rigid and narrow occupational expectations.

Correspondingly, individuals with the same amount of schooling but with differing academic experiences do not necessarily have the same chances of joining manual and nonmanual sectors of employment.

Regardless of such difficulties, there are sharp contrasts in the educational qualifications of manual and nonmanual populations. Half of the current manual workers have never attended school, but half of their nonmanual colleagues have completed their primary schooling (Table 9). Further, over 7 percent of the latter have gone beyond primary school, as against less than 1 percent of the manual workers. Thus, as expected, there are differences not only in the average amount of formal schooling acquired by the two populations but also in the profile of the corresponding distributions. In addition, the technical qualifications of the two types of wage earner are also different. The percentage of manual workers who have not followed any type of vocational training program is slightly higher than that of their nonmanual counterparts (90 versus 84 percent), and the technical qualifications acquired by manual workers are lower than those obtained by their nonmanual counterparts. No less than 37 percent of white-collar wage earners who *did* attend a technical school have completed the first cycle of the corresponding studies, as against 10 percent of their blue-collar counterparts. In the first category, over 10 percent went beyond that stage, against only less than 1 percent in the second category. In short, nonmanual workers have attained a higher level of both academic and vocational training.

TABLE 9

Educational Characteristics of the East Cameroun Labor Force
(percentages)

Level of formal education	Manual workers	Nonmanual workers	Total
Did not go to school	49.6	3.3	42.2
Some primary schooling	35.1	35.8	35.1
Completed primary school	11.5	50.9	17.8
First cycle of post-primary school	0.3	5.9	1.2
Second cycle of post-primary school	0.1	0.7	0.2
Postsecondary schooling	0.0	0.6	0.1
Other primary[a]	1.7	1.2	1.7
No answer	1.7	1.6	1.7
Total	100.0	100.0	100.0
N	(30,582)	(5,696)	(36,278)

[a]Largely primary education acquired in West Cameroun.

However, an evaluation of the formal qualifications of the manual and nonmanual labor forces is made more difficult not only by the differential *nature* of the postprimary studies they have undertaken, but also by the differing characteristics of the institutions they have attended. Increased demand for formal schooling has favored the development of a large number of private—both religious and secular—educational institutions. Similarly, this demand has also stimulated the growth of correspondence courses or special training programs sponsored by local employers. The government does not necessarily accord formal status to the diplomas awarded by certain academic or technical private schools.[5] Similarly, both the government and local employers do not necessarily recognize qualifications acquired through correspondence courses. Finally, whereas certain programs of vocational training favor mobility *within* the firms which sponsor them, others stimulate as well mobility *across* sectors.[6]

Insofar as manual and nonmanual populations entertain differing educational aspirations and do not similarly internalize the requirements of their future jobs, they do not make the same use of nonaccredited schools and correspondence courses. Almost 18 percent of those white-collar workers who have had some vocational training prior to their entry into the labor force acquired the corresponding skills from these two kinds of institutions as against less than 1 percent of manual wage earners.

In spite of the differential meaning attached to academic and vocational training acquired in distinctive contexts, it is still possible to rank such experiences on a unidimensional scale. Obviously, the simplest solution consists in translating these experiences in terms of their relative duration. I have thus devised a continuous scale ranging from scores of zero for individuals who do not speak French and have no vocational or academic training up to scores of twenty for individuals who hold a doctorate.[7]

---

[5] A number of schools have no accreditation agreements with local educational authorities, which limits the occupational choices of individuals who graduate from these institutions.

[6] For instance, in the Ivory Coast, the night courses sponsored by the Chamber of Commerce and financed by local enterprises were aimed at preparing individuals for technical examinations that enabled them to change skill categories as defined by collective bargaining agreements. By contrast, the courses offered by the local Federation of Mechanical Industries were aimed at the award of diplomas, the value of which was recognized only by the current employer of the students in question. This suggests that employers do not have the same response to a situation of scarcity. Certain firms will be willing to play the laissez-faire game and compete freely for the services of the most desirable labor force, whereas others will seek to restrain the mobility of their manpower.

[7] The construction of this aggregate training score takes into account the incidence of repeating classes within the primary system, where this phenomenon is most frequent, and I have thus given the equivalent of four years of schooling to individuals who read and write French, although the acquisition of this skill should formally take no more than three years. I have similarly taken into account the variable duration of the specific vocational training programs and of the distinct formal institutional streams and cycles followed by the sample population. Finally, as the gains derived from noninstitutionalized training programs vary with

An inspection of the mean aggregate training scores obtained by the two populations confirms the validity of the first basic proposition. The aggregate average training score of current nonmanual workers is significantly higher than that of blue-collar wage earners. Whereas the former average 6.3 years of aggregate academic and vocational training, the latter have a mean score of only 2.9. White-collar workers have been longer at school than their blue-collar counterparts, and they have also higher technical credentials.

Educational Prerequisites to Manual and Nonmanual Employment

As I have suggested that the definition of nonmanual activities is more universalistic in nature than that of manual tasks, the aggregate training score distribution of the first population should have not only a higher mean but also a lower variance. In spite of similarities in the standard deviations of the two distributions (2.6 for nonmanual and 2.7 for manual), it is still possible to infer from the major hypothesis discussed here that the educational profile of nonmanual population will be more independent of age (and, hence, time), ethnic origin, and place of residence.

Age and aggregate training scores.

In developing nations, age is an equivocal variable, for individuals do not necessarily know their age nor do they attach the same significance to this variable as Europeans. In addition, among societies affected by high rates of societal change, age mirrors both the particular life cycle of an individual and specific historical factors. Despite the equivocal meaning of the data, it is still evident that the proportion of manual workers with a low aggregate training score (less than 1.5) decreases from 87 percent among those forty-six years old and over to 9 percent for those under twenty years of age (Table 10). Symmetrically, the proportion of individuals with a score of 7.1 or more increases from 0.3 percent for the oldest segments of that particular population to 13 percent for the youngest. Similarly, the percentage of nonmanual workers with low educational qualifications (under 7.0) decreases from 55 to 11 percent among the oldest and youngest individuals, whereas the proportion of those with a score of 7.1 or more increases from 12 to 29 percent between these two groups.

Two conclusions can be derived from this short analysis. First, as hypothesized, the relationship between age and educational attainment is more marked in the case of manual than nonmanual wage earners. Individuals with a maximal aggregate training score are over *forty times*

---

the highest level of formal schooling attained, I have accorded a differential weight to the corresponding experiences acquired by individuals with varying levels of educational attainment.

TABLE 10
Aggregate Training Score of the East Cameroun Labor Force by Age
and Category of Worker
(percentages)[a]

Age	0	0.1-1.5	1.6-6.0	7.0	7.1-11.9	12	Total	N
			Aggregate training score					
Below 20								
Manual	4.5	4.9	40.3	37.1	13.0	0.2	100.0	(834)
Nonmanual	0.0	0.0	10.9	59.8	29.3	0.0	100.0	(174)
21-25								
Manual	5.6	11.6	45.1	26.3	11.3	0.1	100.0	(3,888)
Nonmanual	0.0	0.0	17.0	51.2	30.7	1.1	100.0	(1,165)
26-30								
Manual	14.8	1.8	48.6	10.2	4.5	9.1	100.0	(5,450)
Nonmanual	0.0	0.0	36.4	40.0	20.6	3.0	100.0	(1,123)
31-35								
Manual	25.3	26.1	41.9	5.1	1.5	0.1	100.0	(4,709)
Nonmanual	0.0	0.0	49.3	37.8	10.6	2.3	100.0	(1,001)
36-40								
Manual	36.1	27.7	32.2	2.8	1.1	0.1	100.0	(3,562)
Nonmanual	0.0	0.0	48.3	37.8	10.2	3.7	100.0	(662)
41-45								
Manual	50.7	24.0	23.9	1.7	0.5	0.2	100.0	(2,042)
Nonmanual	0.0	0.0	58.8	30.8	8.3	2.1	100.0	(340)
46 and over								
Manual	68.8	18.1	12.0	0.8	0.3	0.0	100.0	(2,612)
Nonmanual	0.0	0.0	55.2	33.2	6.6	5.0	100.0	(337)
Total								
Manual	27.6	21.0	37.4	9.9	3.9	0.2	100.0	(23,097)
Nonmanual	0.0	0.0	38.0	41.5	18.0	2.5	100.0	(4,802)

[a]For purposes of clarity, all "no answer" categories with respect to age, category of worker, and aggregate training have been deleted from the table.

more numerous in the younger than in the older age categories of the manual population. In the nonmanual sector, individuals with high qualifications are less than *three times* more numerous in the first than in the last age category.

Second, contrasts in the aggregate training scores of the two populations are less pronounced for younger than older cohorts. Half of the youngest manual workers have an aggregate training score of 7.0, as against 90 percent of the nonmanuals, but the corresponding figures are 14 and 62 percent, respectively, among individuals over forty-five years of age. Thus, educational development narrows occupational choices. Whereas older individuals with a score of between 1.6 and 6.9 (corresponding to some primary schooling) are concentrated in nonmanual occupations, newcomers to the labor market who possess these modest qualifications are currently more numerous in the blue-collar sector. As a result of the growing disparities betwen the rates of educational and economic development, young job seekers are obliged to revise their occupational expectations and aspirations. To be sure, they may be initially tempted to delay their entry in the labor market, as long as the opportunities available to them do not match the models they have internalized.[8] As this wait-and-see strategy is made more problematic both because of the growing output of local school systems and of the declining hospitality of urban residents, an increasing number of young job seekers tend to lower their occupational choices and to content themselves with blue-collar employment.[9] No less than 69 percent of the younger individuals with a postprimary education are currently engaged in manual work, as against 15 percent of their older counterparts.

Ethnicity and aggregate training scores.

As one might expect, the Douala enjoy a disproportionate share of available nonmanual occupations. They have been exposed more intensely than any other group to modernizing processes, and their home territory is located in the heart of the regions touched by economic development. In contrast, the less educated Northerners and politically more marginal foreign-born Africans are proportionately more numerous in blue-collar jobs.[10]

[8] See J. Sween and R. Clignet, "Urban Unemployment as a Determinant of Political Unrest: The Case Study of Douala, Cameroon," *Canadian Journal of African Studies* 111(1969):463-488. No less than 39 percent of the individuals who never entered the labor market (the unemployed) have completed at least primary school, as against only 12 percent of those who have left the market (the deemployed). In the first case, to be jobless mirrors conflicts between opportunities and expectations. In the second case, it results from a lack of adaptation to the changing needs of an urban labor market.

[9] Similarly, the author has observed that in the Ivory Coast an increasing number of young individuals with one or two years of postprimary schooling were employed in unskilled positions in one of the textile firms of Abidjan. They were reported to be unwilling to look for a more appealing job because they wanted to reenter the school system later on. In Ghana, 25 percent of the unskilled manual workers included in Peil's sample had entered but not completed a middle school education. See *The Ghanaian Factory Worker: Industrial Man in Africa* (Cambridge: Cambridge University Press, 1972), pp. 65-66.

[10] Clearly, there are cross-cultural variations in the relationship between migratory experiences and occupational placement. In the early phases of economic development in French-speaking Africa (notably in the Ivory Coast), employers were likely to import their qualified clerical labor force from Senegal, Ghana, Togoland, and Dahomey. It was only after the riots of 1958 that local authorities decided to restrict the participation of foreigners in key administrative positions within the modern sector of the economy. To the degree that Camerounian populations have been able to achieve a higher level of formal schooling and to obtain a greater political independence, they have also been able to impose controls on the kinds of employees they are willing to accept in the country.

TABLE 11
Aggregate Training Score of East Cameroun Workers by Ethnicity and Category of Employment
(percentages)

	Aggregate training score							
	0	*0.1-1.5*	*1.6-6.9*	*7.0*	*7.1-11.9*	*12+*	*Total*	*N*
Ewondo								
Manual	22.5	20.6	42.8	10.6	3.5	0.0	100.0	(3,512)
Nonmanual	0.0	0.0	35.5	46.2	15.5	2.8	100.0	(456)
Other Beti-Fang[a]								
Manual	17.2	14.2	56.4	15.2	6.4	0.0	100.0	(1,409)
Nonmanual	0.0	0.0	25.0	53.9	17.5	3.6	100.0	(308)
Bamileke								
Manual	29.5	24.7	33.3	7.1	5.3	0.1	100.0	(6,040)
Nonmanual	0.0	0.0	42.3	36.8	19.6	1.3	100.0	(1,245)
Bassa								
Manual	26.0	20.0	41.6	9.4	2.9	0.1	100.0	(5,654)
Nonmanual	0.0	0.0	37.9	41.7	18.5	1.9	100.0	(1,095)
Douala								
Manual	6.3	13.3	61.5	11.9	6.4	0.6	100.0	(1,474)
Nonmanual	0.0	0.0	38.0	41.2	16.6	4.2	100.0	(1,090)
Other[b]								
Manual	39.7	22.4	24.3	11.2	2.3	0.1	100.0	(5,011)
Nonmanual	0.0	0.0	37.8	42.0	18.3	1.9	100.0	(608)
Total								
Manual	27.5	21.4	37.3	9.8	3.9	0.1	100.0	(23,100)
Nonmanual	0.0	0.0	38.0	41.5	18.0	2.5	100.0	(4,802)

[a]This cluster includes the ethnic groups residing in the Mefou, outside the city of Yaoundé.

[b]These include the Mbam, the northerners, and the foreigners.

As anticipated, ethnic variations in levels of formal schooling are less marked among white- than blue-collar workers (Table 11). At the upper end of the educational continuum, the proportions of manual workers with aggregate training scores of over 7.0 vary from 2 percent in the case of Northerners, Mbam and foreigners to 7 percent in the case of the Douala, whereas the corresponding figures for nonmanual wage earners only range from 18 percent in the case of the Ewondo to 21 percent for other Beti-Fang. The same pattern obtains at the lower end of the educational continuum. Although the proportion of manual workers with a score of zero, and hence with a total lack of formal qualifications, varies broadly from a minimum 6 percent for the Douala to almost 40 percent for the

Northerners, the corresponding range is narrower for white-collar workers. The proportion of those with scores lower than 7.0 (and, hence, with minimal qualifications) only varies from 25 percent in the case of Bete-Fang other than Ewondo to 42 percent in the case of the Bamileke.

Yet the influence of formal schooling on occupational placement varies along ethnic lines. First, high qualifications do not uniformly provide access to nonmanual activities. Only 31 percent of the Douala with an aggregate score of over 7.0 are currently engaged in manual activities, compared with no less than 56 percent of their Bamileke counterparts. But does such a difference suggest that the rewards employers accord to similarly high qualifications depend on the ethnic affiliations of job seekers or alternatively, that ethnic contrasts in the occupational aspirations of secondary school students persist in spite of their similar exposure to the values of the educational environment?

The influence of ethnicity on the relationship between schooling and occupational placement reflects in part the differential overall involvement of Camerounian peoples in modernizing processes. Although Douala and Bamileke blue-collar individuals tend to have a proportionately higher aggregate training score than their counterparts from other ethnic groups, they probably joined the manual labor force for different reasons. The intense exposure of the Douala people to urban, educational, and occupational structures enhances their sensitivity to the declining rewards traditionally attached to formal schooling, and to the opportunity resulting from the expansion of the manual labor market. Their sensitivity in this respect is likely to be enhanced by the location of major industrial organizations, which enables them to preempt the most attractive positions in the blue collar sector.[11]

The reasons underlying the occupational placement of educated Bamileke are different. As this people entered the process of modernization relatively late, ambitious Bamileke enjoy fewer occupational choices. However, as the overall involvement of this people in modernizing processes becomes more marked, the proportion of highly educated Bamileke entering manual occupations should decline. The widening of the networks used by these educated individuals should enable them to satisfy more easily their occupational aspirations.

Thus far, however, the analysis remains more revealing of the *extent* than of the *determinants* of ethnic variations in the profile of the modern labor force. The aggregate training score of Bamileke wage earners is higher than the overall level of modernization of this particular people would have led one to predict, and the educational selectivity underlying access to the modern labor market is steeper in the case of the Bamileke

---

[11] Thus, my findings suggest that the processes of modernization are not cumulative and that the most modernized ethnic groups are able to play a particularistic game more efficiently.

than it is for the Bassa or the Douala.[12] Does this mean that Bamileke are the victims of discrimination and that in order to be employed they must have proportionately higher qualifications than individuals coming from more modernized groups? Or does it mean alternatively that Bamileke urban migrations are characterized by a marked selectivity and that only the most modernized individuals in this particular group are attracted by an urban life style and more specifically by the prospect of work in the modern sector? As this people is characterized by a complex system of stratification, it is plausible to hypothesize that individuals who enter modern jobs are selected from among narrow segments of the overall Bamileke population and are particularly enterprising.

To sum up, ethnic variations in the educational and vocational background of Camerounian workers are less marked in the white- than the blue-collar sector. In addition, the determinants of such variations are rather complex: they may involve particularistic hiring practices, but they also reflect contrasted cultural orientations and differential patterns of migrations, as well as differential overall ethnic involvement in modernizing processes.

Residence and aggregate training scores.

The demand for white collar work is maximal among the enterprises of the tertiary sector of the economy, usually located in the largest urban centers of the Cameroun.

Thus, no less than 90 percent of the nonmanual labor force is employed by urban concerns, as opposed to only two-thirds of manual workers (Table 12). Further, even though urbanization is associated with an overall rise in the credentials of the Camerounian labor force, variations in the educational qualifications of nonmanual workers by type of residence are proportionately more limited than corresponding contrasts among manual wage earners. Nonmanual workers with an aggregate training score over 7.0 are only *three* times more numerous in the largest cities than in the hinterland, but their qualified manual counterparts are *eleven* times as many in the urban than in the rural context. In brief, the educational profile of the manual labor force varies more markedly by type of environment, but differences between manual and nonmanual workers are less marked in the urban than in the rural context. Even though individuals who have had any kind of postprimary education are more often holding currently nonmanual positions in urban than in rural areas (46 against 37

---

[12] By selectivity, I refer to differences between the characteristics of wage earners and those of the population at large. As over 30 percent of Bamileke wage earners have completed at least their primary studies, as opposed to 14 percent of the adult residents of Douala of that origin, one can argue that educational selectivity is particularly sharp. It is even sharper if one considers the entire Bamileke population, for an analysis of current enrollments suggest that the educational level of Bamileke rural adults is even lower. The enterprising spirit of Bamileke migrants is also noted by W. Johnson in *The Cameroun Federation*, p. 50.

TABLE 12

Training Scores of East Cameroun Workers by Location of Employment
(percentages)

Aggregate training score	Rural		Semiurban		Urban	
	Manual	Non-manual	Manual	Non-manual	Manual	Non-manual
0	46.2	0.0	34.5	0.0	19.4	0.0
0.1 to 1.5	19.1	0.0	20.3	0.0	21.9	0.0
1.6 to 6.9	28.3	56.9	33.2	48.2	41.4	36.1
7.0	5.9	36.0	9.4	40.2	11.6	42.0
7.1 to 11.9	0.5	7.1	2.5	11.2	5.5	19.1
12 and above	0.0	0.0	0.1	0.4	0.2	2.8
Total	100.0	100.0	100.0	100.0	100.0	100.0
N	(6,552)	(267)	(789)	(276)	(15,759)	(4,259)

percent), the large concentration of educated individuals in cities still erodes the rewards initially attached to formal schooling. This concentration may also be associated with a decrease in the differential value that various cultures attach to nonmanual and manual jobs.

Aggregate training scores: an overview.

In the introduction to this chapter, I proposed complementary interpretations of the relationship between schooling and occupational placement. On the one hand, there could be a rational and objective interdependence between educational and economic institutions, in which case the hierarchy of the courses taught at school is the legitimate reflection of the differential contribution of various occupations to the overall productivity of the entire economy. On the other hand, educational differences between manual and nonmanual workers may primarily reflect contrasts in both the values and resources of various segments of the population at large and, hence, social or cultural inequalities in the patterns of access into various types of educational institutions.

In the first perspective, the composition of school populations should be open, for the rationality of the economic system requires a maximal amount of inter- and intragenerational mobility. In the second perspective, conversely, emerging social and ethnic stratifications should introduce significant skews in the characteristics of students: the higher educational level acquired by current cohorts of nonmanual workers should reflect only the privileged status of their family. It is therefore important to determine whether educational development facilitates a more equal participation of all segments of the Camerounian society in educational structures, and, hence, whether differences in the imputed attributes of manual and nonmanual workers are independent of educational inequalities.

In many developing countries, individual educational attainment remains moderately determined by familial background.[13] But chances of reaching the highest rungs of the academic ladder are still influenced by the size of the community of origin, the socioeconomic profile of the region where individuals have grown up, and parental education and occupation.[14] It would be necessary to test empirically whether the observations made along these lines may be generalized to the Camerounian scene. And it would be equally necessary to see whether the proprietorship status of Camerounian educational institutions is associated with contrasts in the composition of their student body.[15] Unfortunately, data concerning the background of Camerounian wage earners are limited, and one can assess only the impact of cultural origin, current type of residence, and

[13] Unfortunately, I did not have access to the information regarding the parental background of the workers studies here. Indeed, it would have been interesting to compare the results obtained in the Cameroun with those reported by Blau and Duncan in *The American Occupational Structures*. Nevertheless, it can be hypothesized that as the complexity of a society increases, the influence of stratification and of parental characteristics on individual occupational placement becomes more apparent. Thus, about three-quarters of wage earners in the modern sector of Dakar had fathers engaged in farming. See A. Hauser, *Les Ouvriers de Dakar: Etude psycho-sociologique* (Paris: Orstom, 1958), p. 49. The same holds true of Ghanaian workers, even though clerical wage earners differ from their manual counterparts in this regard. Only half of the former originate from farming families, as opposed to 80 percent of blue-collar workers. See Peil, *The Ghanaian Factory Worker*, p. 80. Most relevant to my concern here is the already quoted study of Bàlan, *Men in Developing Society*. The educational level of the Mexican gainfully employed population is highly correlated with paternal levels of education and occupations. Thus, the average number of years of schooling varies between 2.9 for the sons of illiterate individuals and 12.3 for those whose fathers attended a post-primary institution; similarly the same measurement of educational attainment varies between 3.7 for the sons of manual workers with low skill levels to 19.5 for those whose fathers have reached the upper rungs of the educational ladder.

[14] Mexican data suggest that educational attainment is independent of family size. Indeed, one may hypothesize that the relationship between these two variables is negative only when individuals perceive social mobility to be at variance with familism. In Africa, as in many other developing countries, many people feel that chances to move upward in the social structure are not as much influenced by the intensity of the care given to a child as by statistical factors. "The more children an individual has, the greater the chances that at least one of them will hit the jackpot." Further, in contrast to the West, educational attainment is often associated with an increase in the number of children. See, for instance, R. Clignet and J. Sween, "Type of Marriage and Family Size in Two African Urban Centers," *American Ethnologist* 1(May 1974):221-241.

[15] I am currently engaged in an examination of variations in the composition of the student populations enrolled in the second, fourth, and final years of the public and private institutions of East and West Cameroun. I want to see whether the implications of variations in proprietorship status on selectivity are culturally relative, and whether the populations attending public institutions in East Cameroun tend to originate from more narrow segments of the population than their classmates attending private institutions and whether the pattern is reversed in the Western part of the country.

educational development (as indirectly measured by the age of the respondents) on individual level of schooling.[16].

The task remains to ascertain not only how these various components of the selectivity underlying access into educational institutions interact with one another, but also whether the patterns for white- and blue-collar populations are alike. Comparisons between the results of the relevant multiple regressions should enable one to determine whether one accounts for a same percentage of the variance in the distributions of formal schooling among manual and nonmanual labor forces and whether the relative contribution of the independent variables are analogous in the two instances.

However, the use of this particular technique is subject to a number of limitations. It rests on a linear model which does not necessarily correspond to the reality of the phenomena investigated. Thus, it is not sure that the construction of an aggregate training score scale with equal intervals is meaningful, nor for example, that the requirements and rewards attached to a score of 7.0 are really one unit greater than those attached to a score of 8.0. Similarly, it is not clear that the relationship between age and the aggregate training score is linear. An additional unit in age might be associated with a decrease in one unit in aggregate training for certain segments of the distribution, but this might cease to be the case for other portions of that same distribution.[17] As a result, the value of zero-order correlations might be lowered and so could be the validity of the entire regression analysis.

[16] Even though current type of residence is a result of educational attainment, it may also be conditioned by significant aspects of the familial environment and notably by the influence of parental behaviors on propensity to migrate. Many studies of inequalities in educational enrollment involve the use of path analyses. In the present case, this particular technique was inappropriate not only because of the limited number of independent variables available but also because their intervention in time is rather problematic. For example, one may ask whether educational level determines or is determined by current place of residence. In the present argument, I am taking the view that variations in the environment of destination of migrants reflects the characteristics of their environment of origin and, for instance, that although individuals currently living in rural areas are unlikely to come from a city, those currently living in cities may come from other ciites as well as from traditional villages. In brief, I am aware of the limitations of my inferences and of the shortcomings of the analysis.

[17] In fact, the association between age and educational attainment tends to be curvilinear. Although the recent growth of Camerounian educational structures is associated with a lowering in the age of individuals with a postsecondary education, this particular type of education, by definition, tends to delay the point of entry in the labor force. As a result, individuals graduating from a university tends to be as old as those wage earners who only speak French (34.4 versus 34.1 years of age, as an average) but older than those who completed only the first cycle of their postprimary studies (34.4 against 28.2). Further, university graduates have been an average of 2.6 years in their current occupational activity, but the average seniority is 5 years among those wage earners who hold their baccalaureate and 3.6 years among those who have completed their primary studies and have begun their occupational life thereafter.

The three independent variables considered here jointly account for almost one-third of the variance in the distribution of aggregate training scores among manual workers, but for less than 9 percent of the corresponding variance among white-collar wage earners (Table 13). Education seems to be more randomly distributed in the case of the second population. Further, although the requirements of nonmanual activities prevent individuals with minimal educational and vocational qualifications from entering this particular sector of employment, the nature of manual work does not prevent individuals with high aggregate training scores from entering blue-collar jobs. Correspondingly, the second distribution is more "statistically normal" than the first.

Moreover, age (and, hence, educational development) is the most significant predictor of the formal credentials acquired by both manual and nonmanual wage earners. In both cases, the influence of ethnicity is also the same, and to be a Douala or a non-Douala seems to command differential access both to the educational and modern occupational structures of the country. As already indicated, this results from the particularly significant role played by this ethnic group in the development of the country. It also mirrors the relative concentration of modern industrial and commercial activities in the home territory of this people. For both historical and spatial reasons, the Douala have a privileged access to the modernized spheres of the contemporary Camerounian society, and the same historical and spatial reasons enable individuals currently living in urban centers to enjoy a higher level of educational attainment than other segments of the local society.

Modes of Entry into the Modern Labor Force

Thus far, I have examined the educational profile of populations *currently* engaged in manual and nonmanual work. This, or course, does not say anything about the mechanisms used by individuals with differing levels of formal schooling to actually enter the labor force. In fact, the association between educational achievement and occupational placement is likely to be more marked in the initial than in the subsequent phases of the adult life of an individual. As an individual gets older, factors other than his formal training affect his occupational status.[18]

Obviously, there are sharp differences in the initial occupational experiences of manual and nonmanual wage earners. About 75 percent of the blue-collar individuals are still engaged in the same activity as when they first joined the labor force, as against only 56 percent of the adult males currently engaged in white-collar work.[19] Further, there are also

---

[18] As an individual becomes more committed to the industrial discipline, he is more likely to follow his particular employer when the latter changes employment himself.

[19] The population of workers who have performed only one particular job since their entry in the labor market includes individuals who have directly entered the labor force wihtout any

TABLE 13
Multiple Regression Analysis of Aggregate Training Score

	Manual Workers		
N[a]	23,210		
Mean	2.7		
Standard deviation	2.7		
Intercepts	4.67		
R^2	0.303		
Variables	*Beta*	*t*	R^2[d]
Age	-0.14	87.50	0.252
Urban-rural	0.32	32.85	0.290
Douala[c]	1.88	20.48	0.303
	Nonmanual Workers		
N[a]	4,915		
Mean	6.3		
Standard deviation	2.6		
Intercepts	5.87		
R^2	0.088		
Variables	*Beta*	*t*	R^2[d]
Age	-0.08	20.01	0.062
Douala[c]	0.73	8.17	0.077
Urban-rural	0.32	7.83	0.088

[a] After elimination of incomplete individual data.

[b] The sequential order in which the variables are introduced reflects their level of significance; the equation was discontinued when the additional amount of variance explained by the introduction of a new variable fell below the 1 percent level.

[c] Ethnicity has been treated in terms of a series of dummy variables.

[d] As in the following tables, the R^2 indicated correspond to the successive steps of the equation.

Note: The program adopted was the B34T Library Program of Northwestern University's Vogelback Computing Center.

sharp contrasts in the educational attainment of individuals *initially* employed in blue- or white-collar activities. Among populations initially engaged in maual work, aggregate training scores vary between 2.8 for individuals who have retained the same type of job, and 5.7 for those who have transferred into nonmanual activities. Conversely, among the populations initially engaged in white-collar activities, aggregate training scores decline from 6.5 for those individuals who have remained in the

particular training and those who learned their current job *at school* before joining the labor market.

same sector of employment to 6.1 for those who are currently participating in the manual sector of employment. Thus, differences in the educational level of the individuals who cross the boundaries between manual and nonmanual markets are more limited than the contrasts between their counterparts who have not changed activities.

Finally, formal schooling affects the type of employers with whom job seekers begin their occupational lives. As expected, the percentage of manual workers who begin their careers with parents or friends is relatively higher than the corresponding proportion among nonmanual workers (21 versus 16 percent). Further, although the role of parents and relatives in this regard is more marked for individuals with minimal education, the significance of the corresponding relationship has declined over time.[20] Among older individuals currently engaged in manual jobs, no less than 97 percent of those who began their occupational life with friends or relatives have low educational qualifications, as against only 56 percent of their counterparts less than twenty-five years old. The pattern is the same in the case of nonmanual workers; among the individuals over forty years of age, 52 percent of those who began their occupational lives with friends or relatives have aggregate training scores under 7.0 as compared with 19 percent of those less than twenty-five years old. In other words, increased disparities in the growth patterns of educational and occupational markets enhance the educational standing of the job-seeking population initially attracted by the murky sector. As time passes, boundaries between "modern" and "traditional" labor markets decline, and young cohorts of highly educated job seekers cease to have the same choices as their elders.

At the same time, only one-third of the individuals currently engaged in nonmanual work who had prior occupational experience began their occupational career with a large-scale organization, as against over 45 percent of their counterparts currently engaged in manual activities.[21] To the extent that large-scale organizations frequently offer on the job training programs to newcomers, it is important to identify the educational profile of the job seekers who take advantage of such opportunities.

This should facilitate better assessment of the changing policies adopted by the enterprises of a developing country, such as the Cameroun, with

---

[20] In the sampled population of wage earners examined in the Ivory Coast by the author, no less than 25 percent of the illiterate individuals who began their occupational life in another job than the one they were holding at the time of the study were initially employed by African artisans or traders, as against only 9 percent of those who had some postprimary education. In contrast, only 13 percent of the illiterate individuals who had prior employment began their occupational lives in government services, but this characterized no less than 32 percent of their counterparts who had at least completed the first cycle of postprimary studies.

[21] These large-scale organizations include the army. Indeed, many Camerounian workers learned their jobs during a stay in the colonial army. Of course, the role played by the army along these lines makes it even more difficult to accurately evaluate the returns that individuals obtain from their educational investments.

regard to the training of their workers and, more specifically, to examine the relevance of the distinction between the specific and general types of training discussed in the introduction.[22] As long as an economic system is simultaneously characterized by a large supply of available job seekers and a low overall level of technological development, entrepreneurs should be reluctant to invest in general forms of training, for their definition of the ideal productivity to be achieved by their employees is largely independent of educational attainment. Thus they should refuse to bear the costs of general programs which should be subsidized either by individual wage earners or by the community at large, but they should alternatively be more inclined to support nontransferable, specific forms of training. However, they should reverse their policies and participate both in specific and general programs whenever technological changes make it necessary to hire educated workers.

An examination of the changing policies followed by large-scale enterprises in this regard involves an analysis of the educational characteristics of the job seekers admitted in on-the-job training programs. Whenever participation in such programs is highest among individuals with relatively high educational qualifications, educational and vocational qualifications may be regarded as *complementary;* employers prefer to offer specific rather than general training. Alternatively, whenever such participation prevails among job seekers with low academic credentials, vocational and educational qualifications should be regarded as *substitutes,* and the distinction between general and specific training should cease to be operative.

In the nonmanual labor market, on-the-job training and formal schooling tend to act as substitutes for each other during the initial phases of educational development, because of the scarcity of candidates with appropriate qualifications. Thus, the percentage of nonmanual workers with low academic credentials who have participated in on-the-job training programs is significantly greater among the cohorts of over forty-five years of age than among newcomers in the labor market under twenty-five years of age. To give an example, almost 65 percent of the older individuals with an aggregate training score of under 7.0 initially participated in such programs, as against only 47 percent of their younger counterparts (Table 14).

Alternatively, on-the-job training programs and formal schooling serve complementary functions only after educational development reaches a critical threshold and, hence, only after employers are in a position to be more selective in their hiring practices. Thus, only 5 percent of the individuals over forty-five years of age who completed the first cycle of

---

[22] For a discussion of the distinction between specific and general training and its economic implications, see L. Thurow, *Poverty and Discrimination* (Washington, D.C.: Brookings Institution, 1969), p. 88.

TABLE 14

Percentage of Workers Undergoing Formal On-the-Job Training With
Firms by Aggregate Training Score and Age

Aggregate training score	Manual		Nonmanual	
	Workers age 25 and below	Workers age 45 and over	Workers age 25 and below	Workers age 45 and over
0	28.3	45.3	--	--
0.1-1.5	36.7	56.8	--	--
1.6-6.9	48.3	70.0	47.3	64.8
7.0	48.3	78.3	39.0	72.3
7.1-12.0	8.0	27.7	15.6	32.0
12.1 and above	--a	--a	23.1	0.0

aFewer than ten cases in the category -- too few to be meaningful.

their postprimary studies before joining the labor force initially
participated in *any* kind of on-the-job training program, as against no less
than 39 percent of their counterparts under twenty-five years of age. In
other words, although employers used to consider ten years of formal
schooling as both a necessary and sufficient prerequisite for performing
clerical activities at a level deemed acceptable, they currently expect the
more numerous new entrants in the labor market with similar
qualifications to supplement their academic experiences with the
acquisition of more specific skills.

The relationship between formal schooling and the on-the-job training
programs offered to manual workers is necessarily more complex. On the
one hand, industries recruit their manual labor forces from broader
segments of the population, and although a lack of literacy does not
prevent the performance of manual tasks, it still restricts the range of
communication that can take place within an industrial organization.[23]
Therefore, employers have incentives to act as a substitute for schools in
the case of specific segments of their blue-collar labor force. Second,
academic experience is less consistent with the performance of manual than
of nonmanual tasks. The definition of white-collar jobs is more
standardized and more markedly influenced by metropolitan models,
whereas the definition of manuals tasks is much more dependent on local
conditions. Insofar as schools are uniformly influenced by European
models, they may inhibit the successful adaptation of candidates to blue-
collar jobs, and employers may claim that is it necessary to socialize their
manual workers to the specific environment of the firm.[24]

[23] In Senegal, Hauser notes that only 14 percent of his respondents used French and only
French at work. *Les Ouvriers de Dakar*, p. 50.

[24] Indeed, vocational schools in Africa tend to use machinery employed in the Metropole

As was the case for nonmanual workers, the extent to which formal schooling and on-the-job training programs provided by firms act as substitutes for each other has declined over time. Regardless of their level of formal schooling, older manual workers are more likely to have undergone on-the-job training, and this results from the greater scarcity of qualifications among older age groups. Yet, regardless of age, the percentage of individuals having taken advantage of on-the-job opportunities offered by large-scale firms increases with their educational level, at least up to the completion of primary studies. In this sense, formal schooling and on-the-job training are complementary to each other. In effect, whereas formal schooling often operates both as a necessary and sufficient condition for satisfactory performance in nonmanual activities, formal schooling was and is often considered as a necessary but insufficient condition for occupational achievement within the system of manual work.

Conclusions

The major thrust of this chapter has been to assess the impact of education on participation in manual and nonmanual activities. Whereas the level of formal schooling attained by white-collar workers is both higher and more independent of age, ethnic origin, and current place of residence than that for blue-collar workers, such contrasts result from the differential "productivity" of the two kinds of jobs and, hence, from the varying requirements that employers attach to manual and nonmanual activities.

But the preference for white-collar employment may also reflect the culturally specific orientations of individuals with higher academic credentials. This does not appear to be the case. For one thing, Camerounian schools seem to serve relatively large segments of the school-age population. For another, schools do not necessarily contribute to the emergence of a system of social stratification based on occupational roles. Even when they have similarly high levels of schooling, individuals with differing ethnic origins and places of residence do not necessarily join the same occupational families.

Further, educational contrasts between manual and nonmanual populations are declining. The conjunction of high rates of educational development and of increased disparities between school output and the needs of the labor market is associated with a rise in the educational prerequisites underlying access to manual and nonmanual labor markets. As this rise exerts greater pressures on the nonmanual labor market, educated job seeekers change their occupational aspirations and

---

because of the prestige that this adds to the status of the teaching force. In addition, the relationships between such schools and the labor market are always bureaucratic and rigid in nature, which means that there is always a time lag between the demands of the market and the nature of the training programs developed by the schools. As a result, the period of unemployment is often longer for the graduates of technical than academic schools. For an illustration, see Clignet and Foster, *The Fortunate Few*, chap. 8.

expectations and, more specifically, their evaluation of the rewards derived from manual activities.

Such a reevaluation characterizes not only younger individuals but all those social groups that have obtained more than their "fair share" of access to educational and vocational opportunities. Thus, contrasts between the educational background of manual and nonmanual workers are also less marked among urban ethnic groups with maximal involvement in modernizing processes. In this sense, there is increased convergence in the structures of manual and nonmanual labor markets.

Finally, there are changes in the individual modes of entry into the two types of occupational roles. Although in earlier colonial days formal schooling was more attuned to the needs of the local economy, the scarcity of qualified manpower induced employers to play the role of surrogates for schools, a responsibility that they are now more unwilling to perform.[25] Thus, there seems to be a decline in the importance of on-the-job training programs defined as tools of compensatory education.

Hence, the influence of industrialization on the modernization of individual skills and aspirations is not necessarily cumulative. In early colonial days on-the-job training programs sponsored by large-scale firms were important tools of socialization to the demands of nonmanual and manual roles, but current newcomers into the labor market tend to acquire their initial occupational experience through contacts with an African artisan or entrepreneur. As a result, their socialization to the requirements of an industrial order might be slower than that of their predecessors. In brief, patterns of commitment to an industrial order vary over time.

---

[25] Changes in the attitudes of employers in this regard are striking, for the educational institutions of the early phases of the colonial period were more anxious to satisfy the needs of public or private enterprises than the schools of today. See Clignet and Foster, *The Fortunate Few*, chap. 2.

Chapter 4

OCCUPATIONAL ACHIEVEMENT OF MANUAL
AND NONMANUAL POPULATIONS

To show overall differences in the profile of white- and blue-collar populations constitutes a necessary but insufficient condition for identifying
the processes of segmentation operating in the Camerounian labor market. If
this segmentation exists, the rules of the game should differ in the two cases and
there should be sharp contrasts in the extent and determinants of the rewards
that manual and nonmanual wage earners derive from the exercise of their
occupational activities. These rewards are twofold: individuals are entitled to
gain access to a particular skill level within the specific hierarchy to which they
are attached, and they are entitled to a particular income.

As in the previous chapter, I continue to assume that employers hold
common views on the rewards they control. In other words, I am positing
that differences in the skills or income of blue- and white-collar workers as
well as in their respective determinants result primarily from contrasts in
individual productivity. But the uncertainties underlying the definition of
individual productivity *within* a same occupational family are the same as
those underlying the definition of this term across branches of activity.
Thus, the placement of wage earners in distinct skill and income categories
may involve varying criteria. It may reflect the relative contribution of an
individual to the output of the firm or office for which he works, but it
may also depend on the *kind* rather than on the *quality* of the work
performed.[1] Regardless of their actual performance, accountants may be
entered in higher skill levels than typists. Similarly, this placement may
also be affected by the conformity of wage earners to industrial discipline.
In spite of his performance, an individual may also remain in a low skill
category whenever employers deem his behavior to jeopardize the internal
social order of the organization.[2]

Thus, boundaries between skill or income categories are necessarily
culturally relative, and they tend to reflect as much the bargaining power of
varying segments of the labor force as their relative contribution to the

---

[1] See Lambert, *Workers, Factories, and Social Change in India,* p. 223.

[2] From the "rational" viewpoint allegedly adopted by employers, it can be argued that if
individual workers are conflict prone, they disrupt the activity of the gang or workshop to
which they are attached and lower its overall productivity in spite of the quality of work they
may perform themselves.

profits of employers. With the development of strong labor organizations, crossing such boundaries depends as much on overcommitment as on commitment per se.[3] This situation obtains in countries where educational development tends to precede economic growth and where, correspondingly, the most educated segments of the labor force influence political processes. In such cases, boundaries between skill categories tend often to be fixed, self-perpetuating, and resistant to crossing.[4]. Such characteristics should be more characteristic of the white- than of the blue-collar labor market. The higher educational level of the former population facilitates their organization into powerful labor unions. Further, the concentration of white-collar workers in governmental bureaucracies obliges private employers to ultimately make the same concessions as those initially made by colonial authorities.

Independent of the uncertainties underlying the definition of individual productivity within a same job family, the first goal of the present chapter is to demonstrate that the influence of education on occupational attainment is both stronger and more independent of ascriptive forces in the white- than the blue-collar labor market. Yet the differential relationship between the educational and occupational achievements of manual and nonmanual workers does not remain stable over time. Because of the educational development of the country as a whole, contrasts in the educational qualifications of skilled manual and nonmanual wage earners are more marked among older than younger cohorts.

But formal qualifications only influence general patterns of adaptation to the industrial scene. Current occupational attainment and occupational mobility depend also on individual commitment as measured by the *duration* and the *diversity* of past occupational experiences. If manual and nonmanual labor markets are distinct, the consequences of these experiences on the achievement of the two populations should be different. Thus, the second goal of the present chapter is to demonstrate that because nonmanual workers can easily negotiate their skills across the board, the amount of time they have spent in the labor force or on the job is a more powerful predictor of their current occupational attainment.

Further, because white-collar activities are standardized and hence cosmopolitan, clerical workers should be able to use *interchangeably* their educational credentials and the occupational experiences they have acquired in the labor force as a whole or in the context of a particular

---

[3] It seems possible to argue that far from succeeding one another, stages of commitment may characterize simultaneously distinct segments of the labor force. In addition, the historical patterns underlying the growth of labor organizations differ between these two major occupational families. Under these conditions, it is difficult to understand why so many sociologists distinguish three skill levels within the manual population but treat the nonmanual population as an undifferentiated whole. Of course, the output of nonmanual workers is more difficult to evaluate, and so are their productivity and skill level.

[4] Lambert, *Workers, Factories and Social Change in India,* p. 244.

occupational role to reach the higher rungs of the occupational hierarchy and earn higher incomes. In contrast, blue-collar activities are place-bound and whereas seniority in the firm should be a more significant determinant of manual achievement than educational attainment, these two forms of experience should be unlikely to *substitute* for one another. In short, the third goal of the present chapter is to compare the patterns of interation between educational and occupational credentials as determinants of achievement between manual and nonmanual populations.

Finally, the diversity of past occupational experiences cannot have the same meaning or the same implications for the two categories of workers. Thus the fourth goal of the present chapter is to demonstrate that nonmanual workers more frequently change jobs and that the resulting diversity of their experiences is more often rewarded. Changes of occupation enable white-collar wage earners to get ahead in the occupational hierarchy, but the reasons underlying the mobility of their blue-collar counterparts are more diverse.

As noted at the beginning of the present chapter, occupational attainment refers both to the skill level attained by an individual and to his earnings. To be sure, the institutionalized constraints exerted on Camerounian labor markets lead these two aspects of occupational achievement to be highly correlated. Zero-order correlations between skill level and annual income are 0.618 for manual workers and 0.647 for their nonmanual counterparts. In spite of convergences in the determinants of these two facets of achievement, they are analytically distinct and their examination should be made separately.[5]

Measures of Occupational Attainment

The study of occupational attainment may involve two distinct strategies. The first one relies on an examination of the legal systems of classification adopted by developing countries. In former colonies, employers and employees have often borrowed a metropolitan legal framework to define skill levels in

---

[5] Although skill level acts as a filter regulating the influence of occupational or educational background, the consequences of variations in skill level are not necessarily greater than those attached to background factors. When one compares the effects of variations in skill level and variations in seniority within the same firm on annual individual earnings, the data indicate that variations in skill level have more important financial consequences for workers with maximal seniority than for those who have only spent one year in their current employment. I have also asserted that the influence of education on income is institutionalized and that the level of formal schooling of an individual controls his access to a particular skill level. Although education seems to be a necessary condition for entering higher skill levels and achieving a high income, it by no means is a sufficient condition. Thus, among individuals with the equivalent of twelve years of education the earnings of unskilled nonmanual workers average 475,000 CFA per year as against 1,300,000 CFA for their counterparts who have reached the top of the skill hierarchy. By contrast, among workers with an aggregate training score of below 7, the unskilled nonmanuals earn 136,000 CFA per year as against 501,000 CFA for their highly skilled counterparts.

bureaucratically oriented terms.[6] However, the meaning of these skill levels is generalizable only across the various firms of *a same* branch of activity, and the relevant analysis may concern only a limited segment of the economic scene. The second strategy involves the establishment of a more universal system of classification to account for the differing activities of the entire wage-earning population. The second solution, adopted in the present study, rests on the construction of a tridimensional scale which takes into account the number and complexity of the tasks performed by an individual and the degree to which these tasks are associated with the exercise of supervisory functions. The status of a wage earner in the modern sector of the economy varies not only with the technical skill involved in his work but also with the amount of autonomy and authority to which he is entitled.[7]

The scale used here includes seven levels. The first involves the execution of one simple unskilled task performed under direct supervision. The second involves the execution of a complex task also performed under direct supervision. The third, fourth, and fifth correspond to low-level supervisory roles accompanied by the performance of tasks which increase both in number and complexity, and level six is defined by the exercise of middle-range supervisory functions, whereas the top one involves the performance of managerial and executive functions.

Sharp contrasts are observable in the central measures and the profile of the distribution of skill-level scores among manual and nonmanual populations. The average score is only 1.70 for the first category, as against 3.08 for the second. Almost 40 percent of the nonmanual labor force has currently reached a skill level superior or equal to 4 (involving at least the performance of a number of relatively qualified tasks with low-level supervisory functions), as against hardly 8 percent of manual workers. Because of the low degree of division of labor operating in industrial and agricultural activities in the Cameroun, a large number of manual workers remain at the bottom of the occupational hierarchy as unskilled laborers, whereas the status of white-collar wage earners is significantly more differentiated.

---

[6] Clearly, occupational hierarchies vary across cultures. In Senegal, Hauser noted that 34 percent of the individuals he interviewed in selected firms were highly skilled. (See Hauser, *Les Ouvriers de Dakar,* p. 48). In a sample of 802 workers employed by seven firms in Abidjan (Ivory Coast), the author of the present study observed that whereas 37 percent of the individuals engaged in white-collar work were highly skilled or qualified, this characterized less than 15 percent of their manual counterparts. Cross-cultural variations in the proportion of highly skilled African workers reflect contrasts both in the nature of the different activities present in countries and in the relative development of their political and educational systems. Indeed, the highly significant position occupied by Senegal in French West Africa enabled local unions to be more demanding of employers than Ivory Coast labor organizations.

[7] One may question whether a skill scale based on (a) the number of tasks performed, (b) their relative complexity, and (c) the degree to which they involve supervisory functions is entirely valid. Yet the fact is that this scale yields significant results.

As anticipated, the association between skill level and aggregate training score is higher for nonmanual than for manual workers (Table 15).[8] However, zero-order correlations do not tell one whether this relationship is more independent of ascriptive factors such as ethnicity for white- than for blue-collar workers.

Ethnic origin, aggregate training score, and skill level.
Nonmanual work involves more "cosmopolitan" orientation, and access to the top rungs of the corresponding hierarchy is relatively independent of ethnic factors. Relationships between the ethnic origin and skill level of manual and nonmanual workers are hardly significant. There are, however, two exceptions to this general pattern. First, the Douala more easily reach the top of *both* hierarchies, and this is not surprising in view of the earlier and

TABLE 15
Zero-Order Correlations between Skill Level and Other Demographic and Social Variables

	Manuals	*Nonmanuals*
1. Aggregate training score	0.296	0.345
2. On-the-job training with firms	0.260	0.064
3. Number of jobs learned or performed	0.317	0.248
4. Age	0.071	0.323
5. Seniority on present job	0.184	0.287
6. Seniority in the firm	0.108	0.262
7. Ethnicity		
Ewondo	0.038	0.035
other Beti-Fang	0.026	0.020
Bamileke	-0.057	-0.180
Bassa	-0.056	0.049
Douala	0.221	0.184
Others	-0.061	-0.024
8. Urban-rural	0.230	0.058

[8] Although correlation coefficients provide quick and synthetic information, they may be somewhat misleading for a number of reasons. First, the intervals between the various points on the scale are not necessarily equal; it cannot be argued, for instance, that the skill level of individuals engaged in managerial and executive functions is seven times greater than that of workers located at the bottom of the occupational hierarchy. Second, the relationships between skill level and the independent variables are not necessarily linear, and this lack of linearity might correspond to the very nature of the association I am seeking. Thus, as similar coefficients may reflect different slopes, it is indispensable to examine *both* correlation coefficients and cross-tabulations of the variables under analysis.

more intensive participation of this ethnic group in modernizing processes. Alternatively, Bamileke are underrepresented at the summit of the nonmanual hierarchy, and although this may be attributed to their delayed exposure to modernizing forces, this form of ethnic particularism apparently operating within the nonmanual sector of employment still runs counter to my general argument.[9]

Further, the association between skill level and formal qualifications is less affected by ethnicity in the case of white- than of blue-collar populations. The proportion of nonmanual individuals in top skill levels (5 to 7) with more than seven years of aggregate training varies within relatively narrow limits, from a minimum of 36 percent for the Douala to a maximum of 51 percent for the Beti-Fang and the Bamileke. The range of corresponding variations is broader among manual populations and the corresponding figures decline from 69 percent for the Beti-Fang (excluding the Ewondo) to only 20 percent of the Douala.[10]

Age, aggregate training score, and skill levels.

In developing nations with high rates of change, it is difficult to compare the occupational and educational characteristics of individuals with *similar* skill levels but *differing* ages. They have not necessarily enjoyed the same opportunities. And even though their age may primarily reflect their overall seniority in the labor force and more specifically in the modern labor market, its effects on occupational attainment are not necessarily consistent or cumulative. To be sure, an individual spends the initial years of his career learning job patterns, establishing credentials and preparing himself to move ahead in the occupational hierarchy.[11] Although experiences which go with aging might initially facilitate access to the higher rungs of the occupational hierarchy, their benefits are likely to decline later on. The negative effects of age are particularly visible for manual workers; many employers assume that older persons have more rigid patterns of behavior as well as a greater propensity to fatigue. In addition, manual tasks are more frequently affected by the introduction of

---

[9] Variations in the differential access of distinctive ethnic groups to the highest rungs of the occupational hierarchy do not only characterize the Camerounian scene. In Ghana, it is quite clear that Ga, Akan, and Ewe peoples preempt the most desirable jobs in the manual labor market. See Peil, *The Ghanaian Factory Worker,* p. 44.

[10] Similar variations were observable in the Abidjan sample studied by the author. For example, the incidence of illiterate skilled manual workers varied from a maximum of 82 percent for the Malinke Voltaic to 54 percent for individuals migrating from countries located in the Gulf of Benin. Similarly, the population of white-collar workers with postprimary education varied from 11 percent for the Agni and related peoples to a high of 35 percent for the peoples coming from outside the Ivory Coast. In all cases, it is not clear whether the educational prerequisites used by employers vary along ethnic lines or whether the differential educational attainment of skilled individuals with differing ethnic origins reflect the distinctive educational and migratory experiences acquired by various peoples.

[11] For further elaboration, see Thurow, *Poverty and Discrimination,* p. 181.

new technologies. Finally, although occupational experiences increase uniformly with age, they are still less easily negotiable in the case of blue-collar wage earners.

Thus, zero-order correlations between skill level and age are 0.323 for the nonmanual population, against only 0.071 for blue-collar workers. The differential percentage of unskilled individuals between oldest and youngest cohorts is much sharper in the case of white- than of blue-collar workers. Almost three-quarters of individuals under twenty years of age belong to the lowest skill categories of the nonmanual population, as against only 13 percent of those over forty-five years of age. Among manual workers, the relevant figures vary only between 92 and 77 percent. Symmetrically, the percentage of individuals with higher skill levels (4 and above) rises from 9 percent for the youngest age group to 69 percent of their elders within the white-collar sector, but only from 4 to 8 percent for the relevant groups in the manual population. Hence, overall occupational experience is more often a necessary condition for occupational achievement in the first than the second case.[12]

As expected, however, age or overall seniority and aggregate training tend to substitute for each other as determinants of skill level. None of the youngest manual workers placed in skill level 4 has an aggregate training score lower than 1.5, against 17 percent of those between thirty-one and thirty-five years of age and 58 percent for their oldest counterparts. The corresponding figures for individuals with top skill levels (between 5 and 7) increase similarly from 0 to 7 and 30 percent, respectively. Symmetrically, the proportion of individuals in the same top skill levels who have had more than seven years of formal educational and vocational training drops from 80 percent for the cohort under twenty-five years of age to 23 percent for the cohort between thirty-one and thirty-five years of age, and reaches a minimum of 5 percent among the oldest segment of that population (Table 16).

Parallel trends are observable among nonmanual wage earners. None of the youngest nonmanual individuals in top skill levels has had less than seven years of aggregate educational and vocational training, against 16 percent for the group between thirty-one and thirty-five years of age and 34 percent for the oldest segment of that particular population. Symmetrically, the proportion of individuals placed in the top rungs of the hierarchy

---

12 This, of course, does not necessarily obtain in other countries. In Abidjan, for example, it is clear that the association between age and skill level is higher for manual than for nonmanual workers. Thus, the incidence of highly qualified nonmanual workers varies from 51 percent among those under twenty-nine years of age to 71 percent among those over fifty years old. Among manual workers, the corresponding figures are 29 and 10 percent. In relative terms, age is therefore a better predictor of manual achievement. In Ghana, M. Peil suggests the same phenomenon when she notes that among the manual population no less than one-half of the individuals over forty years of age are highly skilled, against about one-fifth of their counterparts under twenty-four years old. See Peil, *The Ghanaian Factory Worker*, p. 44.

TABLE 16

Relationship between Age, Aggregate Training Score and Skill Level
among Manual Workers
(percentage distribution)

Aggregate training score	15-20	21-25	26-30	Age 31-35	36-40	41-45	Over 45
				Skill level 4			
0	0.0	0.6	0.7	1.8	5.8	9.7	27.5
0.1-1.5	0.0	0.6	10.2	15.2	21.4	24.8	30.3
1.6-6.9	0.0	12.4	50.1	67.9	62.9	57.9	38.2
7.0	0.0	9.3	14.4	10.8	6.1	5.5	2.8
7.1-12.0	100.0	76.4	24.1	4.5	3.7	2.1	1.1
Over 12.0	0.0	0.6	0.4	0.0	0.0	0.0	0.0
Total	100.0	99.9	99.9	100.2	99.9	100.0	99.9
N	(27)	(161)	(278)	(336)	(294)	(145)	(178)
Percentage in skill level 4	3.2	4.1	5.1	7.1	8.3	7.1	6.8
				Skill levels 5-7			
0	--[a]	0.0	0.0	1.7	0.0	6.4	7.5
0.1-1.5	--	0.0	0.0	5.3	6.9	19.3	22.5
1.6-6.9	--	13.3	25.4	55.3	66.6	38.8	62.5
7.0	--	6.6	18.6	14.2	6.0	9.6	2.5
7.1-12.0	--	53.3	44.1	12.5	12.1	9.6	2.5
Over 12.0	--	26.7	11.8	10.8	9.2	16.1	2.5
Total	--	99.9	99.9	99.8	99.9	99.9	100.0
N	(5)	(15)	(59)	(56)	(68)	(31)	(40)
Percentage in skill levels 5-7	0.6	0.4	1.0	1.1	1.9	1.5	1.5

[a]The figures are too small to be converted into percentages.

who have had more than seven years of total vocational and educational
experiences declines from 64 percent for the youngest cohort to 47 percent
for their middle-aged counterparts and reaches a minimum of 24 percent
among the oldest workers (Table 17).

Even though the influence of formal qualifications on skill level is
uniformly more marked among younger wage earners, the effect of
educational credentials in this regard is more visible in the manual labor
market. The youngest workers who have reached the top of the blue-collar
occupational hierarchy and have had more than seven years of formal

TABLE 17

Relationship between Age, Aggregate Training Score, and Skill Level
among Nonmanual Workers
(percentage distribution)

Aggregate training score	15-20	21-25	26-30	Age 31-35	36-40	41-45	Over 45
				Skill level 4			
Less than 7.0	6.7	6.4	23.2	37.9	39.3	49.6	53.7
7.0	26.7	36.9	46.5	50.6	48.7	39.8	36.2
7.1-12.0	66.7	55.6	27.8	10.3	10.3	10.6	4.7
12.1 and above	0.0	1.0	2.5	1.2	1.7	0.0	5.4
Total	100.0	99.9	100.0	100.0	100.0	100.0	100.0
N	(15)	(203)	(284)	(324)	(235)	(124)	(152)
Percentage in skill level 4	8.6	17.4	25.3	32.2	35.3	36.2	44.2
				Skill levels 5-7			
Less than 7.0	--	9.0	13.1	16.3	21.8	30.5	34.1
7.0	--	27.5	28.6	36.3	38.1	47.2	41.5
7.1-12.0	--	54.5	42.7	34.8	25.3	13.9	15.8
12.1 and above	--	9.0	15.6	12.6	14.7	8.3	8.6
Total		100.0	100.0	100.0	99.9	99.9	100.0
N	(0)	(44)	(128)	(137)	(143)	(173)	(84)
Percentage in skill levels 5-7	0.0	3.8	10.9	13.5	21.4	21.2	24.3

training are sixteen times more numerous than their elders, but the corresponding ratio is less than three in the case of the nonmanual labor force.

However, the declining scarcity of qualified job applicants changes both the magnitude and the direction of differences between the aggregate training scores of highly skilled white-collar and blue-collar workers. Among the oldest cohorts (over forty-five years of age), formal qualifications are not only rare but they are also relatively more significant determinants of access to the top of the nonmanual than of the manual hierarchy. Within that age group, a little over 24 percent of the white-collar workers in skill levels 5 to 7 have had more than seven years of formal training, against 5 percent of their manual counterparts. Yet as one moves lower on the age continuum and as educational development becomes more apparent, there is a uniform rise in the educational qualification of *all* skilled wage earners and a corresponding decrease in the differential aggregate training scores of white- and blue-collar skilled populations. The direction of these contrasts is *reversed* at the lower end of the age continuum, and 80 percent of manual workers under twenty-five years of age in top skill levels has a maximal aggregate training score, against only 64 percent of their nonmanual counterparts.

Thus, the expectations that both employers and employees hold about the occupational implications of formal training are not independent of the supply of qualified personnel. Formal schooling appears to become both a necessary and sufficient condition for the occupational achievement of *young* blue-collar workers. In contrast, it remains necessary for entering nonmanual activities, but ceases to be the exclusive determinant of subsequent occupational achievement.[13]

Training on the job, aggregate training, and skill level

Differences between manual and nonmanual tasks are associated with contrasts in the influence of on-the-job training on the occupational attainment of the two populations. The correlation between participation in on-the-job training programs and current skill level is higher for blue- than white-collar workers (0.260 against 0.064).[14]

With the growth of educational institutions, larger firms cease to view on-the-job training as a *substitute* for formal schooling.[15] The highly skilled individuals who have begun their occupational life with large-scale organizations in spite of limited educational and vocational qualifications (below 7) are proportionately less numerous among younger than older cohorts of manual and nonmanual workers. Younger individuals with inadequate credentials encounter increasing difficulties not only in being initially hired by large-scale organizations but also in reaping the rewards stemming from corresponding experience. The younger a skilled manual or nonmanual worker is, the more likely he is to have *both* more than seven years of formal training and on-the-job training with a larger firm. No less than 29 percent of the youngest blue-collar workers in the top skill levels have followed this particular path, as against only 4 percent of their elders. Similarly, this route characterizes 10 percent of the highly skilled young nonmanual wage earners but only 5 percent of their elders (Table 18). In

---

[11] Students react quickly to changes in the occupational structure, and although secondary school students enrolled before independence were most often attracted by white-collar jobs, their successors enrolled in the first years of the postindependence period realized the increased opportunities offered in the blue-collar sectors. See, for instance, Clignet and Foster, *The Fortunate Few*, chap. 7.

[14] Participation in such programs varies markedly along ethnic lines. The Bamileke employed both in manual and nonmanual activities are more likely than any other group to have followed this particular path. This suggests that these Bamileke are likely to enter the labor market as wage earners in large-scale companies which give them preferential treatment.

[15] This raises once more the problem of the distinction between general and specific forms of training. See Chapter 3 of this study.

TABLE 18

Relationship between Total Training, Age, and Skill Level for Manual and Nonmanual Workers
(percentage distribution)

Total educational and On-the-Job training	15-30 Manual	15-30 Nonmanual	Age group 31-40 Manual	31-40 Nonmanual	Above 40 Manual	Above 40 Nonmanual
Skill level 4						
No formal education and no on-the-job training	0.0	0.0	0.1	0.2	2.7	0.0
Formal education of 7 years and above, but no on-the-job training	24.0	26.1	3.1	7.5	0.9	6.5
Formal education up to 7 years and on-the-job training with a modern firm	33.7	28.2	69.9	59.2	70.6	62.3
Formal education of 7 years and above and on-the-job training with a modern firm	13.6	7.7	9.2	2.7	4.0	2.5
Other[a]	28.7	38.0	17.7	30.4	21.8	28.7
Total	100.0	100.0	100.0	100.0	100.0	100.0
Skill levels 5-7						
No formal education and no on-the-job training	0.0	0.0	0.0	0.0	2.8	0.6
Formal education of 7 years and above but no on-the-job training	37.1	35.0	17.2	30.0	15.5	15.3
Formal education up to 7 years and above but no on-the-job training with a modern firm	17.9	25.3	27.0	34.7	57.7	58.6
Formal education of 7 years and above and on-the-job training with a modern firm	29.4	10.2	14.8	3.4	4.2	5.0
Other[a]	15.6	29.5	41.0	31.9	19.8	20.5
Total	100.0	100.0	100.0	100.0	100.0	100.0

a Includes on-the-job training with nonaccredited schools, correspondence courses, parents, or African entrepreneurs in conjunctions with or in lieu of formal education.

this sense, employers become more interested in offering *specific* rather than *general* forms of training to the young wage earners they intend to place in highly skilled positions.

To sum up, there is a tightening up of the prerequisites for access to the higher rungs of the manual or nonmanual hierarchy. This tightening up implies not only a rise in the level of formal qualifications expected from candidates to higher positions but also a more consistent initial exposure to the discipline of large-scale organizations.

Yet this tightening up does not always take similar forms in the two sectors of employment. The increased severity of academic hurdles perhaps leads a growing number of younger job applicants to take correspondence courses or to attend nonaccredited educational institutions in order to meet the expectations of their employers. Yet whereas this marginal form of vocational training is still rewarding in the case of young nonmanual workers (30 percent of the youngest individuals placed in skill levels 5 to 7 have learned their trade by this method, as against only 21 percent of their elders), the rewards attached to the unorthodox educational endeavors of blue-collar workers are increasingly elusive (the corresponding figures have dropped from 20 to 16 percent between older and younger cohorts).

Alternatively, however, initial experiences in the murky sector are more rewarding than they used to be, and this is particularly evident in the case of manual workers. Only 1 percent of the oldest manual workers in skill levels 5 to 7 began their occupational lives with friends and relatives, against 10 percent of the youngest ones. Among the corresponding nonmanual population, the corresponding figures are 4 and 7 percent, respectively. Thus, the erosion of boundaries between murky and modern sectors is selective.

Occupational seniority, aggregate training score, and skill level

Thus far, I have established that age and, hence, overall occupational experience influence the career profile of both groups of workers. Yet this concept remains ill-defined. An individual may have performed the occupation in which he is currently engaged for a large number of years with different employers. Alternatively, he may have spent most of his active working life with the same company in a variety of jobs. As manual skills are not easily transferable, seniority *in the firm* should be a more significant determinant of manual occupational attainment. In contrast, seniority on the job (independently of where it has been practiced) should be a better predictor of nonmanual skill levels.

Even though the two forms of seniority are not independent of age, and hence of *overall* occupational experience, these three aspects of job experience are analytically distinct.[16] Overall occupational experience and

---

· [16] In the manual population, the correlation between age and seniority on the job is 0.656, between age and seniority in the firm is 0.538, and between the two forms of seniority is 0.649. Among nonmanual workers, the three correlation coefficients are 0.675, and 0.595, and 0.579.

seniority on the job depend primarily on individual abilities and motivation but seniority in the firm depends as much on the characteristics of the labor market, the general patterns of economic development, and more specifically the age of the firm.[17]

Whereas seniority on the job is uniformly a better predictor of current skill levels, seniority in the firm is unexpectedly more closely associated with nonmanual than manual attainment.[18] In addition, *disparities* between the amount of time spent in a job and in a firm increase as one moves up in the hierarchy. Thus, three-quarters of highly skilled nonmanual workers have spent differing amounts of time in their current job and with their current employer, as against only 56 percent of those placed lower in the hierarchy. Although less marked, the pattern is similar among manual workers, and the corresponding figures are 61 and 52 percent, respectively. But does a worker who stays longer in a particular *job* than with a particular *firm* have proportionately better chances to achieve a high skill level, and are there contrasts between manual and nonmanual wage earners along these lines?

In spite of my assumption, a high degree of commitment toward employers rather than toward jobs is more characteristic of highly skilled nonmanual workers. Almost one-half of highly skilled nonmanual workers have been longer with their current employer than on their current job, but only one-fourth of them have had the reverse experience and stayed longer on the job than in their current employment. Conversely, 30 percent of highly skilled manual wage earners have spent more time in their current firm than on their current job or, alternatively, more time in their current

[17] A multiple regression analysis was run to analyze the distribution of seniority in the firms among the two populations. A combination of selected independent variables accounts for 42 percent of the variance in seniority among manual workers and for 48 percent of its variance among nonmanual wage earners. In both cases, age has the highest raw regression coefficient of all variables entered in the equation (0.359 and 0.341, respectively). Among manual workers the next highest coefficients are those associated with age of firm (0.021) and branch of activitiy (with construction industries entered as a dummy variable 2.1). The significant influence of the characteristics of the firm on worker seniority is explainable in terms of the particular patterns of economic development in the Cameroun and other African countries: different types of industry and organization have come to Africa at very different periods of time. Initial phases of development were dominated by plantations and export/import companies. A second period saw the growth of transportation, banks, and insurance, whereas the postindependence period has witnessed the emergence of processing industries. Clearly, individuals in processing industries cannot have more than a few years' seniority; those employed in banks are unlikely to have more than fifteen years' seniority; whereas employees in plantation activities can achieve relatively higher levels of seniority.

[18] For nonmanual workers, the relevant zero-order correlation coefficients are 0.287 and 0.262. For manual wage earners, the corresponding figures are 0.184 and 0.108. A similar relationship between seniority on the job and occupational attainment is observable among the manual workers in Ghana. In the sample studies by M. Peil, the proportion of individuals with five years' and more experience on the same job increases from 18 percent among unskilled workers to 34 among their highly skilled counterparts. See *The Ghanaian Factory Worker,* p. 44.

job than with their current employer. In this sense, nonmanual achievement is more influenced by particularistic factors than the nature of the work would have led one to believe.

The next step of the analysis is to evaluate the combined effects of the two types of seniority and of formal qualifications on the differential occupational attainment of the two segments of the modern labor force. Although the percentage of individuals in skill level 4 with more than the equivalent of seven years' formal training uniformly declines as a function of their experience on the job, the extent of this decline is proportionately less marked in the case of nonmanual workers (Table 19). Among the individuals placed in the fourth category of the nonmanual hierarchy, those with substantial educational and vocational qualifications are 4.4 times more numerous in the group with less than five years of experience than in the group with at least ten years of occupational seniority, whereas the corresponding ratio increases to 25 for manual workers. Yet the influence of academic credentials on access to top skill levels is uniformly more independent of occupational experience. Thus in the two sectors of employment, highly skilled workers with an aggregate training score over 7 are less than three times more numerous among the groups with minimal seniority than among those with maximal experience.

But if *high* educational qualifications compensate for *low* occupational seniority, does *long* commitment to a specific occupational role override the negative impact of *low* formal training? The proportion of highly skilled nonmanual workers with less than seven years of formal qualifications increases from a minimum of 13 percent for those with minimal job experience to 31 percent for those with at least 10 years of seniority in their profession. Greater in absolute terms, the range of variation is proportionately narrower among manual wage earners, and the corresponding figures are 35 and 74 percent, respectively. In brief, the combined influence of job experience and formal training on occupational attainment varies between the two categories of workers. As hypothesized, educational and occupational credentials are more likely to act as substitutes for each other in the nonmanual labor market.

The combined influence of formal qualifications and seniority in the firm on occupational attainment follows a different pattern. A lack of seniority in the firm does not prevent nonmanual workers with high formal qualifications fron gaining access to top positions, and the percentage of highly skilled individuals with an aggregate training score of 7 and more increases from 24 percent among those with more than ten years in the same firm to 61 percent among those who entered their current employment during the two years preceding the survey. In contrast, the proportion of highly educated manual workers in skill levels 5 to 7 is independent of variations in seniority and remains uniformly below 25 percent.

TABLE 19

Aggregate Training Score of Nonmanual and Manual Workers by Skill level and Seniority on the Job
(percentage distribution)

Aggregate training score	Below 5 years' experience		5-10 years' experience		Over 10 years' experience	
	Manual	Nonmanual	Manual	Nonmanual	Manual	Nonmanual
	Skill Category 4					
0	1.7	--	2.1	--	10.9	--
0.1-1.5	7.3	--	13.5	--	21.8	--
1.6-6.9	26.7	19.3	61.1	33.7	59.5	48.2
7	12.1	40.6	10.7	51.7	5.7	42.8
7.1-12	52.2	38.3	12.3	12.7	2.1	7.1
12 and above	0.0	1.8	0.3	2.0	0.0	1.9
Total	100.0	100.0	100.0	100.1	100.0	100.0
N	(364)	(530)	(372)	(359)	(673)	(448)
	Skill Category 5-7					
0	0.0	--	1.4	--	3.9	--
0.1-1.5	0.0	--	2.8	--	15.6	--
1.6-6.9	34.5	12.8	49.3	21.2	54.7	31.0
7	16.5	31.1	11.2	34.2	7.8	42.2
7.1-12	31.4	36.2	28.2	35.7	7.8	20.3
12 and above	17.6	19.9	7.0	8.9	10.1	6.5
Total	100.0	100.0	99.9	100.0	99.9	100.0
N	(74)	(241)	(71)	(146)	(119)	(216)

Alternatively, the amount of time spent with a same employer does not compensate for a lack of appropriate educational and vocational qualifications. Among highly skilled nonmanual workers, the proportion of individuals with *low* aggregate training scores hardly increases from 21 percent among those with a *minimal* seniority to 27 percent among those with more than ten years in the same firm. Among their manual counterparts, the range of variations is even narrower, and the corresponding figures are 64 and 65 percent, respectively.

To sum up, educational qualifications and occupational seniority uniformly compensate for each other in the influence they exert on patterns of access to top jobs because these two variables reflect "universalistic" and congruent processes. However, to the extent that nonmanual skills are more easily transferable throughout the entire labor market, the trade-off between educational qualifications and experience on the job is more flexible in the case of white- than of blue-collar wage earners.

Although in a more limited way, the trade-off between seniority in the firm, educational qualifications, and experience on the job is also more flexible in the case of nonmanual workers. In this sense, nonmanual achievement depends as much on particularistic factors. As employers have more frequent and more intense contacts with their white-collar personnel, they rely more often on a direct evaluation of individual performance than on abstract educational or occupational credentials to identify the type of worker they want to enter supervisory roles. In addition, the exercise of nonmanual supervisory functions is not devoid of political considerations, and the amount of time spent with a firm becomes, therefore, an important indicator of the loyalty that an African supervisor might display toward the interest of management.[19]

The meaning attached to the exercise of supervisory functions in manual work involves greater technical autonomy and responsibility. As many European employers tend to hold negative stereotypes about the mechanical ability and orientation of their African labor force, they are inclined to attach a relatively greater weight to educational and vocational credentials as conditions for access to the higher levels of the manual hierarchy; but they are also less likely to use such credentials as substitutes for the more direct experience they have of the skills displayed by their manual workers. In absolute terms, seniority in the firm remains the major passport to the highest rungs of the manual hierarchy.

---

[19] At the same time the differential importance that employers attach to the combined influence of formal training and seniority in the firm or occupational experience may also reflect the distinctive pressures exerted toward a greater Africanization of skilled jobs within the nonmanual sector; hence, the organizational ability of white-collar workers may be more threatening. For an analysis of the stereotype held by Europeans of African workers, see, for instance, R. Cruise O'Brien, *White Society in Black Africa* (Evanston: Northwestern University Press, 1972), chaps. 5 and 6.

Diversity of occupational experience,
aggregate training score, and skill level

Occupational experience reflects not only the *stability* that an individual displays in his occupational role or his specific employment, but also the *diversity* of jobs he has held since his initial entry into the labor market. This diversity is particularly important to analyze in the African context, for many European employers are tempted to hold negative views about changes in occupation, which they view as symbolic of a lack of commitment to the requirements of industrialization and modernization. The view that changes in occupation reflect occupational instability is probably particularly true of countries formerly dominated by France, as French traditions minimize the importance of alternative channels of upward mobility and emphasize the influence of loyalty to the organization on promotion.[20]

Nonmanual skills are nevertheless easily transferable, and white-collar workers frequently have held more than one job after their entry into the labor market. They have learned and/or held an average of 1.62 occupations against only 1.14 for the manual workers. About 30 percent of the former have held or learned more than three jobs, against only 15 percent of the blue-collar labor force.[21]

In addition, the determinants of occupational diversity are not alike for the two populations. Although the total number of jobs varies with the structure of existing opportunities and is greater in urban than rural areas, the differential opportunities offered by distinct environments are not alike for the two categories of wage earners (Table 20). The proportion of nonmanual individuals who have held more than one job varies from 72 percent in the rural hinterland to 90 percent in the largest cities of the Cameroun, but the corresponding proportions among blue-collar workers only increase from 64 percent in the rural areas to 74 percent in urban centers. Thus, contrasts in the occupational experiences of nonmanual and manual populations are most marked in the largest labor markets.

Diversity of experiences also depends on age. To be sure, older individuals are more likely to take advantage of the alternative opportunities offered by the labor market, but the effect of age in this respect still depends on societal rates of change. As Table 20 shows, the association between age and number of jobs held is curvilinear and remains positive *only* within certain limits. The low rate of change characterizing the Camerounian economy before World War II did not provide the

---

[20] For a description of the psychological traits associated with the French form of this pattern, see M. Crozier, *The Bureaucratic Phenomenon* (Chicago: University of Chicago Press, 1964).

[21] This evaluation remains gross, for I am dealing only with the first and second jobs learned or performed after the entry of the individuals into the labor force and the occupation they had immediately prior to their current employment.

TABLE 20
Influence of Age and of Residence on the Occupational Experience
of Manual and Nonmanual Workers

| Age | Percentage of individuals having held more than two Jobs since their entry into the labor market | |
	Manual	Nonmanual
15-20		
Rural	2.9	33.1
Urban	18.0	31.3
21-25		
Rural	17.6	52.6
Urban	29.5	42.2
26-30		
Rural	26.4	35.2
Urban	36.3	42.5
31-35		
Rural	22.4	41.7
Urban	35.8	52.8
36-40		
Rural	23.9	50.1
Urban	34.1	70.2
41-45		
Rural	22.9	70.4
Urban	29.7	59.6
Above 45		
Rural	22.4	40.0
Urban	26.7	51.1

individuals entering the labor market at that date with many occupational alternatives, and the oldest African wage earners have not changed occupations as often as their immediate successors.

Most important, time lags in the expansion of manual and nonmanual activities across the country explain the differential occupational mobility of the various age cohorts of the Camerounian labor force. Thus, the percentage of manual workers who currently live in the hinterland and have held more than two jobs since their entry in the labor force begins to decline among the cohorts over thirty years of age, who probably entered the labor market before 1950. In contrast, among urbanized nonmanual workers, the decline occurs only for the cohort over forty years of age who entered the labor market before 1940. In other words, there is an apparent minimal lag of ten years in the relative take-off points of the tertiary sector of the urban economy and of the primary and secondary sectors in rural areas. Because of this differential growth, contrasts in the relative mobility of blue- and white-collar workers do not remain constant over time, nor between urban and rural areas.

Dependent on the structure of the local labor market, diversity of prior occupational experience is also affected by educational and vocational attainment. Within each age group, the percentage of individuals who have held or learned more than two jobs since their entry in the labor force increases with their educational and vocational credentials (Table 21). In other words, willingness to take occupational risks increases with educational attainment.[22] Yet the differential influence of formal schooling

TABLE 21
Percentage of Workers Who Have Learned or Performed More than One Job Prior to Present Job, by Training Score and Age

| Age | Aggregate training score | | | | | |
	0	0.1-1.5	1.6-6.9	7	7.1-12	12.1 & above
15-20						
Manual	2.9	7.1	8.9	10.3	33.3	*
Nonmanual	--	--	5.3	23.0	74.5	--
21-25						
Manual	11.1	17.4	24.1	22.1	55.6	*
Nonmanual	--	--	37.4	37.5	55.7	76.9
26-30						
Manual	13.7	28.8	42.6	29.7	58.3	*
Nonmanual	--	--	48.6	47.6	62.7	55.8
31-35						
Manual	15.7	26.1	43.3	38.2	61.2	*
Nonmanual	--	--	47.6	52.1	78.5	81.8
36-40						
Manual	15.3	34.0	42.9	43.0	72.2	*
Nonmanual	--	--	52.8	55.2	77.6	72.0
41-45						
Manual	16.1	28.9	47.1	45.4	63.6	*
Nonmanual	--	--	55.0	67.7	74.0	100.0
Above 45						
Manual	18.0	31.4	50.7	42.8	66.6	*
Nonmanual	--	--	45.2	59.9	72.7	76.5

*Fewer than ten cases. The figures are too small to be translated into percentages.

[22] The data presented by M. Peil suggest marked contrasts between the number of jobs held by Ghanaian manual and nonmanual workers. No less than 54 percent of the latter group had three or more jobs, against less than 30 percent of the former. Among manual workers, there

on the diversity of experience acquired by manual and nonmanual populations is not stable over time. Among the youngest cohorts, the association between formal qualifications and number of jobs previously held is more marked among nonmanual than manual workers, but the pattern is reversed among their elders. This may reflect the differential growth of the two sectors of activity and hence the differential risks associated with changes of jobs at various points in time. Because initially the manual labor market was narrower and tended to follow more particularistic patterns of organization, manual workers needed proportionately greater skills to change jobs.

But if the determinants of the diversity of occupational experience achieved by manual and nonmanual workers are not alike, can one expect parallel contrasts in the consequences attached to their prior experience? In general terms, and in contrast to my assumption, diversity of occupational experience has a stronger influence on manual than on nonmanual skill levels. The relevant zero-order correlation coefficients are 0.317 in the first instance, as opposed to 0.248 in the second. However, the influence exerted by diversity of experience is not the same when one considers the entire distribution of manual and nonmanual skill levels or their upper segments. Over half the nonmanual populations who have learned or performed at least four jobs since their entry in the labor force are currently engaged in highly qualified tasks which require at least junior supervisory functions, against only 14 percent of their manual counterparts. Yet the *relative* effect of diversity of occupational experience remains more evident in the case of manual wage earners. An increase of from zero to three in the number of jobs held prior to the current position is associated with a *fortyfold* increase in the proportion of skilled manual workers, but with only a *threefold* increase among nonmanual employees.

However, the effects of the diversity of occupational experience also depend on academic credentials. Formal qualifications and diversity of occupational experience seem to act as *joint conditions* for gaining access to highly skilled manaual and nonmanual positions (Table 22). Put in other terms, no less than 28 percent of white-collar workers who have both higher academic qualifications and have held over three jobs since they

---

seems to be a negative association between number of jobs performed and access to the highest rungs of the hierarchy. Thus, only 8 percent of unskilled manual workers have had only one type of job, against 40 percent of their skilled counterparts. See Peil, *The Ghanaian Factory Worker,* p. 50. Alternatively, however, changes in job seem to be associated with upward mobility among the manual workers of Abidjan in the Ivory Coast. Although only 57 percent of the sampled unskilled workers had some experience prior to the job they had at the time of the study (1963), this characterized 88 percent of their skilled counterparts. However, such a relationship was not observable among the nonmanual population. The incidence of individuals with prior occupational experience was 67 percent among the lowest skill categories, 82 percent among the intermediate rungs of the nonmanual hierarchy, and 69 percent among the top skill echelons.

TABLE 22
Distribution of Formal Qualifications and Diversity of Occupational Experiences among Skilled and Highly Skilled Manual and Nonmanual Workers
(percentage distribution)

	Aggregate educational score						
	0	0.1-1.5	1.6-6.9	7	7.1-12	12.1 and above	Total
Manual, skill level 4							
No jobs before present	39.1	13.0	43.5	4.3	--	--	99.9 (23)
More than two jobs before present	2.4	14.6	59.3	6.8	16.9	--	100.0 (383)
Nonmanual, skill level 4							
No jobs before present	--	--	48.7	43.6	6.4	1.3	100.0 (78)
More than two jobs before present	--	--	31.5	41.3	24.0	3.3	100.0 (429)
Manual, skill levels 5-7							
No jobs before present	14.2	14.2	57.4	7.1	7.1	--	100.0 (14)
More than two jobs before present	2.5	10.4	51.9	7.8	18.2	9.1	99.9 (77)
Nonmanual, skill levels 5-7							
No jobs before present	--	--	61.5	50.7	7.8	0.0	100.0 (13)
More than two jobs before present	--	--	18.4	33.9	33.1	14.6	100.0 (212)

Note: Figure in final column in parentheses is the number of workers in the sample.

began to work have reached the top of the hierarchy, as against only 2 percent of those with minimal credentials and no prior experience. Among manuals, only 5 percent of the individuals with maximal educational qualifications and many prior experiences are currently engaged in highly skilled positions, as against 0.7 percent of those with minimal educational and occupational experiences. Thus, high formal qualifications *and* diversity of occupational experience considered jointly seem to constitute a more important prerequisite for gaining access into the top positions of the nonmanual rather than the manual hierarchy.

Patterns of mobility and skill level

As diversity of occupational experiences refers not only to the *number* but also to the *nature* of jobs previously held by wage earners, it is necessary to make a more detailed assessment of occupational trajectories.

There are significant differences in the job histories of manual and nonmanual workers. Few in number, crossovers between these two types of employment are asymmetric; no less than 19 percent of white-collar workers entered the labor market as manual wage earners, whereas only 3 percent of their blue-collar counterparts began their career by learning or performing a nonmanual job.[23] The same patterns of crossover between the two sectors of employment characterize as well individuals who have held another job between their current role and the one they performed at the time of their entry in the labor force. No less than 34 percent of the white-collar workes with at least two jobs before their current employment were previously involved in manual work, but only 12 percent of manual wage earners with similar characteristics had a clerical job before being currently involved in blue-collar activities. Thus, nonmanual employment seems to be more attractive than manual work.[24]

This, however, provides only a gross approximation of the occupational history of the two populations. The complexity of the codes used to describe the occupations performed or learned by individuals during their active life facilitates a more detailed analysis of occupational shifts. After

---

[23] In Ghana, the situation tends to be reversed, and although only 4 percent of clerical workers began their careers as manual workers, about 7 percent of their manual counterparts entered the labor market as clerks. Yet if one takes the overall profile of the jobs performed by these two types of worker, 57 percent of clerical workers have at one point in their career been employed in a manual capacity, whereas conversely less than 26 percent of blue-collar employees have had white-collar jobs. In this sense, the patterns of mobility are comparable in the two countries. See Peil, *The Ghanaian Factory Worker,* p. 50. In the Ivory Coast, similarly, although only 12 percent of manual workers had begun their career in the white-collar sector, no less than 26 percent of their white-collar counterparts had been initially employed in a manual occupation.

[24] It would have been interesting to see whether the forms of mobility experienced by Camerounian respondents varied with the nature of the employer for whom they initially worked. In the Ivory Coast the data suggest that access to the top of the manual or non-manual hierarchy was easier for individuals who had initially worked for the government.

having eliminated those individuals who are still performing the same job they had on entry into the labor market, one can distinguish those wage earners who have experienced upward mobility (with or without transfer from manual to nonmanual activities) from those who have experienced downward mobility and from those who have changed jobs but have not moved up or down the status scale. Although subjective, this evaluation of mobility is based on the prestige, pay, and the skills attached to specific occupations.[25]

Differences in the nature and desirability of nonmanual and manual work are associated with parallel contrasts in the mobility pattern prevailing in the two sectors of employment. One-fourth of nonmanual workers are upwardly mobile between their *first* and current occupations, as against 11 percent of the blue-collar wage earners. Similarly, 23 percent of the former are upwardly mobile between *prior* and present jobs, against 12 percent of the latter.

But what are the determinants of upward mobility? Although educational and vocational experiences determine the point of entry into the manual or the nonmanual hierarchy, subsequent movements within the labor market depend more closely on actual performance. Correspondingly, the relative influence of formal qualifications declines as a direct function of the length of time spent in the labor force; thus, the relationship between aggregate training scores and mobility experienced between first and current jobs is tighter than that between formal qualifications and the mobility between prior and current occupations.

Regardless of age, a lack of vocational and educational qualifications is significantly associated with downward mobility between first job learned or performed and current occupation. Further, the effects of such a lack are more significant among nonmanual workers. About 16 percent of those white-collar workers with less than seven years of formal schooling have moved downward in the occupational ladder, as against 7 percent of those who had more than seven years of educational and vocational training. Among their manual counterparts, the corresponding figures are 85 and 78 percent, respectively. Put another way, 60 percent of the downwardly mobile nonmanual workers have minimal academic credentials as opposed to only one-half of their upwardly mobile counterparts. At the same time, similarly low credentials characterize 84 percent of the downwardly mobile manual individuals, but 88 percent of those who are upwardly mobile.

The picture becomes clearer when one takes age into account. With an increase in the time span between first and current jobs, variations in aggregate training scores are more closely related to the particular form of mobility studied here (Table 23). Opportunities for upward mobility are proportionately more numerous for all the educated individuals who have

---

[25] For a discussion of the difficulties associated with the definition of mobility, see Peil, *The Ghanaian Factory Worker*, pp. 53-59.

TABLE 23
Mobility between First Job Performed and Present Job
by Category of Worker, Age, and Aggregate Training Score
(percentage distribution)

Aggregate training score	Mobility			
	Downward	Lateral	Upward	Total
Below 7.0				
Less than 25 years old				
Manual	84.2	5.4	10.4	100.0
Nonmanual	13.5	61.0	15.5	100.0
Over 35 years old				
Manual	87.4	4.9	7.7	100.0
Nonmanual	34.7	48.8	16.5	100.0
7.0				
Less than 25 years old				
Manual	73.0	4.5	22.5	100.0
Nonmanual	20.0	66.0	14.0	100.0
Over 35 years old				
Manual	64.6	9.6	25.8	100.0
Nonmanual	7.7	62.8	29.5	100.0
Above 7.0				
Less than 25 years old				
Manual	80.6	12.9	6.5	100.0
Nonmanual	8.1	79.8	12.1	100.0
Over 35 years old				
Manual	60.0	20.0	20.0	100.0
Nonmanual	6.7	50.0	43.3	100.0

spent a long time in the labor force than for those who have just entered the labor market. Among the oldest age groups, the proportion of upwardly mobile manual workers rises from 8 percent for those with low academic credentials to 20 percent for those with maximal aggregate training scores; this proportion climbs from 17 to 43 percent among the oldest white-collar workers with the corresponding educational characteristics.

In brief, vocational and educational credentials influence both the point of entry into the manual or nonmanual hierarchy and the subsequent moves within these two labor markets. Yet the relative influence of such credentials also varies with the scarcity of educated job seekers. During the early phases of development, it was difficult for employers to find workers with adequate qualifications, and older individuals encountered few difficulties in successfully negotiating their skills, and particularly so in the white-collar market. Conversely, current high rates of educational development lead to a decline in the premium attached to formal schooling, and this trend works against white-collar workers.

Thus, the degree to which educated individuals who have just entered the labor force are able to preempt the jobs offering many opportunities for advancement depends on the stability of the economy.[26] In developing countries, time lags between the early growth of the tertiary sector and the later processes of industrialization lead to parallel contrasts in the rewards that nonmanual and manual workers derive from their formal schooling. As the scarcity of educated job seekers declines, nonmanual workers with high academic credentials are obliged to wait for longer periods of time before reaping the rewards associated with their educational attainment. Conversely, as industrialization maintains the demand for educated manual workers at a high level, blue-collar workers with high academic qualifications are more frequently in a position to reap immediately the rewards which go with a relatively high level of schooling.

Yet the effects of formal education on mobility patterns decline when one shortens the time span used for defining levels of occupational achievement and when one compares in this regard current and immediately preceding job experiences.

Because such a comparison emphasizes the importance of past occupational experience, there is a corresponding decline in the role that formal schooling plays in upward mobility between *prior* and current occupations, and this decline is particularly evident among the oldest cohorts of wage earners. Thus, a low training score does not prevent older manual workers from experiencing upward mobility between their last and their present jobs twice as frequently as between their first and current ones (the relevant figures are 16 against 8 percent), whereas the corresponding difference is much smaller for their youngest counterparts (11 against 10 percent). Among young nonmanual workers with similarly low qualifications, the proportions of upwardly mobile individuals climbs from 16 percent when one takes the first job as a point of reference to 20 percent when one compares their current roles with their immediately preceding occupation, whereas among their elders the corresponding proportions increase more markedly from 17 to 26 percent (Tables 23 and 24).

To summarize, occupational experience compensates more often for a lack of academic credentials as a determinant of upward mobility among older than younger cohorts and among nonmanual than manual workers. The place-bound character of manual skills often prevents blue-collar workers from negotiating as successfully as their white-collar counterparts the variety of occupational experience they have acquired in the past.

---

[26] See Thurow, *Poverty and Discrimination,* p. 181.

TABLE 24
Mobility between Previous and Present Job
by Category of Worker, Age, and Aggregate Training Score
(percentage distribution)

Aggregate training score	Mobility			
	Downward	Lateral	Upward	Total
Below 7.0				
Less than 25 years old				
Manual	80.0	9.2	10.7	99.9
Nonmanual	15.2	65.2	19.6	100.0
Over 35 years old				
Manual	73.1	11.2	15.7	100.0
Nonmanual	10.7	62.8	26.4	99.9
7.0				
Less than 25 years old				
Manual	87.4	9.1	3.4	99.9
Nonmanual	3.9	64.7	31.3	99.9
Over 35 years old				
Manual	78.3	18.3	33.3	99.9
Nonmanual	4.0	78.9	17.0	99.9
Above 7.0				
Less than 25 years old				
Manual	75.1	16.2	8.6	99.9
Nonmanual	23.1	76.9	0.0	100.0
Over 35 years old				
Manual	58.3	22.2	19.4	99.9
Nonmanual	5.3	56.8	37.9	100.0

As the overall profile of the entire white- and blue-collar populations differs from that of the segments of the labor force that have reached the top rungs of the occupational ladder, are there similar contrasts in their respective mobility patterns? Three-quarters of top manual personnel entered the labor market at their present skill level, as against less than one-half of their nonmanual counterparts. In addition, 31 percent of the most skilled nonmanual workers have experienced upward mobility between the job they learned or performed at the time of their entry into the market and their current position, as against 5 percent of their manual counterparts. Similarly, 22 percent of the former experienced upward mobility between prior and present activities, as against 7 percent of manuals. In brief, access to the highest rungs of the nonmanual hierarchy is more fluid than access to the equivalent rungs in the manual ladder.

However, the influence of formal education on the mobility of highly skilled workers is far from clear. To be sure, formal qualifications favor the upward mobility of highly skilled nonmanual workers between first job learned or performed and current occupation. Over one-half of the individuals who have moved upward toward such skill levels have an aggregate training score superior to 7, as against only 25 percent of their counterparts who have experienced downward mobility.[27] The corresponding figures are 21 and 15 percent for the equivalent groups in the blue-collar population.

At the same time, the influence of a high level of formal training on mobility between immediately prior and present job is more problematic. Among highly skilled nonmanual populations, high aggregate training scores are more frequent among downwardly than upwardly mobile individuals, and two-thirds of the former have had more than seven years of vocational and educational training, against only 32 percent of the latter. Thus, the fit between the educational qualifications and the job histories of highly skilled white-collar workers ceases to be perfect, and conflicts are likely to occur betwen the aspirations of these individuals and the evaluation that employers make of their performance. To quote an ancient adage: "The Tarpeian rock is close to the Capitol."

Skill Level of Manual and Nonmanual Populations: An Overview

In the preceding analysis, I have considered only a limited number of factors that influence the occupational attainment of Camerounian workers. I can now turn to an examination of their combined effects.

This analysis requires a variety of preliminary steps. First, the statistics involved presuppose a linear association between dependent and independent variables. As already indicated, this assumption may prove to be unwarranted, and the effects of formal schooling or of seniority on occupational attainment are not always stable. That is, the influence of an additional year of training may be more powerful at the lower than at the upper end of the educational scale, and it can be hypothesized that the difference between twelve and thirteen years of formal schooling is less significant than the contrast betwen six and seven years of training, for the second example corresponds to effective graduation from the primary school system.[28] Yet the exact form of the association between formal schooling and dependent variables is not known, and this requires a transformation of aggregate training scores to determine in which forms

---

[27] Here I am considering individuals who moved down from categories 6 or 7 to category 5.

[28] For an illustration of this phenomenon in the United States, see P. Andrisani, "An Empirical Analysis of the Dual Labor Market Theory" (Center for Human Resource Research, Ohio State University, 1973).

they yield the highest correlations. Therefore, I have compared raw aggregate scores with their squared and their logarithmic values.[29]

Second, the model on which multiple regression analysis is based is purely additive, and simple independent variables are successively introduced in the equation as if their respective influences were independent of one another. Yet in certain instances it may be argued that some variables act according to a multiplicative rather than additive pattern.[30] In such cases, the variance in the dependent variable explained by the *product* of these two variables is larger than that accounted for by their *sum*. In subsequent multiple regressions, I have therefore attempted to define which independent variables operate according to a multiplicative rather than additive pattern. For example, I have established that the zero-order correlation coefficient between skill level and the *product* of aggregate training scores and seniority in the firm is higher than that between skill level and the *sum* of these two latter variables. Accordingly, I have introduced the product of these two measures as a separate variable in the equations.[31]

Finally, certain variables appear to be insufficiently distinct from one another both in statistical and substantive terms. For example, age, seniority in the firm, and seniority on the job are highly interrelated and tend to cover somewhat similar parts of the social universe in which individual workers move. Accordingly, I have retained in the equation only the one variable that correlates most highly with skill level.

Although the theme of my argument has been that the white-collar labor market is more structured and hence more easily predictable, the results of the multiple regression analysis presented in Table 25 suggest that educational, ethnic, and occupational backgrounds only account for one-third of the variance in the distribution of manual and nonmanual skills. In this sense, my ssumptions are not valid and access to higher white-collar positions seems to be as randomly distributed as access to top manual jobs.

In spite of these disappointing results, the structure of the multiple regression seems to confirm some of my hypotheses concerning the differential determinants of occupational attainment in the two spheres of activity. First, the number of variables needed to account for a maximal variance in skill level distribution is *smaller* in the case of nonmanual workers. This suggests that the structure of occupational attainment is simpler for this particular population than for its manual counterpart.

[29] Of course, the use of dummy variables employed here to deal with qualitative variables (ethnic status and so forth) may be extended to quantitative variables. Thus, the transformation of educational categories into such dummy variables would have enabled one to assess the contribution of each level of formal schooling to the career of an individual. Although this technique would have enabled one to determine the exact nature of the slope of the association between education or seniority and the dependent variables, it would have been quite costly.

[30] See Thurow, *Poverty and Discrimination*, chap. 5.

[31] Of course, the procedure is legitimate only insofar as the correlation between the two independent variables remains moderate.

TABLE 25
Multiple Regressions of the Determinants of Skill Levels

	Manual Workers		
N	23,210		
Mean	1.707		
Standard deviation	0.586		
Intercept	0.414		
R^2	0.343		

Variables	Beta	t	R^2
1. Joint seniority in the firm aggregate training scores[a]	0.012	42.90	0.177
2. Number of jobs learned or performed	2.410	43.39	0.237
3. Upward mobility (second job learned or performed and current occupation)	5.001	46.36	0.301
4. Douala origin	9.440	24.46	0.320
5. Aggregate training score^2	0.008	27.04	0.330
6. Age	0.138	21.00	0.343

	Nonmanual workers		
N	4914		
Mean	3.027		
Standard deviation	1.309		
Intercept	0.744		
R^2	0.330		

Variables	Beta	t	R^2
1. Joint seniority in the firm and aggregate training score^2	0.010	18.39	0.189
2. Aggregate training score^2	0.008	24.48	0.256
3. Age	0.366	16.68	0.302
4. Number of jobs learned or performed	2.223	14.28	0.330

[a]*Joint* means the multiplication of educational and seniority scores.

Second, the independent effect of formal training is more powerful for the first than the second group. This variable ranks second in terms of significance for the nonmanual population, but only fifth for blue-collar workers. Third, although ethnicity enters as a significant factor for manuals, it has no significant predictive power for the distribution of nonmanual skills. Alternatively, age enters as a significant variable in the nonmanual equation, and the effects of overall occupational experience seem to be more cumulative in the white- than the blue-collar sector.

Despite these contrasts, the fact remains that formal academic credentials, seniority, and diversity of occupational experience are uniformly the most critical determinants of the position currently achieved by wage earners in the modern sector of the economy. The salience of occupational mobility in this regard is remarkable. Although commitment (as measured by achievement) is deemed to depend as much on stability as on mobility, jacks-of-all-trades have more chance than highly specialized individuals to successfully meet the challenges of the industrial world. This probably mirrors the relatively low degree of division of labor operating in the Camerounian market. Finally, the effects of formal education and occupational experience are multiplicative more than additive. Although I do not have the appropriate longitudinal data, I may hypothesize that increased disparities between rates of educational and occupational developments will constrict the structure of occupational rewards and opportunities even more. Accordingly, the combined effects of high academic credentials and prolonged occupational experience on attainment should be even more powerful tomorrow than today.

Camerounian Salary Structures: The Legal Framework

Because of the large number of individuals employed in the public sector and of their frequent intervention in economic and political planning, Camerounian authorities tend to give a strict definition of the components of income and of their determinants. Thus, legislation determines variations in pay scales in function of the place where people work, the period over which their tasks are to be performed, the nature and the quantity of the work to be done, and the characteristics of the workers themselves.

First, the government has drawn up distinctive salary zones based on the assumption that costs of living vary across regions. There are four such zones: the first comprises the cities of Douala, Yaoundé, and Edea; the second includes the cities of Ebolowa, Kribi, Mbalmayo, and Nkongsamba as well as the region of the Wouri; the third comprises the remaining urban centers in the country, the Nyong and Sanaga, the Sanaga Maritime, the Mungo, the Ntam, the Nkem; and the last covers the remaining parts of the Cameroun. Workers in the second zone are entitled to receive approximately 80 percent of the salaries earned by their counterparts in the first zone, and the corresponding figures decline to 66 and 55 percent, respectively, for the two remaining parts of the country.[32]

---

[32] For a description of the regulations governing salaries in the Cameroun, see *Développement industriel au Cameroun, rapport préliminaire 1964-1965* (Paris: Société d'études pour le développement économique et social), pp. 54-56. Although more general, see also B. C. Roberts and L. Greyfie de Bellecombe, "Les négociations collectives dans les pays d'Afrique," *Cahiers de l'Institut international d'études sociales* l(April-June, 1967).

However, the development of such zones is not necessarily based on reasonable assumptions. Authorities suppose that African wage earners maintain a traditional life style which is obviously less costly to keep up in the hinterland. Yet as nonmanual workers have a higher level of formal qualifications and as these qualifications lead them to adopt a "Western" life style, their cost of living is likely to be lower in the largest cities and particularly in Douala, the port through which the majority of imported goods are routed.[33] In addition, the differential knowledge that urban and rural wage earners have of the laws governing their status may be associated with a variable enforcement of governmental regulations regarding the definition of salaries and wages.[34]

Second, the government establishes an institutional relationship between pay scales and the period of time during which work is performed. Thus, enterprises are obliged to grant twenty-one days of paid vacation to their labor force and to pay their workers on those days that have been defined as official holidays (Christmas, for example). In addition, firms using the services of workers on Sundays and other regular holidays are required to increase regular basic pay rates by 40 percent. Should work be performed on holidays defined as official, the gross pay rate is then supposed to be doubled. As I shall indicate, however, the benefits that workers derive from such legislation vary with their pay status. While an individual paid on an hourly basis is not remunerated for the days during which he does not work because his enterprise is legally closed (Sundays, for example), his counterpart paid on a monthly basis is entitled to an income the terms of which are defined independently of Sundays and other vacations. In other words, the amount of work that the two categories of workers are expected to perform in order to obtain comparable incomes is not the same.

Third, the definition of minimal guaranteed hourly wages is not identical in agricultural and industrial sectors. At the time of the survey, for example, this minimum stood at 26.5 CFA for agricultural enterprises in the first zone, as against 36.0 CFA for the industrial organizations similarly located.[35] In addition, the definition of salaries whose level exceeds this minimal threshold is negotiated in the context of collective bargaining agreements, whose extent of application is determined by the government. There are thirty-three such agreements operating in the Cameroun; some of them cover an entire branch of activity (banks, for example), whereas

---

[33] This, of course, constitutes a good illustration of the contradictions implicit in policies based on assimilation. For a critical review of such policies, see R. Clignet, "Inadequacies of the Notion of Assimilation in African Education," *Journal of Modern African Studies* 8 (1971).

[34] Pay scales, however, vary not only by region but also by work environment. Thus, the local labor code stipulates that to work in an industrial or agricultural locale more than five kilometers distant from any village entitles a wage earner to receive a premium equal to 2.5 percent of his gross remuneration in order to cover housing expenses.

[35] By 1964, a U. S. dollar was worth 245 CFA.

others apply to a single enterprise (Shell, SAFA—a particular banana plantation).[36]

Fourth, government defines the rates to be paid for work performed beyond the legal requirements imposed on the worker. Thus, an individual is entitled to a 15 percent increase in his hourly salary for the first eight additional hours during which he works, if these hours are performed during daytime. For the eight succeeding hours, the increase is 30 percent, and it reaches 40 percent for the next four-hour period. Should overtime work occur at night, the increase in basic pay rate is 50 percent.

Finally, the government determines which categories of wage earners are entitled to special treatment with regard to pay scales. For example, workers employed by concerns with more than ten employees are entitled to be represented by elected union stewards in their negotiations with management. These representatives are paid for their union activities. Moreover, workers are entitled to a special premium, the value of which varies with seniority in the firm. Further, workers are entitled to family allowances, the value of which varies with the number of their dependents.[37]

To sum up, the conditions under which employers and employees are entitled to negotiate salaries and wages are strictly determined by local authorities, and this affects the extent and determinants of variations in the wages and salaries paid to different groups in the Camerounian labor force.

Variations in Income: An Overview[38]

The annual mean income of manual workers is 140,550 CFA, whereas that of their nonmanual counterparts is 305,000 CFA; the latter earn more than

---

[36] These agreements not only define the pay rates associated with a particular type of work but also the conditions under which a wage earner can move from one skill category to another. Such conditions might be met as the result of an evaluation of an individual's ability to perform certain activities regarded as appropriate for a particular skill level. In other instances, however, access to a higher skill level is automatically guaranteed to wage earners able to successfully pass examinations administered by government itself. In short, an increase in vocational and educational qualifications enhances both the formal and informal bargaining power of workers, for the links between such qualifications, skill levels, and salaries are negotiable within an institutionalized framework. In addition, collective bargaining agreements define the procedures to be followed for terminating employment and severance pay owed.

[37] This fringe benefit is of importance when one considers the family behavior of various types of wage earners, and should be kept in mind also when one compares the patterns of family behavior of the most modernized segments of the populations of French- and English-speaking nations. As family allowances are nonexistent or less substantial in the latter case, it is not surprising to note that in such countries, participation in modern occupational structures is often associated with a decline in the incidence of polygyny and, more generally, in family size. All together, the fringe benefits paid wage earners represented about 20 percent of the salaries paid by employers.

[38] From this point onward, I shall use this term to refer to both salaries and wages. I shall use interchangeably, however, the words income and earnings to facilitate reading.

twice as much on the average as the former. Prior to an assessment of the determinants of such differences, one must evaluate the accuracy of these figures and identify the three sets of difficulties involved in generating them. First, one must ascertain the significance of seasonal variations in work and determine whether it is legitimate to extrapolate the data obtained for a full year. Second, wage earners are not remunerated on the same time basis: some are paid by the month, others by the day, an additional group is remunerated at an hourly rate, whereas a final group is paid in terms of bonuses computed by reference to sales or output. To compare the incomes of various types of workers requires one to standardize their respective earnings. Finally, incomes vary by zone, and comparisons necessitate their translation within a single framework.

Significance of seasonal variations.

Developing economies are usually characterized by the preeminent importance of their primary sector, and much economic and social activity is focused around the harvesting of export products (coffee, cocoa, bananas, rubber, and so forth). This harvesting directly influences the level of activity in other sectors such as transportation and export. In addition, it affects the direction and magnitude of cash flows both between individuals and firms. This effect is amplified both by the sharp fluctuations which characterize the world markets and by the lack of local capital facilities which obliges many individual farmers, traders, and exporters to rely heavily on credit.

This situation should lead to marked seasonal variations in the levels of activity of particular sectors and hence in their payments to workers. In the Ivory Coast, for example, the volume of economic transactions and the amount of litigation reach a peak in the period following the harvesting of coffee and cocoa, that is, at the time when individuals have a maximal amount of cash in hand.[39] It is during this period that law firms, for example, are most likely to be most active and to pay their employees accordingly. It is during this same period that construction firms are most active and the demand for labor is most marked. Hence, it is at this time that construction workers should receive the highest incomes.

Obviously, the Camerounian economy is subject to similar seasonal variations, even though their impact is certainly not alike for manual and nonmanual employees. White-collar work is more evenly distributed throughout the year, and this category of wage earners is remunerated on a monthly basis, which reduces claims to overtime. By contrast, although blue-collar workers can be expected to work overtime, the number of hours varies with the needs of the particular enterprises. As overtime work is rewarded in terms of bonuses, to extrapolate data obtained at the time of

[39] See, for instance, A. Kobben, "Le Planteur noir," *Etudes éburnéennes* 5(Abidjan: Institut francais d'Afrique noire, 1956).

interview over the whole year is a risky procedure, for the contrasts between manual and nonmanual earnings may not be independent of the season during which the data were gathered.

Accordingly, I have taken the potential significance of seasonal variations into account by distinguishing workers for whom pay data were collected at the peak of Camerounian activities from those for whom such data were collected during months characterized by lower levels of activity. Although the importance of this distinction probably varies by branch of activity (being more marked for agricultural enterprises than for industrial concerns, for example), zero-order correlation coefficients between annual income and the season at which pay was calculated (treated as a dummy variable) were equally low for the two populations: -0.069 for manual workers and 0.057 for their nonmanual counterparts.[40] In addition, the contributions of this variable to the various multiple regression analyses that were undertaken were never significant. Therefore I have no reason to believe that the results have been significantly affected by seasonal variations in employment.

Modes of payment.

As suggested, the possibility of extrapolating the annual income earned by individual workers depends on the basis of their remuneration. These modes of remuneration fall into four categories (month, day, hour, pro rata) with varying profiles. Monthly payment covers a number of days that government regulations define as legal vacations and during which no work is performed, but such privileges do not apply to other categories of wage earner. In other words, individuals paid by the month require fewer working days than any other category of wage earner in order to obtain a same annual income. Accordingly, I took this fact into consideration in estimating individual earnings. The first step in this evaluation consisted in assessing the hourly pay rate of *all* workers, and I defined the number of hours effectively worked per day as eight in the case of individuals paid on an hourly basis, 6.931 in the case of those remunerated on a daily basis, and 5.778 in the case of those paid by the month.[41] This step was necessary in order to obtain comparable yearly figures for each subgroup of wage earners.

In addition, distinctions among modes of payment correspond to the distinction between manual and nonmanual employment: about 69 percent of blue-collar workers are paid on an hourly basis, as against only 19 percent of their white-collar counterparts. Similarly, 11 percent of the first group are paid by the day, as against less than 3 percent of the nonmanual

---

[40] I divided the calendar year into two parts: the first and final three months are characterized by a higher level of economic activity than the remainder of the year.

[41] The numbers correspond to the legal duration of the work period per day. They are obtained by deducting from 365 days the appropriate number of Sundays, religious, and national holidays. As noted, the number of days to be deducted is not the same for individuals paid on an hourly, daily, and monthly basis.

population. Distinctions among modes of payment are significantly associated with contrasts in annual earnings, even when the number of hours effectively performed is controlled. Thus, for the manual population, the zero-order correlations between annual income and hourly, daily, and monthly modes of payment (treated as dummy variables) are respectively -0.11, -0.16 and 0.26. For nonmanual workers, these coefficients are respectively -0.16, -0.09 and 0.19. In both cases, therefore, it pays to be paid on a monthly basis.[42]

Many labor unions and management associations are increasingly aware of the implications of differential modes of payment, for these distinctions affect the solidarity that binds various categories of workers together, both *within* and *between* the manual and nonmanual sectors of employment. Furthermore, they affect the relative integration of individual workers into an enterprise, as a monthly basis of payment has been long considered a privilege to be granted to the most faithful segments of the labor force. Finally, distinctions among modes of payment affect the attitudes that individuals entertain toward stability, because their mode of remuneration determines the amount of resources they enjoy when they leave their current employment.[43] It is no surprise, therefore, that at least in France labor unions have been anxious to obtain from management the extension of monthly based status to all categories of wage earners.

Salary zones.

The last difficulty concerns the implications of the division of the country into four zones characterized by distinct levels of minimum guaranteed wage. The influence of this division on the differential earnings of manual and nonmanual populations is at least twofold. First, these populations are differentially concentrated in the three salary zones included in the sample; as no less than 28 percent of manual workers are employed by concerns located in the rural zone, as against only 6 percent of nonmanuals, contrasts in the annual earnings of the two populations may result partly from the differential geographic location of their work.

At the same time, the actual application of these regulations remains problematic and depends both on the level of information and the number of alternative opportunities open to various categories of wage earner. Employers are probably less likely to respect regulations in the case of their

---

[42] The labor code indicates that severance pay must be computed on the basis of mode of payment. An individual paid by the month will obtain at least a full month's pay, whereas his counterpart paid by the hour will normally obtain only eight days' compensation.

[43] Obviously, there are also significant relations between modes of payment and individual occupational roles. For example, among manual workers, a monthly mode of payment is negatively associated with direct participation in production processes (-0.432). Conversely, a monthly mode of payment is positively associated with skill level (0.238). Among nonmanual workers, monthly modes of payment are positively associated with participation in peripheral services (0.205) and with skill level (0.250).

manual workers who enjoy fewer occupational alternatives. In addition, the lower level of formal schooling of such workers often prevents them from being as well-informed of their rights.

This hypothesis can be tested by comparing the annual median incomes of manual and nonmanual workers with differing aggregate training scores and working for enterprises located in rural, semiurban, and urban zones (Table 26).[44] As a whole, independently of the work they perform, wage earners living in the rural hinterland as well as in secondary centers do *not* earn as much as what they are legally entitled to. Thus, median incomes in the hinterland are only one-half of what they are in Douala, Yaoundé, or Edea. Similarly, workers employed in secondary towns only earn about 70 percent of the salaries of their counterparts in the largest cities. Most strikingly, however, the differential earnings of manual and nonmanual populations do not vary markedly when one moves from the hinterland to the largest cities.

To sum up, seasonal variations probably do not affect estimates of the differential annual median earnings of the two segments of the Camerounian labor force; distinct *modes* of payment influence such differentials, even though for both populations, monthly modes of payment are associated with higher earnings. Finally, nonmanual workers are perhaps less numerous than manual workers in the hinterland, but they do not obtain more favorable treatment.

Influence of educational and vocational background on earnings

The association between aggregate training scores and annual earnings is not linear; additional schooling is not uniformly associated with a commensurate increase in income. For example, urban manual workers with the equivalent of more than twelve years of formal schooling earn three times as much as their counterparts in the immediately preceding educational category. Similarly, their nonmanual counterparts earn twice as much as those in the immediately preceding category, but in both cases differences between the earnings of lower educational categories are less marked.[45]

As the association between qualifications and earnings is not linear, zero-order correlations between these two variables are misleadingly low.

---

[44] In the subsequent tables, I have divided incomes into a number of classes whose size differs. At the lower end of the continuum these classes are small in order to obtain a maximal differentiation of the earnings of the majority of individuals; these classes become larger whenever the number of individuals they contain is limited. For analysis I have added a subroutine to the existing cross-tabulation programs to obtain the mean income scores of each subcategory of workers examined. This mean, however, refers to income classes and not to the incomes themselves. For each table, I have then been obliged to transform the mean obtained back into raw values.

[45] The situation is exactly the same in India, where R. Lambert reports that education unevenly affects income distribution.

TABLE 26
Mean Adjusted Annual Income of Workers by Aggregate Training Score and Salary Zone
(thousands CFA)

Aggregate training score	Rural		Semiurban		Urban	
	Manual	Nonmanual	Manual	Nonmanual	Manual	Nonmanual
0	61.5	--	88.1	--	128.8	--
0.1 to 1.5	71.5	--	38.4	--	134.7	--
1.6 to 6.9	74.0	123.6	110.8	186.5	138.2	239.6
7.0	71.0	131.5	97.7	208.5	131.8	275.3
7.1 to 12.0	121.5	165.2	132.0	261.0	186.7	323.1
Above 12.0	*a	*a	*a	*a	565.4	738.4
Total population	68.3	128.4	99.2	197.8	136.0	279.4
Percentage earning more than overall average[b]	3.8	4.8	12.4	18.0	39.2	35.6
N	6,552	280	789	283	15,759	4,447

[a]Fewer than ten cases.

[b]More than 140,000 CFA per year for manual workers and more than 305,000 CFA per year for nonmanual workers.

One obtains better results when one takes into account the irregular nature of the monetary rewards derived from an additional amount of formal schooling and training by *squaring* aggregate training scores.[46] For the nonmanual population, I obtain a zero-order correlation of 0.343 when such scores are squared, as opposed to 0.272 when they are entered at their face value. For manual workers, the corresponding values obtained are 0.258 and 0.218, respectively. Regardless of the specific technique by which one measures the association, the influence of educational attainment on income appears, however, to be more marked for the nonmanual than for the manual population. But does this association remain more stable in the first case; in other words, is it less affected by ascriptive factors such as place or residence, or ethnic affiliation, and does it vary over time?

The distribution of annual median earnings by salary zone and educational category does not have the same profile for blue- and white-collar workers. For both categories of workers, the differential earnings of individuals with distinct levels of education increase as one moves toward the largest towns. The income of the most educated manual workers is twice as large as that of their illiterate counterparts in rural zones but over four times larger in the largest towns. For the nonmanual population, the corresponding ratio climbs from 1.3 in the first environment to only 3.0 in the second.[47]

In addition, the profile of the association between income and educational or vocational qualifications differs between the two segments of the labor force. In the case of manual workers, the gamma coefficients of association between aggregate training score and salary decline from 0.272 in the rural hinterland to 0.119 in the largest cities in the country, but among nonmanual workers these gamma coefficients increase regularly from 0.102 in the hinterland to 0.231 in Douala, Yaoundé, or Edea.[48] Thus

---

[46] I should have tested for the linearity of the association between the variables. Unfortunately, at the time that this study was undertaken, no appropriate ready-made program was available. Therefore I tried to determine whether better results were obtained by using the simple value, the squared value, the square root, or the logarithmic expression of variables such as age, education, or seniority. For example, the zero-order correlation between manual income and aggregate training score is 0.218. When I square this score, I obtain a correlation of 0.258. When I take its logarithmic expression, I obtain a correlation of 0.188 and of 0.203 if I consider the square root of the score. Thus, the squared value of that particular score seems to yield the best results. Of course, I could also have dummied various educational categories to determine at which point of the distribution the monetary rewards were maximal. Here I have preferred to make an overall assessment of the contribution of education to annual earnings.

[47] In contrast to what happens in rural areas, however, the relative earnings of manual workers in smaller towns are independent of their academic credentials, and the number of educated job seekers anxious to find manual employment in such centers probably far exceeds the capacity of the local labor market. This, of course, should affect the *direction* of migration flows and hence the differential distribution of unemployment in a variety of urban centers.

[48] These gammas are computed on the frequency distributions of income classes among various subgroups of individuals. Whereas the means and medians do not tell one anything

variations in the relative number of educated individuals do not similarly affect the two labor markets. The scarcity of highly qualified job seekers in the rural hinterland regularizes the association between levels of qualifications and levels of earnings in the case of manual workers, but not in the case of their nonmanual counterparts.

Further, the association between vocational or educational qualifications and annual income tends to be more independent of ethnic factors in the case of white- than of blue-collar populations. Because of the uniformly high influence exerted by educational credentials on their productivity, nonmanual workers with *similar* aggregate training scores but *differing* ethnic origins tend to enjoy the same income. Although Beti-Fang individuals with high educational credentials, for instance, earn substantially more than their Douala counterparts, ethnic variations in the association between educational or vocational qualifications and income are still more moderate for nonmanual than manual workers (Table 27). In the first case, gamma coefficients vary from a high of 0.307 for Mbam, foreigners, and northerners to a low of 0.168 for the Beti-Fang (excluding the Ewondo). In the second case, the coefficients range more broadly from 0.337 for the Bassa to 0.030 for the Douala. Similarly, the differential earnings of individuals with varying aggregate training scores but similar ethnic backgrounds are more widely spread in the manual labor market. In this sector, the salaries earned by Bamileke individuals with high credentials are almost *eight times* greater than those earned by their illiterate counterparts. In the white-collar sector, the maximal range observed is more limited. Beti-Fang individuals with *maximal* qualifications earn a little less than *four times* as much as their counterparts with less than seven years of formal schooling.

The relationship between aggregate training score and earnings does not only vary between urban and rural labor markets or among the ethnic groups present in the labor market, it also changes over time. Because of divergences in the relative growth rates of educational and occupational opportunities, the relationship between formal qualifications and annual earnings is higher among older than younger age groups. Competition among employers over access to the scarce qualified available manpower was keener in early phases of development than it is today. Although this competition was particularly salient in the nonmanual labor market, disparities between the annual incomes of individuals with minimal and maximal formal qualifications tend still to be proportionately greater among older manual than nonmanual wage earners.

In effect, the influence of age on the association between aggregate training score and median annual salary is not fully cumulative: manual

about the number of individuals present in the appropriate cells, gammas take such numbers into account.

TABLE 27
Mean Adjusted Annual Income of Workers by Aggregate Training Score and Ethnic Origin
(in thousands CFA)

Ethnic Group	0	0.1-1.5	1.6-6.9	7.0	7.1-12.0	Above 12.0	Percentage of total population earning more than overall average	N
Ewondo								
Manual	104.5	123.2	132.4	125.7	163.4	*	31.4	3,512
Nonmanual	--	--	232.5	210.8	304.7	218.6	27.8	475
Other Beti-Fang								
Manual	104.2	134.8	130.7	124.2	163.2	*	30.2	1,409
Nonmanual	--	--	267.4	253.2	318.1	928.6	33.8	315
Bamileke								
Manual	88.3	121.3	120.6	124.5	177.8	628.1	25.3	6,040
Nonmanual	--	--	177.5	197.6	263.6	674.6	19.1	1,321
Bassa								
Manual	77.4	109.8	124.0	120.8	199.1	*	23.9	5,654
Nonmanual	--	--	232.6	285.4	330.4	869.4	36.5	1,117
Douala								
Manual	137.8	173.4	163.0	138.8	213.5	549.0	59.9	1,474
Nonmanual	--	--	294.5	328.7	345.4	676.1	47.8	1,101
Others								
Manual	94.3	121.8	124.6	121.8	179.6	*	24.3	5,011
Nonmanual	--	--	178.5	252.4	361.6	659.4	31.4	681

*Fewer than ten cases.

earnings vary maximally betwen *one* for individuals between twenty-five and thirty years of age without academic credentials and *six* for their counterparts with twelve years of formal training, but the range tends to decrease among older age groups. Among the nonmanuals, highly educated individuals earn up to *four* times as much as their counterparts with low credentials for the cohort between thirty-one and thirty-five years of age (899,000 CFA versus 225,000), but the relevant ratios decline thereafter (Table 28).

Contrasts in the peaks of the association between schooling and income reflect the differential development of the two labor markets. Because the technology of manual work has changed more recently, the returns derived from formal qualifications have reached an optimal value in that sector at a later date than in the case of the nonmanual sector. Beyond these peaks, both labor markets are characterized by a certain amount of rigidity. Accordingly, formal qualifications become less negotiable, and older workers probably deem security of employment to be more valuable than opportunities for upward mobility and additional income.

Last, the influence of modes of entry into the labor force on the incomes of the two populations is uneven. Initial employment in the context of larger firms only influences the earnings of *manual* wage earners (the zero-order correlation betwen these two variables is 0.143 in the case of blue-collar workers as opposed to 0.002 for nonmanuals). Among manual workers, entering the labor market in the context of a large firm after having attended a postprimary academic or technical institution exerts a more powerful positive effect on income than either one of these two experiences taken separately (Table 29). Thus, among illiterate individuals, contrasts in initial occupational experiences are not associated with differences in earnings. Nor are there contrasts in the incomes of manual workers with the equivalent of seven years of formal schooling but with differing forms of initial contact with the occupational world. But there are still sharp differences between the earnings of illiterate manual wage earners who have never learned a particular trade and those of the individuals who, having completed the equivalent of seven years of schooling, have participated in a training program sponsored by a large firm. The first mean adjusted annual income is 83,100 CFA, as compared with 234,100 CFA for the second. In this sense, formal schooling and participation in on-the-job training programs serve complementary functions. In other words, manual earnings reflect the acquisition of both *general* and *specific* skills.

Among nonmanual workers, however, the situation is more complex. In the lower educational categories, *any* form of on-the-job training as an initial occupational experience is associated with an increment in salary. At the same time, among individuals who have reached the higher rungs of the educational and vocational ladder, it is more profitable to enter directly in the labor force than to learn a trade, and particularly so with a large-scale

TABLE 28
Mean Adjusted Annual Income of Workers by Age and Aggregate Training Score
(thousands CFA)

Age	0	0.1-1.5	1.6-6.9	7.0	7.1-12.0	Above 12.0	Percentage of total population earning more than overall average	N
15-20								
Manual	64.1	72.4	81.5	94.2	143.1	*a	12.7	833
Nonmanual	--	--	121.6	145.7	206.7	*a	5.6	174
21-25								
Manual	71.2	87.1	101.4	112.6	156.4	*a	18.5	3,888
Nonmanual	--	--	164.2	184.6	255.7	357.8	15.4	1,185
26-30								
Manual	83.5	116.2	125.1	129.4	212.4	509.2	28.0	5,450
Nonmanual	--	--	191.5	259.8	327.4	679.4	28.9	1,161
31-35								
Manual	87.5	124.1	137.2	154.3	215.2	354.0	34.0	4,709
Nonmanual	--	--	224.6	325.6	426.4	899.5	38.3	1,001
36-40								
Manual	30.1	124.9	155.2	157.8	272.6	*a	33.7	3,562
Nonmanual	--	--	239.4	470.6	487.6	579.4	46.9	699
41-45								
Manual	101.2	133.5	144.8	205.4	279.0	*a	31.7	2,042
Nonmanual	--	--	276.5	415.7	429.6	586.0	49.1	363
Over 45								
Manual	84.1	138.4	157.2	182.8	243.1	*a	27.3	2,612
Nonmanual	--	--	327.5	429.4	614.8	527.6	61.2	378

*aFewer than ten cases.

Mean Adjusted Annual Income of Workers by Aggregate Training Score and Vocational Training Program (in thousands CFA)

Aggregate training score	None	With friends and relatives	With nonaccredited schools or by correspondence courses	With a large-scale firm	Percentage of total population earning more than overall average	N
Percent total population earning more than overall average						
Manual	16.2	29.0	26.7	36.0	--	--
Nonmanual	28.0	32.2	30.8	33.0	--	--
0						
Manual	83.1	111.1	*	99.5	13.3	6,373
Nonmanual	--	--	--	--	--	--
0.1 to 1.5						
Manual	111.4	121.6	*	128.5	28.8	4,862
Nonmanual	--	--	--	--	--	--
1.6 to 6.9						
Manual	115.1	123.6	130.9	136.7	34.8	8,636
Nonmanual	157.1	175.2	181.1	176.8	22.2	2,054
7.0						
Manual	105.6	122.0	120.6	130.6	28.3	2,284
Nonmanual	157.4	194.5	197.7	234.1	33.5	1,995
7.1 to 12.0						
Manual	150.4	216.6	*	224.7	74.9	909
Nonmanual	256.8	285.1	327.1	297.2	43.9	863
Beyond 12						
Manual	466.2	*	*	*	91.6	36
Nonmanual	524.4	462.7	437.6	353.8	84.7	118

*Fewer than ten cases.

organization. In this sense, the two types of experience are *substitutes* for each other. In other words, the distinction between general and specific skills has fewer apparent implications.

Influence of occupational experience on earnings

Up to this point, I have examined the impact of what the individual wage earner brings with him in the labor market. To be sure, I have indicated how the association between aggregate training score and earnings varies with age, but I have nevertheless treated age in this regard as a proxy variable for economic and social development.

To evaluate the influence of age on earnings assumes that individuals enter the labor market right upon their graduation from educational institutions. In developing countries, however, individuals stay for varying periods of time out of the modern sector either because they are unemployed or because they participate in the so-called murky sector of activities.[49] Further, as already noted, the occupational experience associated with age does not necessarily exert a cumulative influence on the earnings of individual wage earners.[50] Employers may be less interested in rewarding the overall occupational history of an individual than in rewarding the amount of time spent in a particular job, or in the enterprise, or the diversity of past jobs held by the individual. In this sense, to rely on age rather than seniority may lead to misleading conclusions.

Variations in the transferability of manual and nonmanual skills are associated with contrasts in the association between earnings and occupational experience. The correlation between the annual estimated income of manual workers, on the one hand, and their age, seniority in the firm, and seniority on the job, on the other, are respectively 0.091, 0.185, and 0.157. In contrast, the corresponding figures are 0.226, 0.228, and 0.164 in the nonmanual sector. In brief, the three forms of seniority examined here seem to be more crucial determinants of nonmanual earnings. Further, in the case of this particular population, chronological age seems to be a more powerful predictor of annual earnings than seniority in the firm, for the range of variation by row (that is, by age) is substantially larger than the corresponding range by column (that is, by seniority, Table 30). Because of their greater mobility, nonmanual workers derive greater rewards from their overall "universalistic" experiences.

But can one take the same line of reasoning when one compares the effects of seniority on the job and seniority in the firms on the differential earnings of the two populations? Among nonmanual populations, the

---

[49] For an illustration of this pattern, see, for example, Clignet and Foster, *The Fortunate Few,* chap. 7.

[50] For a development of this argument, see Thurow, *Poverty and Discrimination.* In the Tunisian shoe industry J. Simmons notes that whereas a combination of education and age accounts for only 10 percent of the variance in individual earnings, the percentage of variance accounted for increases to 24 percent when age was replaced by time spent in the present firm.

TABLE 30
Mean Adjusted Annual Income of Workers by Age and Seniority in the Firm
(in thousands CFA)

Seniority in the firm	15-20	21-25	26-30	31-35	36-40	41-45	46 and above	Percentage of total population earning more than overall average	
Less than 1 year									
Manual	104.3	108.1	120.1	120.2	121.3	117.3	113.5	17.9	5,771
Nonmanual	151.2	165.2	200.1	201.5	279.6	437.1	214.1	12.3	781
1-2 years									
Manual	81.6	120.6	122.8	122.6	127.4	115.4	107.6	24.5	3,003
Nonmanual	175.4	175.3	219.8	273.0	276.1	258.3	175.1	18.7	572
2-5 years									
Manual	98.0	106.8	120.6	124.6	124.3	124.2	118.1	26.3	5,106
Nonmanual	178.3	219.3	247.5	255.8	291.6	265.1	291.4	28.2	1,242
5-10 years									
Manual	*	110.7	127.1	130.1	128.9	126.1	111.1	37.5	4,426
Nonmanual	*	261.8	273.2	297.6	331.6	293.8	336.1	42.1	1,051
10-15 years									
Manual	*	111.6	126.3	131.6	132.1	130.1	129.2	42.2	2,590
Nonmanual	*	*	291.6	303.4	277.1	333.5	576.2	44.9	741
Over 15 years									
Manual	*	85.4	105.8	117.2	111.6	126.1	113.8	29.4	2,204
Nonmanual	*	*	*	366.1	366.4	407.6	425.6	64.8	489

*Fewer than ten cases.

influence exerted by seniority in the firm is more salient than the influence of seniority on the job, and the range of variations in nonmanual earnings by row (that is, by seniority in the firm) is greater than the range of variation by column (that is, by seniority on the job, Table 31). Whereas an increase in experience on the job only moderately influences the earnings of individuals with *minimal* seniority in the firm, *minimal* experience on the job does not prevent individuals with more than ten years in the same firm from having significantly higher wages than their counterparts who have only spent a year with their current employer.

In contrast, for manual workers the influence of the two types of seniority on annual earnings is significantly more modest. To be sure, variations in the relative amount of time spent in a particular job by manual workers with low seniority in the firms are systematically associated with contrasts in annual median earnings (the gamma coefficient between seniority on the job and annual pay is 0.302 for individuals with less than one year of experience in the same firm), but the association between these two variables declines as one allows seniority in the firm to increase. Indeed, the gamma coefficient between seniority on the job and annual earnings declines to 0.022 for the manual subpopulations who have spent between ten and fifteen years in their current firm, and in the case of manual populations with maximal seniority in the firm the association between annual earnings and job experience becomes negative with a gamma coefficient of -0.239.

To summarize, the differential earnings of manual and nonmanual workers are not independent of the two forms of occupational experience discussed here. Contrasts are much greater in the case of populations who have maximal seniority *both* in their current job and in their current employment than among their counterparts who are just beginners in their current job as well as with their current employer. Differences in the incomes of the two populations reflect differences not only in their respective patterns of recruitment and upward job mobility but also in the social definition of the work they perform respectively.

The last form of occupational experience that I will consider concerns the number of jobs learned or performed by individuals. Although the diversity of jobs learned or performed by Camerounian workers is uniformly associated with an increase in their income, this increase appears to be higher for manual than nonmanual workers: the zero-order correlation coefficients between the two relevant variables are 0.205 in the first case but only 0.113 in the second.

Influence of educational and occupational background on income

Thus far, I have shown that when considered independently of each other, educational and occupational experience are significant determinants of annual earnings. In Table 32 I examine the *combined* effect of these two factors. In both cases, the association between aggregate training scores and earnings increases with seniority. Manual incomes vary from 89,100

TABLE 31

Mean Adjusted Annual Income of Workers by Seniority in the Firm and on the Job

(in thousands CFA)

Seniority on the job	Less than 1 year	1-2 years	2-5 years	5-10 years	10-15 years	Over 15 years	Percentage of total population earning more than overall average	N
Less than 1 year								
Manual	100.1	117.8	125.1	120.1	146.5	101.8	15.5	4,908
Nonmanual	166.2	191.4	241.6	230.6	449.0	464.6	16.0	1,029
1-2 years								
Manual	118.1	111.0	109.1	135.4	127.0	98.2	21.2	5,439
Nonmanual	204.8	207.2	221.7	350.4	339.7	360.2	26.7	908
2-5 years								
Manual	124.2	126.2	127.5	122.5	136.0	131.6	32.9	5,567
Nonmanual	224.9	250.1	279.6	281.4	294.8	426.7	37.6	1,117
5-10 years								
Manual	119.3	120.4	105.6	121.9	129.3	125.8	24.4	2,875
Nonmanual	224.3	256.1	244.3	247.6	343.5	573.2	31.5	602
10-15 years								
Manual	129.3	133.4	136.3	154.7	123.6	136.9	41.1	3,731
Nonmanual	211.9	267.9	284.6	345.7	279.8	390.6	39.7	762
Over 15 years								
Manual	127.2	126.2	137.4	136.2	199.2	101.5	32.8	2,570
Nonmanual	209.0	189.0	315.6	378.4	390.6	402.5	56.3	458

TABLE 32
Mean Annual Adjusted Income of Workers by Seniority in the Firm and Aggregate Training Score

Seniority in the firm	Aggregate Training Score											
	0		0.1-1.5		1.6-6.9		7.0		7.1-12.0		Above 12.0	
	Manual	Nonmanual	Manual	Nonmanual	Manual	Nonmanual	Manual	Nonmanual	Manual	Nonmanual	Manual	Nonmanual
Less than 1 year												
Mean	89.1	--	111.6	--	116.2	163.8	108.1	172.1	136.8	222.1	*	425.1
Percentage earning more than overall average	6.2	--	16.7	--	20.0	8.3	13.5	9.0	46.0	16.1	*	61.9
Between 1 and 2 years												
Mean	93.1	--	117.6	--	122.6	171.8	121.4	191.6	177.1	277.6	*	944.2
Percentage earning more than overall average	9.2	--	20.6	--	26.2	13.0	27.2	12.3	60.4	29.2	*	52.8
Between 2 and 5 years												
Mean	33.7	--	121.1	--	121.8	194.1	125.1	233.5	204.8	325.6	*	854.1
Percentage earning more than overall average	9.8	--	26.9	--	28.8	12.4	30.8	23.5	69.5	50.8	*	96.5
Between 5 and 10 years												
Mean	82.5	--	125.7	--	139.0	210.8	169.9	340.1	251.6	417.2	*	532.6
Percentage earning more than overall average	13.5	--	40.1	--	50.8	21.3	64.1	52.9	93.6	68.0	*	74.1

TABLE 32 (continued)
Mean Annual Adjusted Income of Workers by Seniority in the Firm and Aggregate Training Score

Seniority in the firm	Aggregate Training Score											
	0		0.1-1.5		1.6-6.9		7.0		7.1-12.0		Above 12.0	
	Manual	Nonmanual	Manual	Nonmanual	Manual	Nonmanual	Manual	Nonmanual	Manual	Nonmanual	Manual	Nonmanual
Between 10 and 15 years												
Mean	102.8	--	134.2	--	178.6	244.2	239.0	368.1	284.3	556.5	*	826.1
Percentage earning more than overall average	21.2	--	43.8	--	67.2	25.6	96.8	57.6	95.4	87.2	*	88.9
Over 15 years												
Mean	84.7	--	126.5	--	177.4	346.5	218.6	518.7	1,036.5	582.4	1,034.5	1,024.1
Percentage earning m more than overall average	15.3	--	37.8	--	63.5	48.4	77.5	80.0	100.0	82.6	100.0	100.0

*Fewer than ten cases.

CFA for individuals with minimal seniority in their current employment and minimal educational qualifications to 1,034,500 CFA for those who have had the equivalent of twelve or more years of formal schooling and have been in their current employment for a period of sixteen years of more.[51] Thus, the latter earn almost twelve times as much as the former. Contrasts in the annual income of nonmanual workers with maximal educational and occupational experiences are less marked: individuals with an aggregate training score of above 12.0 and more than fifteen years' experience in the same firm earn almost nine times as much as their counterparts with minimal educational, vocational, and occupational qualifications. An examination of gamma coefficients also suggests that the influence of formal qualifications on earnings is more stable in the case of nonmanual workers.

Among blue-collar workers, such coefficients range from 0.162 for the populations with less than one year of experience with the same firm to 0.560 for those with fifteen years' seniority or more, but among nonmanual workers such coefficients only increase from 0.322 in the first instance to 0.428 in the second.

Finally, there is reason to suspect that the effects of the combination of seniority and aggregate training scores on salaries are multiplicative rather than additive. Indeed, the zero-order correlation between income and the *product* of years of formal schooling and of years of seniority is 0.476 for manual workers and 0.456 for their nonmanual counterparts, and such values are higher than those obtained when one simply adds those two variables. More important, the greater scarcity of manual workers with top educational and occupational qualifications enables them to obtain proportionately more significant economic rewards from their employers than their white-collar counterparts.

At this point, the data can be treated in a more systematic manner. In spite of the institutional factors affecting income, and more specifically in spite of the role played by collective-bargaining agreements in this regard, it is still possible to ascertain the variance in the distribution of individual earnings accounted for by variables mirroring what individuals bring them at the time of their entry in the labor force or in their current positions. In the first case, I consider successively age, ethnicity, residence, educational, and vocational experiences, regardless of their level of statistical significance. This is because I wanted the analysis to mirror the sequential order in which these various traits are acquired. In the second case,

---

[51] It also remains to determine the relative influence of education and seniority on earnings. In his examination of blue-collar workers in the metal repair shop of a Soviet oil refinery, Zhiltoz found that production experience explained four times more variance in workers' performance than formal schooling. See "Statistical Methods of Evaluating the Complexity of Labor," in H. Noah, ed., *The Economics of Education in the USSR* (New York: Praeger, 1969). It is not sure, of course, that the same results would be obtained in another country and another branch of activity.

however, it does not seem feasible to force the variables which reflect what a wage earner brings with him in this current position, and they have been treated according to their level of significance.

In either case, the amount of variance in the distribution of manual and nonmanual incomes accounted for are different (Table 33).[52] Considered separately, background variables explain over one-fourth of the variance in the distribution of nonmanual earnings but only for 15 percent in the case of manual incomes. In this sense, what workers bring with them in their employment is more significant in the case of the white- than of the blue-collar labor market. With the addition of occupational experiences, the amount of the first variance accounted for increases to one-third in the first case but only to 26 percent in the second instance. In this sense, the nonmanual labor market remains slightly less imperfect. Thus, the relative importance of educational or vocational background is higher in that particular case than in the blue-collar labor market. Further, age and hence overall occupational experience affect nonmanual incomes independently of other factors, but in the case of manual earnings this particular variable is contaminated by other determinants and its effects are correspondingly washed out. Finally, ethnicity (which can be treated as a form of particularism) enters as a significant factor in the blue-collar equation only.

Conclusions

I have reached the objectives defined at the outset of the chapter in that I have shown that the rules of the game differ between manual and nonmanual labor markets and that the determinants of occupational attainments are not alike for the two populations. First, nonmanual workers reach higher skill levels and, hence, earn better incomes. In addition, formal schooling is a more significant determinant of their skill level and their earnings. The influence that academic credentials exert in this regard is also less variable.

Second, overall occuptional experience yield more significant rewards in the white-collar than in the blue-collar labor market. In addition, and in contrast to what was inferred from the negotiable nature of nonmanual skills, seniority in a same firm is a better predictor of nonmanual attainment than experience acquired on the job, and in fact the predictive power of seniority in the firm is more salient in the white- than in the blue-collar labor market. Further, nonmanual wage earners may substitute high

---

[52] In all subsequent multiple regression analyses, the reader should be aware that I have tried to eliminate variations reflecting salary zones and have multiplied rural and semiurban zone earnings by appropriate constants (1/0.66 in the first case and 1/0.80 in the second). I was not interested in examining the contribution of institutional factors to the variance in the distribution of annual earnings. For these earnings, I have incorporated in their annual evaluation basic pay rates, basic bonuses, and premiums. I have at the same time eliminated such factors as family allowances when appropriate.

TABLE 33
Multiple Regression Analysis of the Annual Income of Workers
(personal variables only)[a]

Nonmanual population

N	4,915
Mean	305.00
Standard deviation	249.58
R^2	0.257
Intercept	168.35

Overall experiences

Variables	Beta	T	R^2
1. Interaction of aggregate training score and seniority in firm	0.002	21.13	0.211
2. Aggregate training score[d]	0.002	26.10	0.282
3. Age	0.636	14.93	0.313

Educational and social antecedents

Variables	Beta	T	R^2
1. Bamileke[c]	-3.268	4.37	0.029
2. Douala[c]	2,408	3.01	0.042
3. Age	1.022	26.20	0.101
4. Aggregate training score[d]	0.003	32.10	0.257

Manual population

N	23,210
Mean	140.50
Standard deviation	107.23
R^2	0.147
Intercept	110.11

TABLE 33 *(continued)*
Multiple Regression Analysis of the Annual Income of Workers
(personal variables only)[a]

Manual population

Educational and social antecedents[b]				Overall experiences			
Variables	*Beta*	*T*	R^2	*Variables*	*Beta*	*T*	R^2
1. Doula[c]	5,654	21.05	0.029	1. Interaction of aggregate training score and seniority in firm	0.002	73.95	0.227
2. Age	0.257	32.28	0.037	2. Number of jobs learned or performed	1.344	21.61	0.242
3. Aggregate training score[d]	0.002	50.47	0.129	3. Upward mobility between second job learned or performed and current occupation[c]	1.952	16.34	0.252
4. On-the-job training	2.987	24.77	0.147	4. Doula[c]	3.975	15.84	0.263

[a]Expressed in thousands CFA. It should be noted tha individual salaries have been corrected to take into account legal regulations regarding salary zones. Thus, rural salaries have been increased by 1,499/1,000 of their value. Similarly, the salaries of individuals employed in secondary centers have been increased by 117/100 of their initial value.

[b]In these equations, variables are forced in terms of their chronological order.

[c]These variables are treated as dummy variables.

[d]This variable has been squared, as its influence is obviously not linear.

educational credentials for a lack of occupational experience, or vice versa, in order to gain access to the top of the hierarchy or to earn higher incomes, but the degree of freedom enjoyed by their manual counterparts in this regard is more limited.

Third, white-collar workers are more often mobile than their blue-collar counterparts. Although the number of past experiences is more closely associated with occupational rewards in the second than the first labor market, changes of occupation are still more frequently associated with upward mobility in the case of the nonmanual populations.

Whereas past educational and occupational experiences exert differing influences on the relative success of the two populations, these differences are not necessarily stable over time. The corresponding spatial or temporal segmentation of the local labor force reflects fluctuations in the demand for and the supply of labor, which vary themselves with the relative educational and economic development of the distinct regions of Cameroun. In brief, the forms of segmentation operating in the Camerounian economy tend to evolve, and contrasts in the educational or occupational profile of highly skilled manual and nonmanual wage earners or of the best-paid segments of these two populations are not the same across age or ethnic groups or between urban and rural areas.

Finally, the influence of formal schooling or occupational experience on attainment is not necessarily the same when one considers the *overall* manual and nonmanual populations and when one concentrates the analysis on the segments of such populations who have already reached the middle and upper rungs of the hierarchical ladder. Such contrasts are important in assessing the strategies most appropriate for accelerating processes of Africanization. Indeed, the role of education and of the various forms of seniority considered here are not necessarily cumulative.

Chapter 5

TYPES OF EMPLOYMENT:
THE PERSONNEL POLICIES
OF CAMEROUNIAN FIRMS

Thus far the analysis has minimized the significance of variations in the personnel policies adopted by enterprises operating in the Cameroun. To emphasize the influence of the past and current educational or occupational experiences of wage earners on their current achievement is to assume implicitly that this achievement is independent of the views held by employers, or more specifically to posit that employers adopt uniform attitudes and behavior toward labor.

Such an assumption is problematic. The segmentation of the Camerounian labor market cannot be exclusively the result of the particular strategies adopted by wage earners. If the performance of workers may be characterized by a varying amount of rationality, the same holds true of employers. Hence, the major thrust of the chapter is to ascertain the extent and determinants of variations in the personnel policies adopted by firms and individual entrepreneurs. In a first part of the chapter, I will show that economic concerns operating in the Cameroun are not only characterized by differing levels of complexity but are also confronted with varying historical constraints. In the second part, I will show that such contrasts are associated with parallel differences in hiring and promotion practices as well as in wage policies.

Organizational Complexity:
A Review of Its Components

Organizational complexity reflects an interplay of factors defined by reference to *what* firms or enterprise produce of exchange, *where, when,* and by *whom.*

First, firms belong to various sectors of activity, characterized by differing degrees of technological development. Tools and machines are less costly to purchase and maintain in plantations than in the aluminum-processing industry. Similarly, the technology utilized in the shipyards is far more advanced than that employed by construction firms. Yet technological sophistication also varies *within* sectors of activity. To give an example, the bakeries operating in the Cameroun do not all use similarly automated types of ovens, and banks do not uniformly rely on computers to handle their clients' accounts. These variations in the activities of enterprises should be accompanied by similar contrasts in the size and profile of their labor forces.[1]

Second, as firms do not operate in the same environment, they do not enjoy the same degree of freedom in the definition of their personnel policies. Although operating costs are often higher in rural than in urban areas (the purchase of material goods and external services is often more expensive in the hinterland), this is not necessarily so for labor costs. To be sure, the concentration of firms in major urban centers obliges employers to compete for skilled manpower, but the range of the choices they can make is also enhanced by the presence of a large number of educated Africans.

Third, as firms have not simultaneously begun to operate in the Cameroun, they do not use similar strategies. The form and level of investments varies with the date at which an employer has begun his operations in Africa. This date even influences the beliefs held about the potential adaptation of African workers to complex tools and machineries. Long-established colonial firms still tend to think of their production problems in terms of the particularistic aspects of the local labor market, whereas those settled after independence are more influenced by the practices of sophisticated enterprises operating in industrialized nations.[2] Of course, the varying approaches of employers are also affected by the stereotypic views that African workers and officials hold about foreign investors. The high visibility of firms and employers initially settled before

---

[1] As an illustration of this choice, the match factory installed in the Ivory Coast decided to buy secondhand machinery discarded by the most modern plants in Europe. By constrast a company engaged in the processing of soluble coffee used the most advanced machinery available in Europe. To be sure, such choices are not entirely dictated by economic social considerations. Indeed, technological advances in the second field are more recent, which limits the availability of secondhand equipment. Yet the fact remains that these two strategies do not have the same implications for the allocation of wages and salaries to African workers.

[2] Employers operating in Africa before the war were often unwilling to import even the simplest equipment; their decision was based on the reasoning that African workers would not know how to use a wheelbarrow, for example, and would place it on their heads. Even in 1952, one of the most important quarries in the Ivory Coast (Ake Befia) did not have a single wheelbarrow, and stones were transported exclusively in little baskets carried on the heads of laborers. Further, "old-timers" in the Ivory Coast as in the Cameroun are sensitive to ethnic stereotypes and "know" that the Baoule are "industrious," the Voltaics "dedicated" but "stupid," the Bete "quarrelsome," the Douala "conceited," and the Bamileke "eager to succeed." By constrast, the more recently arrived large-scale organization will operate in Africa on the basis of a model of organization which has led to success elsewhere. For example, there are few differences in the organizational chart used by Renault in Africa and in metropolitan France. In 1963, the personnel director of that firm had little knowledge of ethnic factors in the Ivory Coast and discounted them in his hiring practices: "For me, these Africans are all the same."

the war makes them particularly vulnerable to local criticism.[3] This vulnerability may limit the current pool of job seekers to which they have access, but it might also induce them to practice more liberal personnel policies in order to erase the negative aura which still surrounds their activities.

Thus, variations in the nature of the tasks performed by an organization, in its location and its age, affect its organizational structure.[4] Technological development and spatial differentiation of activities entail a greater specialization of tasks, hence a greater need for coordinative functions. As a result, there is a corresponding increase in the number of wage earners engaged in purely administrative functions.

The numerical importance of the administrative personnel depends, however, on other factors.[5] Thus, the bureaucratization of a firm is also affected by its legal status. Because public corporations are vulnerable to the pressures of a larger number of social groups (stockholders, unions, and so forth), the greater range of their coordinative functions requires the services of more numerous white-collar workers. In addition, the bureaucratization of a firm is also influenced by the location of its headquarters. As the distance between the production units of a firm and its headquarters increases, disparities between the views of the managerial staff located at the hub of the system and of their counterparts in direct contact with local realities become more salient. Because of these disparities, there is a greater need to minimize disruptions in the communication system, and the satisfaction of this need entails a greater demand for administrative personnel.

Last, even though complexity leads to a bureaucratic style of organization, its effects still depend on the ethnic background of administrative personnel. In Africa, bureaucratization should vary with the number of Europeans working for the organization.

But is it possible to rank Camerounian firms in terms of their level of organizational complexity, as measured by this variety of indicators? If this

---

[3] Interesting differences exist in this respect between large- and small-scale import/export firms. By 1963, in the Ivory Coast, it was clear that the owners of small, long-established companies were both better known and more sharply criticized than the managers of the more bureaucratized SCOA. The first type of company was frequently used as an example to illustrate the evils of the colonial situation.

[4] For a brief summary of the literature on this question, see Ingham, *Size of Industrial Organization and Worker Behavior*, chaps. 1 and 2.

[5] For a review of the conflicting evidence regarding the influence of size on bureaucratization, see for example, T. Caplow, *Principles of Organization* (New York: Harcourt, Brace, 1964), pp. 25-26; R. Bendix, *Work and Authority in Industry* (New York: Wiley, 1963), pp. 221-226; and J. Woodward, *Management and Technology* (London: Oxford University Press, 1958), pp. 7-17. See also the more recent work of P. Blau and R. Schoenherr, *The Structure of Organizations* (New York: Basic Books, 1971), where they show the extent of variations in the interaction among size, a number of other intervening variables, and administrative ratios.

complexity is really unidimensional, one should be able to demonstrate that contrasts in the organizational profile of Camerounian firms are associated with parallel variations in the experiences, qualifications, and commitment of their workers.

Overall Characteristics of Camerounian Firms

As indicated in Chapter 2, the data were gathered by production unit, that is, by work locations distinct from one another, rather than by firm. Many Camerounian enterprises perform a variety of tasks in a number of different locations, and the first step of the analysis involves, therefore, an aggregation of the data at the level of the unit using the largest number of wage earners.[6]

Geographic distribution of modern firms.

Differences in the relative development of Camerounian regions are associated with contrasts in the number, nature, and age of modern enterprises. At one extreme, the Mungo area is characterized by a relatively high concentration of *older* enterprises mostly engaged in *primary* activities or in the processing of raw material for exports (Tables 34 and 35). At the other extreme, Douala, the earliest focus of industrial development, accommodates one-half of all the organizations included in the sample, the majority of which belong to the secondary sector of the economy. Between these two extremes, there are two additional significant foci of development. In Yaoundé, the government is anxious to diversify local activities and to find additional jobs for the large number of educated adults living in the area. Yet these governmental endeavors are recent, and 60 percent of the organizations located in the capital city have been created after independence.[7] In Edea, alternatively, the presence of industrial activities results from the relatively recent building of a hydroelectric dam and thus from the availability of a reasonably cheap source of energy.

This distribution of Camerounian firms exemplifies the general patterns of economic development in Africa. There is a marked concentration of diversified industrial and commercial activities in a few large urban centers,

---

[6] Of course, *largest* does not refer to an absolute majority. The majority of workers in a particular enterprise might be engaged in a variety of minor activities. One must also recognize that to define the primary function of an economic organization in terms of the number of workers it requires can be misleading. A particular activity can absorb large quantities of manpower because of its low level of technological complexity and minimal profits. Another solution to the problem would have consisted in defining the main activity of an enterprise as the one producing the greatest net profit. Unfortunately, the necessary data were not available.

[7] The case of Yaoundé illustrates conflicts betwen economic and political considerations in processes of development. As industrial activities in the Cameroun involve both exports and imports, to locate them in Yaoundé makes little economic sense, for it raises costs of production and export prices.

TABLE 34
Age and Location of Camerounian Firms
(percentage distribution)

Main Location	Date of foundation				
	Post-independence (after 1960)	Post-W.W. II (1945-1958)	Pre-W.W. II (before 1945)	Total	N
Yaoundé	60.0	32.8	7.2	100.0	101
Douala	49.0	36.4	14.6	100.0	255
Nkongsamba	47.0	28.4	23.6	100.0	17
Mungo	17.4	21.7	60.9	100.0	23
Edea	69.0	31.0	0.0	100.0	13
Sanaga	55.5	22.2	22.2	99.9	9
Others	32.0	36.0	32.0	100.0	23

but enterprises located elsewhere tend both to be generally older and to have a narrower range of functions with a greater emphasis on primary production.

Historical patterns of development of modern firms.
Although the age of a firm is a predictor of its personnel policies, its meaning remains ambiguous. This age may reflect "sociological time," and hence, mere variations in positions that organizations occupy in their life cycle. In this context, size and organizational complexity should increase as a direct function of the number of years that an economic organization has operated. But the age of an organization has also a specific *historical* meaning, and this is why I have divided the sample into three categories, distinguishing firms created before World War II from those having begun their operations between 1945 and 1960 and from those that have established themselves in Cameroun since independence.[8]

As already noted, local economic life until 1945 was dominated by the "colonial pact." Although this pact prevented the development of a large secondary and tertiary sector, the simultaneous limitations imposed on the immigration of lower-class whites facilitated, in the primary sector, the growth of African-owned small-scale enterprises and well-established large-scale plantations controlled by European interests. No less than 42 percent of the firms of the primary sector were created before the war.

During the period between 1945 and 1960, colonial powers became fearful of losing control over African territories. This fear induced the adoption of conflicting strategies. Authorities were perhaps willing to

---

[8] Hence, I am assuming that the influence of time is not unidirectional nor cumulative.

TABLE 35
Location of Firms by Branch of Activity
(percentage distribution)

Branch of activity	Yaoundé	Douala	Nkongsamba	Mungo	Edea	Sanaga	Other	Total	N
				Main location					
Primary[a]	1.1	8.6	0.0	45.6	1.1	11.9	31.6	99.9	92
Processing[b]	25.9	22.2	11.1	27.7	3.9	0.0	9.2	100.0	54
Textile[c]	30.1	60.8	5.9	0.8	0.0	0.8	1.6	100.0	117
Metallurgical[d]	16.0	68.9	10.4	0.0	3.5	0.0	1.2	100.0	37
Construction	33.3	53.0	3.7	3.7	0.0	0.0	1.4	100.1	81
Banks and insurance	17.4	78.3	0.0	0.0	0.0	0.0	4.3	100.0	23
Transport[e]	100.0	0.0	0.0	0.0	0.0	0.0	0.0	100.0	3
Import/export	18.9	55.9	10.0	12.7	0.0	0.0	2.5	100.0	211

[a]Includes forestry and plantations, fishing and husbandry.

[b]Includes slaughterhouses, food, and tobacco-processing as well as mines.

[c]Includes textile, wood, printing, and chemical industries.

[d]Includes auto repair stations, shipyards, aluminum-processing industries.

[e]The three firms indicated belong to the Camerounian Railroad Company, whose headquarters are in Yaoundé.

accelerate educational development and to concede greater political rights in order to satisfy the major aspirations of local populations, but they were also keen to perpetuate the existing economic control of the Metropole. As this perpetuation required a massive development of local technical and financial infrastructures, the period is characterized by the growth of firms engaged in large-scale public works and construction as well as of more adequate local banking and credit facilities. In contrast to what theory would lead one to believe, the development of tertiary activities in the Cameroun has preceded industrialization. At the same time, colonial authorities were keen to counterbalance the centrifugal forces associated with the increased demand for independence by pushing forward the integration of the local economy into the framework provided by large metropolitan concerns. Out of the 151 enterprises created between 1945 and 1960, no less than 78 percent had the status of corporation, which characterizes only 56 percent of the firms created before the war and 61 percent of those founded after independence.

During the postindependence period, the government has been anxious to diversify both economic activities and their organization. Although only 10 percent of all enterprises are African owned, the relevant percentage is higher when one looks at the organizations more recently founded. Thus, there are increasing variations in the legal status of Camerounian firms, and no less than 58 percent of the small-scale privately owned firms and 45 percent of the large semipublic and private organizations have been created after independence.

The growing governmental concern over the economy is also conducive to changes in the proportion of firms with local headquarters, for they are easier to control. Over three-quarters of the enterprises created either after independence or before the war have locally based headquarters, as against only 60 percent of those created between 1945 and 1960. In short, the period between the end of World War II and the gaining of independence has facilitated the opening up of the Camerounian economy to large-scale, internationally based enterprises.

Finally, historical factors influence the form of bureaucratization adopted by employers. The number of Europeans employed by local concerns varies markedly over time. As many large-scale internationally based corporations in the tertiary sector of the economy were established between 1945 and 1960, it is not surprising to note that almost three-quarters of the firms created during that period have more than three Europeans on their staff, against 69 percent of their prewar counterparts and 47 percent of the postindependence concerns.

To sum up, the role that time plays in influencing the organizational profile of firms in a developing nation is both sociological and historical. Variations in the technical, legal, and organizational profile of industrial or commercial concerns reflect as much specific historical incidents as firm maturation and internal dynamics.

Correlates of organizational complexity.

Although there are specific contrasts among Camerounian firms with differing ages and locations, it is still necessary to see whether these contrasts present a consistent pattern and whether their relative complexity results from identical forces.

First, the sheer size of these firms is affected by technological development. All sectors characterized by a low degree of mechanization, and hence a low degree of division of labor, require the services of a large (usually unskilled) labor force. About 52 percent of the primary concerns and 43 percent of construction enterprises have more than fifty wage earners. In contrast, the more advanced technology utilized by some branches of the secondary sector or by the tertiary sector as a whole allows for greater variations in the size of individual firms. Only one-fifth of mechanical and metallurgical concerns employ more than fifty workers. Similarly, one-third of banks and insurance concerns fall into the category of the largest employers (with fifty employees and more), but 27 percent of them are small scale and use the services of fewer than ten individuals.

Second, sheer size is also related to the age of an enterprise. Only 41 percent of the enterprises created since independence employ more than twenty-five workers as against 54 percent of their counterparts created between 1945 and 1960 and 58 percent of those established in the Cameroun before World War II. Older firms are the largest because of both their natural pattern of expansion and of the usually low level of their technology (and hence their need for a large unskilled labor force).

Third, sheer size is associated with the physical dispersion of a firm's activities. Only 32 percent of the 256 concerns that have only one place of activity employ more than fifty individuals, as opposed to 57 percent for those 89 enterprises whose activities are spread among more than two offices, plants, office warehouses, or stores. The effects of physical dispersion on size, however, are greater for locally than internationally based enterprises (Table 36.)

Last, the sheer size of a firm is related both to its legal status and the location of its headquarters. Thus, 85 percent of the concerns with fifty workers or more are public or semipublic corporations, whereas 71 percent of the firms with fewer than ten workers are privately owned and not incorporated. In other words, 43 percent of the public and semipublic corporations employ over fifty workers, but 52 percent of privately owned enterprises have fewer than ten wage earners. Similarly, the percentage of firms with headquarters located outside the Cameroun increases regularly with the number of their workers, from 17 percent for those with fewer than ten workers to 44 percent for those with more than fifty employees.

Yet organization complexity does not refer only to sheer size but also to (a) patterns of division of labor operating within the firms, (b) their level of bureaucratization, and (c) the form this bureaucratization takes.

TABLE 36
Interaction between Size, Number of Units of a Firm, and Location of Its Headquarters
(percentage distribution)

Number of Geographical Units in firm	Size of headquarters							
	Fewer than 10		11-25		26-50		Over 50	
	Local	*International*	*Local*	*International*	*Local*	*International*	*Local*	*International*
1	84.1	47.9	67.6	61.3	69.4	52.6	59.7	20.0
2	8.7	28.6	17.1	12.9	22.4	21.1	16.9	16.7
More than 2	7.2	28.6	15.2	25.8	8.2	26.3	23.4	63.3
	100.0	100.0	99.9	100.0	100.0	100.0	100.0	100.0
N	(69)	(14)	(105)	(31)	(49)	(19)	(77)	(60)

Division of labor entails the relative dispersion of workers across a variety of occupational roles, and thereby firms can be distinguished in terms of the proportion of painters, mechanics, carpenters, and so forth that they use.[9] At the same time, division of labor also conditions the number of services rendered or activities performed by a particular concern. For example, a firm may specialize in the production of one particular product, in which case the bulk of its labor force is concentrated in a single department. In contrast, another firm (for example, the "classical" long-established import/export concerns) may be simultaneously engaged in the processing and sale of locally produced raw materials, the sale of imported goods from the Metropole, the repair of a variety of tools or equipment, and the sale of services such as insurance, in which case its personnel is evenly scattered among a large number of units or departments. In the following analysis, I have retained the second rather than the first definition of division of labor.[10]

When one controls for sector of activity, there is a clear association between the number of workers employed by a firm and their concentration in a particular department or service (Table 37). Among banks, insurance concerns, and export/import enterprises, increase in size implies a greater dispersion of workers and, hence, an accentuated division of labor.[11] In the secondary sector, the relationship between size and level of division of labor varies with technological development. At the upper end of the continuum, the increased size of metallurgical or mechanical enterprises is accompanied by a greater dispersion of their labor force among a variety of services and departments. The larger a garage, for example, the more it tends to develop ancillary services (the sale of second-hand vehicles and of spare parts and the extension of credit facilities and so forth). At the lower end of the continuum, however, an increase in the number of workers present in the less technologically sophisticated construction firms is usually associated with their concentration in a

[9] The author had the opportunity of comparing two repair stations with contrasted characteristics in this respect in Abidjan. The first one was attached to an old, established import/export company. The organizational pattern of the entire firm and a lack of space limited the specialization of the mechanics, who had to be equally prepared to repair the mechanical and electrical equipment of a disabled vehicle. By contrast, in the second garage attached to a worldwide automobile industry, the handling of distinctive types of breakdown was performed by mechanics specializing in the performance of specific tasks.

[10] For a discussion of the two forms of division of labor, see J. Gibbs and M. Browning, "The Division of Labor, Technology, and Organization of Production in Twelve Countries," *American Sociological Review* 31(1966):91-92.

[11] One must also take into account the fact that distinct branches of activity do not have the same legal status nor the same type of headquarters. No less than 73 percent of the banks included in the sample are internationally based, and 90 percent of them have the status of public corporations. By contrast, only 38 percent of timber and textile processing enterprises have this status, and only one-fourth of them are internationally based. Such differences cannot but contribute to differential forms of division of labor.

TABLE 37
Extent of Division of Labor by Size and Branch of Activity
(percentage distribution)

	Index of concentration[b]				N
	High	Medium	Low		
Primary sector					
Small[b] [i]	43.7	31.2	25.1	100.0	(16)
Large	43.7	20.3	36.0	100.0	(64)
Processing raw materials					
Small	0.0	34.6	65.4	100.0	(26)
Large	13.0	17.4	69.6	100.0	(23)
Textiles, wood, furniture					
Small	28.5	53.5	28.0	100.0	(28)
Large	32.5	30.2	37.3	100.0	(43)
Mechanical and metallurgical					
Small	38.4	30.7	30.9	100.0	(26)
Large	20.6	27.6	51.8	100.0	(29)
Construction and public works					
Small	43.4	30.4	26.2	100.0	(23)
Large	54.3	28.2	17.5	100.0	(46)
Banks and insurance					
Small	0.0	33.3	66.7	100.0	(12)
Large	0.0	22.2	77.8	100.0	(9)
Transport					
Small	*	*	*		
Large	0.0	33.3	66.7	100.0	(3)
Import/export					
Small	2.9	27.2	69.9	100.0	(136)
Large	0.0	14.5	85.5	100.0	(48)

*No cases in this category.

[a]Small inclues firms employing twenty-five workers or fewer. Large includes firms including more than twenty-five workers.

[b]This index is derived from a score resulting from the application of the following formula:

$$\text{Index} = 1 - \frac{\Sigma \cdot X^2}{t^2}$$

where X = the number of workers present in each type of activity performed by the firm. t = the sum of workers present in all types of activity undertaken by the firm. This index represents the relative concentration of workers across types of activity.

High = between 0.001 and 0.30. Medium = between 0.31 and 0.59. Low = between 0.60 and 0.99.

limited number of services and, hence, with a decrease in the relative level of division of labor.[12]

Last, division of labor also varies with the legal status of the firm, and it is more marked among large-size public corporations with international headquarters and a European staff than among privately owned and locally based enterprises, even though the relevant association varies by branch of activity (Table 38).

However, an increase in the scalar characteristics of a firm does not only influence its patterns of division of labor but also the number of its workers engaged in coordinative functions. Thus, the percentage of local wage earners engaged in staff functions (general administration) increases systematically as one moves from the plantations to businesses in the tertiary sector, and from privately owned enterprises to public and semipublic corporations (Table 39). Contrasts between public or semi-public corporations and private firms are sharper in the tertiary than in the primary sector.

Similarly, the relative importance of the labor force absorbed in coordinating activities also depends on the location of the headquarters of the firms. However, differences between locally and internationally based concerns in this regard are manifest only among banks, insurance, and import/export firms. Thus, the proportion of tertiary enterprises using *more* than 10 percent of their African personnel in coordinative activities decreases from 89 percent among those whose headquarters are located in Europe to 59 percent among those with headquarters in Douala or

TABLE 38

Percentage of Firms with a Low Index of Concentration by Branch of Activity and Selected Organizational Characteristics

| | Branch of activity | |
Type of firm	Secondary industry	Tertiary industry
Small private firms[a]	29.0	67.0
Large corporations[b]	43.0	86.0
Small, locally based firms	25.0	75.0
Large international firms	60.0	94.0
Firms without Europeans	30.0	60.0
Firms with more than two Europeans	41.0	86.0

[a]Fewer than twenty-five workers (includes franchise units and individual entrepreneurs).

[b]More than twenty-five workers (includes foreign missions, semistate and public corporations.)

[12] For an analysis of the relative division of labor characteristic of construction firms, see A. Stinchcombe, "Bureaucratic and Craft Administration of Production," *Administrative Science Quarterly*, 4(1959):168-187.

TABLE 39

Participation of African Workers in Staff Functions by Sector of Activity and Legal Status of Firms
(percentage distribution)

Percentage of African workers involved in internal coordinating Activities[a]	Primary sector		Secondary sector		Tertiary sector	
	Corporations	Private firms	Corporations	Private firms	Corporations	Private firms
Fewer than 10	86.3	95.4	62.4	86.5	22.4	55.2
Between 11 and 25	9.0	0.0	30.1	10.4	32.0	34.2
26 to 100	4.7	4.6	7.7	3.1	45.6	10.6
Total	100.0	100.0	100.0	100.0	100.0	100.0
N	(44)	(44)	(159)	(159)	(123)	(76)

[a]These are overwhelmingly nonmanual workers concerned with internal accounting, personnel, and general administration.

Yaoundé. In short, the international orientation of an industrial or commercial concern increases the significance of its coordination activities.

The involvement of Africans in coordination activities also varies with the sheer size of the concerns for which they work. To be sure, the concentration of the local labor force in such services is uniformly low in the primary sector. Alternatively, only 21 percent of firms in the secondary sector with fewer than twenty-five employees use more than 10 percent of their African personnel in this kind of activity, as against 32 percent of their counterparts with more than twenty-five workers, and in the tertiary sector the corresponding figures are 59 and 84 percent, respectively. Thus, the influence of size on the salience of bureaucratic functions varies clearly by economic sector and is maximal among commercial and banking enterprises.

Finally, organizational complexity affects the *form* of bureaucratization of Camerounian firms and, more specifically, the number of Europeans present on the staff. European presence varies with the size of local enterprises. No less than 30 percent of the concerns with more than fifty workers use the services of at least ten Europeans, against 4 percent of the enterprises with between twenty-six and fifty workers and none of the smaller concerns. The number of Europeans varies also by sector; few in the enterprises of the primary sector, expatriates are more numerous in the firms engaged in construction and public works (some 45 percent of the 87 firms entered in this last group have more than two Europeans) or in banking and insurance (the corresponding figure rises to 80 percent).[13]

To conclude, economic organizations in the Cameroun do not have the same scale.[14] At one end of the continuum, there are the small locally based, privately owned enterprises with few Europeans, a low level of division of labor, and a low degree of involvement of African workers in coordinative activities. At the other, one finds large public corporations that are internationally based, exhibit a high degree of division of labor, have a number of production units, employ a large number of Europeans, and allow a substantial proportion of their African personnel to undertake staff functions. However, contrasts between these two polar types vary by economic sector and are historically relative. Indeed, independence has been conducive to a greater differentiation of the enterprises operating in the Cameroun.

---

[13] Of course, the actual use of European staff varies by branch of activity. Whereas Europeans employed by banks are most frequently engaged in managerial jobs, those working for construction and public work firms have more differentiated roles. Some of them are draftsmen, some are in charge of the most sophisticated machinery, and some supervise each specific operation in the firm. It would have been interesting to determine whether the distinctive activities of European workers exert differing influences on the occupational careers of their African coworkers.

[14] The word *scale* refers here to the scope of the physical and functional relations established both within the organization and between the organization and the outside world. For a further description of the term, see the introduction to this study.

Personnel Policies of Camerounian Firms

Variations in organizational complexity are paralleled by differences in the expectations that employers entertain about labor. Thus, Camerounian firms do not adopt similar hiring and promotion policies. Nor do they adopt uniform patterns of work organization.

For hiring practices, variations in the organizational complexity of Camerounian economic organizations are paralleled by similar contrasts in the ethnic, educational, or occupational profile of their respective labor forces.

Ethnic composition of Camerounian firms.

As the organizational complexity of a firm increases, its managers become more universalistic in their orientation, and they attach less importance to the ethnic background of their workers. Thus, the extent of the discrimination exerted *against* or *in favor* of a particular people varies both with the size of a firm and its sector of activity (Table 40). Larger firms are uniformly less liable to totally exclude from their labor force job seekers with a particular origin. Symmetrically, they are also less prone than smaller enterprises to recruit more than one-half of their labor force from a single ethnic group. In addition, banks, insurance companies, and export/import firms are more open in their patterns of ethnic recruitment than enterprises in the primary or secondary sector.

Yet these firms are not equally open to the various Camerounian ethnic groups. Regardless of size and sector, the percentage of firms without *any* Bamileke workers is significantly lower than the proportion of firms without any Douala, Bassa, Beti-Fang, or foreign employees. Further, when one controls for organizational complexity and examines the economic concerns of the tertiary sector with more than twenty-five workers, it is clear that no less than 20 percent of employers recruit a majority of their labor force from among Bamileke job seekers, and that none of the other ethnic groups obtains such a preferential treatment. Although Bamileke people have a high level of visibility because of their marginal status in the Camerounian society, they are still often preferred to other groups.[15] Alternatively, many firms totally discriminate against foreigners. Growing disparities between rates of educational and economic development enhance the anxieties of Camerounians over available opportunities. This probably influences the policies of the government and restricts the choices of private employers with regard to the use of aliens.[16]

[15] I have eliminated the groups with the lowest ethnic visibility.

[16] The situation in the Cameroun differs in this respect from that observed in the Ivory Coast. In the latter country, colonial policies led firms to use a great number of alien workers in supervisory roles in preference to Ivory Coasters. This was because ethnic stereotypes led to the belief that Senegalese, Dahomeans, Togolese, Ghanaians, or even Camerounians were more apt at such work than the local population. This colonial legacy still existed in 1963 in certain sectors and firms (notably SCOA).

TABLE 40
Ethnic Concentration of Firms by Size and Sector of Activity

Ethnic concentration within firms	Primary		Secondary		Tertiary	
	Small	Large[c]	Small	Large	Small	Large
Ewondo						
Minimal[a]	80.0	42.0	65.0	20.0	70.0	20.0
Maximal[b]	0.0	0.0	9.0	5.0	1.0	0.0
Bamileke						
Minimal	36.0	10.0	35.0	14.0	21.0	2.0
Maximal	44.0	41.0	25.0	13.0	44.0	20.0
Bassa						
Minimal	80.0	37.0	59.0	14.0	60.0	11.0
Maximal	4.0	13.0	8.0	7.0	6.0	0.0
Douala						
Minimal	76.0	42.0	68.0	24.0	67.0	11.0
Maximal	4.0	0.0	4.0	1.0	5.0	0.0
Foreigners (including West Camerounians)						
Minimal	80.0	37.0	75.0	34.0	80.0	34.0
Maximal	12.0	5.0	3.0	0.0	1.0	1.0

[a]*Minimal* represents zero percent of working force.

[b]*Maximal* represents above 50 percent of working force.

[c]*Small* includes firms employing twenty-five workers or fewer. *Large* includes firms employing more than twenty-five workers.

To conclude, the ethnic cosmopolitanism of Camerounian firms varies with their size and the nature of their activities, but it remains relative, for firms do not adopt similar behavior toward the various ethnic groups present on the local scene.

Educational profile of Camerounian firms.

Enterprises do not require identical educational qualifications from their labor forces. The importance they attach to credentials varies with (1) relative level of technology: firms using sophisticated equipment tend to demand higher educational qualifications than those with a rudimentary level of technological development; and (2) level of bureaucratic organization: an increase in the size and complexity of the network of communications both within and without the firm enhances the dependence of that particular organization on the level of formal schooling of its workers.

Over three-quarters of the concerns engaged in primary activities have a labor force whose average aggregate training score is lower than 3.0. In contrast, over two-thirds of the banks and insurance concerns employ workers whose average aggregate training score exceeds 6.0 (Table 41). As has been noted already industries in the secondary sector of the economy are characterized by differing degrees of technological complexity, and 39 percent of mechanical and metallurgical concerns have a labor force which has an average aggregate training score of 5.0 and above, as against only 9 percent of those firms engaged in public works and construction.

Educational qualifications depend not only on the complexity of the work to be performed, but also on the size of the organization. Yet the association between size and task complexity differs across economic sectors. In the primary sector, the work performed on large-scale plantations is simple enough, whereas the personnel of usually more recent, smaller experimental concerns are expected to perform a larger number of more complex operations. Accordingly, the relationship between the size and the average aggregate training score of the labor force of agricultural enterprises is negative. No less than 94 percent of the firms with more than twenty-five wage earners has a labor force with the equivalent of fewer than four years of formal schooling, against only 68 percent of the smaller concerns. In other words, smaller agricultural experimental stations require a larger number of relatively educated workers.

The situation is analogous in the secondary sector. Thus, 62 percent of the larger secondary concerns have a labor force with the equivalent of less than four years' formal schooling and training, as against 46 percent of the smaller enterprises.

Conversely, task complexity and size are more independent of each other in the tertiary sector, and variations in the size of local firms are hardly associated with contrasts in the average level of qualifications of their workers. Thus, the average aggregate training score of individual workers exceeds 5.0 among 31 percent of the smaller concerns, but this proportion increases to only 36 percent in larger organizations.

However, the relationship between task complexity and the educational or vocational qualifications expected from African workers depends on the ethnic background of the personnel engaged in bureaucratic activities. The presence of Europeans modifies the demand for a highly qualified African labor force. In the primary sector, the proportions of firms whose African labor force has an average aggregate training score of *under* 4.0 declines from 91 percent for those with a European staff to 83 percent for those without. In the secondary sector, the contrasts between the two types of organizations are even sharper, and the corresponding figures are 61 and 36 percent, respectively. In such sectors the presence of Europeans limits the demand for a qualified African labor force, and the involvement of the two populations in bureaucratic functions is mutually exclusive. In contrast, the requirements of bureaucratic work in the tertiary sector lead

TABLE 41
Educational Profile of Firms by Sector of Activity
(percentage distribution)

| | Average aggregate training score of African workers | | | | | |
	Less than 3.0	3.0-3.9	4.0-4.9	5.0-5.9	6.0 and above	Total
Primary	78.2	10.3	9.2	1.1	1.1	99.9 (87)
Processing raw materials	58.5	26.4	13.2	1.9	0.0	100.0 (53)
Textiles and wood	26.9	25.0	29.6	13.9	4.6	100.0 (103)
Mechanical and metallurgical	7.1	19.0	34.5	27.4	11.9	99.9 (94)
Construction and public works	31.6	26.7	22.8	5.1	3.8	100.0 (79)
Banks and insurance	0.0	4.5	4.5	22.7	68.2	99.9 (22)
Transport	0.0	33.3	66.7	0.0	0.0	100.0 (3)
Import/export	19.7	18.8	33.6	17.8	7.2	100.1 (208)

European and African labor forces to perform complementary functions. As a result, the presence of expatriates stimulates the presence of educated African wage earners. Only 27 percent of the firms of the tertiary sector which are without European staff have an African labor force with an average aggregate training score of *over* 5.0, against 35 percent of those which do use the services of European personnel. Thus, the dynamics of Africanization cannot be alike in different branches of the economy, for the presence of Europeans is not evenly detrimental to the hiring and the promotion of educated Camerounians.

Finally, the average qualifications of African labor forces vary with the age of the concerns which employ them. To be sure, as educational development proceeds, all firms should have easier access to the growing number of educated job seekers. This is not so, however, and 51 percent of the enterprises that settled in the Cameroun after independence have African workers with a mean aggregate training score of *over* 4.0, against 44 percent of those created before 1945. In effect, newer firms seem to recruit their labor force from among the younger and, hence, more educated cohorts of job seekers rather than from the mass of individuals already in the labor market. In this sense, the industrial commitment of workers is not independent of the industrial commitment of their employers.[17]

Insofar as analysis of variations in the educational qualifications of African labor forces is only based on means and central tendencies, it may conceal as much as it reveals. Accordingly, it is equally appropriate to examine variations in the proportion of firms which employ African workers with high qualifications, that is, those who have successfully completed at least a long cycle of postprimary technical studies (*Brevet Professionnel*). This examination confirms that the vocational qualifications of African personnel vary with the organizational profile of their enterprises (Table 42). Thus, the proportion of firms employing African workers with at least a *Brevet Professionnel* increases from the primary to the tertiary sector; likewise, this proportion increases with the size of the concerns examined and particularly so in the tertiary secotr. This proportion is also higher in internationally based firms, and large prewar enterprises are more likely to use African personnel with this background than those newly arrived in the market.

Differential importance of on-the-job training programs by types of firms.
Employers with differing characteristics hold differing expectations about the initial occupational experiences of their workers. As has been shown, such experiences are diverse, and although some wage earners learn their trade from friends and relatives, others begin their working life by entering on-the-job training programs within large-scale organizations. Although the second population may be more effectively socialized to an industrial discipline, employers do not attach the same importance to the initial participation of their workers in formal on-the-job programs. The value accorded to the initial learning of an industrial discipline is greater in branches of activity characterized by higher technological development and rationality in work procedures. Thus, the workers of the primary sector tend less frequently to have acquired their first occupational experiences in the context of large-scale organizations. Across sectors, the type of first occupational experience varies with the size of the firms examined: in the primary sector, 36 percent of small concerns have at least one-fourth of their African workers who have been initially employed by large organizations, against 44 percent of the larger companies.[18]. In the secondary sector, the corresponding figures are 71 and 89 percent,

---

[17] See Lambert, *Workers, Factories, and Social Change in India*, p. 57.

[18] The results examined here are analogous to those reported by Peil in *The Ghanaian Factory Worker*. In her sample, half the firms with two hundred workers included in the management survey had some apprenticeship program compared with 13 percent of the organizations with fewer than fifty workers (p. 47).

TABLE 42

**Percentage of Firms with Selected Characteristics Having Some
Representation of Highly Qualified Workers**

Characteristics of firms	Percentage of firms employing workers with at least a brevet professionel
Size and sector	
Small primary[a]	0.0
Large primary	5.0
Small secondary	1.0
Large secondary	9.0
Small tertiary	1.0
Large tertiary	31.0
Location of headquarters	
Large local	5.0
Large international	28.0
Date of foundation	
Large before 1945	23.0
Large 1945-1958	20.0
Large postindependence	6.0

[a]Small includes firms employing twenty-five workers or fewer. Large includes firms employing more than twenty-five workers.

respectively. Finally, in the tertiary sector, half of the firms with fewer than twenty-five workers have at least one-fourth of their African workers who learned or performed their first job with a large-scale enterprise, as against 75 percent of their larger counterparts.[19] In brief, the acquisition of industrial discipline in the context of bureaucratic organizations prevails most often among populations currently attached to large-scale industries in the secondary sector.

Differential importance attached to job experience.
The average job seniority of workers hardly varies with the organizational complexity of their firm. There are no differences in this regard between locally and internationally based enterprises or between firms with differing sizes.[20] Yet occupational stability prevails most often

[19] It should be noted, however, that the importance attributed to on-the-job training programs by firms in distinctive sectors of activity seems to vary over time. In primary and tertiary firms, this stress is more evident among firms newly arrived in the Cameroun. In the secondary sector, however, the pattern is reversed, and it is the oldest companies that are most likely to provide such programs.

[20] Although 32 percent of international firms use an African labor force that averages more than seven years' experience on the same job, this characterizes 30 percent of their locally based counterparts.

among the workers employed by large-scale corporations in the tertiary
sector. No less than 41 percent of this type of concern have a labor force
with an average of at least *seven years* in the same job, as against 30
percent of enterprises with other kinds of legal status and involved in other
activities.

Differential promotion policies of Camerounian firms.

Organizational complexity facilitates the access of African workers into
the higher levels of the occupational hierarchy. Large-scale firms do not
only attach more importance to the vocational qualifications of their
personnel, but their leadership style makes them more likely to reward such
qualifications with an appropriate status. In addition, they have greater
resources with which to reward their personnel in proportion to their
efforts. In contrast, although small-scale enterprises may be willing to
offer competitive salaries, they tend to be more reluctant to base such
salaries on skill levels, for their long-term choices would be limited.

Thus, the representation of African workers in top skill echelons is
maximal in the tertiary sector and among the large-scale, internationally
based, public and semipublic corporations (Table 43). If one combines
indicators of organizational size, no less than 38 percent of the most
complex organizations in the tertiary sector employ African workers in top
skill levels, as opposed to none of the smaller private enterprises in the
primary sector. Similarly, 16 percent of the tertiary internationally based
concerns employ African personnel at these higher levels, against only 2
percent of the locally based primary sector firms. Finally, the access of
African workers to higher skill levels also varies with the form of
bureaucratization of the organization. Firms with European staff are less
likely to have workers in supervisory roles than those without Europeans (4
versus 9 percent).

Firms with differing characteristics do not only offer their workers
varying chances of performing top jobs, they do not offer them similar
opportunities for upward mobility. It has been noted that nonmanual
workers are more often upwardly mobile than their manual counterparts.
As these nonmanual wage earners are concentrated in the tertiary sector, it
is not surprising to note that it is the workers of this sector who enjoy the
largest number of opportunities for upward mobility. In 22 percent of
banks, insurance, and import/export concerns, at least one-fourth of the
personnel have moved upward on the skill scale between their first and
their current occupation. In the secondary sector, the corresponding
proportion is only 12 percent, and it reaches a low of 9 percent among
primary concerns.

However, the effects of organizational complexity in this regard are
inconsistent. Regardless of sector of activity, opportunities for upward
mobility are still greater in the case of smaller and locally based
organizations. The proportion of firms where one-fourth of the workers

TABLE 43
Percentage of Firms with Some African Workers in Skill Categories 6-7

Sector of activity	
Primary	9.0
Secondary	2.0
Tertiary	11.0
Size and status	
Large corporations[a]	10.0
Small corporations	7.0
Large noncorporations	5.0
small noncorporations	2.0
Headquarters	
Local	3.0
International	10.0
Europeans	
Present	4.0
Absent	9.0

[a]Small includes firms with twenty-five workers or fewer. Large includes firms employing more than twenty-five workers.

have experienced upward mobility between their first and current jobs declines from 22 percent in the case of small, locally based enterprises to 7 percent among the larger, internationally based organizations. Two factors may account for these differences. The importance ascribed to educational qualifications by large-scale international organizations may lead them to *directly* appoint qualified African individuals to supervisory roles, whereas smaller units may be more inclined to promote their own internal personnel to such roles. In addition, to move *upward* in the job hierarchy may require some African workers to move *away from* large organizations; small firms may be tempted to attract the more qualified African workers initially trained by larger companies.[21]

Different Patterns of Organization of Work

Firms differ in the procedures they follow to allocate work loads among the various segments of their respective labor forces.[22] To be sure, the amount of overtime work performed by workers has an equivocal meaning. Sometimes

---

[21] Hence the importance of analyzing job histories both in terms of *occupation* and *employment;* upward mobility in terms of job may require downward mobility in terms of employer.

[22] The recording of overtime only concerns workers paid on an hourly basis, that is, the majority of manual wage earners. By contrast, the majority of nonmanual workers are paid on a monthly basis and are usually not rewarded for extra work performed. Hence, they are not included in the subsequent analysis.

it reflects seasonal variations and is affected by the specific necessities of each branch of activity rather than by organizational complexity. Thus, certain activities *are* closely dependent on the harvesting of export products. Sometimes extensive overtime work may also reflect a low degree of technological development as well as poor output planning, and it is therefore an inadequate measure of the relative level of complexity of an organization. Finally, the amount of overtime recorded might merely reflect the differential conformity of employers to the requirements of the local labor code. Indeed, a small concern might demand overtime from its employees without recording the hours, whereas a large firm would be more hesitant to engage in this type of "deviant" activity.

Apparently, the amount of overtime performed varies by sector of activity (Table 44). Industries in the tertiary sector do not demand overtime from their manual employees. Both the mode of payment of their personnel and the rationalization of their work procedures eliminate the need for an increase in the duration of the legally defined work period. Yet there are sharp contrasts along these lines between primary and secondary sectors. The relatively low incidence of overtime work in the primary sector results from two phenomena. As overtime work in this sector is seasonal, interviews in the primary sector may have taken place outside of the peak season. Further, the presence of large numbers of unskilled and usually poorly informed laborers in this sector enables employers to take liberties with the requirements of the labor code.

In contrast, overtime work in the secondary sector is more likely to vary

TABLE 44
Percentage of Firms Using Overtime

Sector of activity	
Primary	39.0
Secondary	58.0
Tertiary	36.0
Size and status	
Large corporations[a]	81.0
Small corporations	44.0
Large noncorporations	42.0
Small noncorporations	19.0
Date of creation of firm	
Postindependence	54.0
1945-1948	61.0
Pre-1945	51.0

[a]Small includes firms employing twenty-five workers or fewer. Large includes firms employing more than twenty-five workers.

with the rationalization of production methods. Because of the low rationalization of the methods used by construction and public work industries, three-quarters of the firms in this branch require an additional one hundred hours of work per year from their workers, against half of the mechanical concerns and 42 percent of the industries engaged in the processing of raw materials. In the same secondary sector, the percentage of firms demanding one hundred hours of overtime work per year also varies with their size and their legal status: no less than 89 percent of the large concerns created between 1945 and 1960 (among which one finds the largest concentration of internationally based, public and semipublic corporations) require overtime work of their personnel, against only 74 percent of concerns founded since independence and 69 percent of the prewar enterprises.

Organizational Complexity and Commitment

Variations in organizational complexity, in personnel policies, and in patterns of work allocation should be associated with parallel contrasts in the commitment of individual workers to the industrial order. Yet the causality underlying such an association remains undetermined. Some sociologists have stressed the feelings of alienation that wage earners experience as a result of the cold and impersonal interaction style prevailing in the most bureaucratically oriented economic organizations, but others have emphasized that participation in large-scale organizations is associated with an increased sense of security which might accentuate feelings of loyalty toward the employer.[23]

In spite of the difficulties surrounding an assessment of individual attitudes in a cross-cultural context, one may still indirectly evaluate the differing degrees of commitment of the labor forces attached to Camerounian enterprises. Thus, absenteeism may be considered an indicator of the alienation experienced by wage earners, whereas the average amount of time spent in a particular firm may reflect their commitment to their employer. If this is so, one can expect absenteeism to prevail among populations with minimal seniority in the firm.

Absenteeism is a particularly crucial variable in the African context. Many European employers have justified low salary policies on the grounds that local workers display a low level of commitment toward work, abandon their job each time they are confronted with familial problems, and, more generally, regard work as an instrument which enables them to achieve a specific and temporary target.

Although absenteeism depends on individual characteristics, it varies also with the characteristics of the environment.[24] First, it is more salient in

---

[23] This sense of security is particularly important for African workers. On this subject, see, for example, Clignet and Foster, *The Fortunate Few*, chap. 7.

[24] Less than 1 percent of the workers interviewed were absent at the time of the survey.

the firms located in the largest towns than in those located in the hinterland. No less than 15 percent of the concerns located in Douala or Yaoundé have absentee workers, against only 7 percent of those situated elsewhere. Second, the percentage of firms with absentee personnel is higher among internationally based enterprises than among those with local headquarters (Table 45). Third, the percentage is significantly higher in large-scale public and semipublic corporations than in any other type of enterprise. Fourth, it varies with sector of activity and reaches a maximum among banks, insurance, and export/import concerns.[25] In this sense, bureaucratic patterns of interaction seem to favor absenteeism and prevent lower individual commitment.

TABLE 45
Percentage of Firms with African Workers Absent without Cause

Sector of activity	
Primary	12.0
Secondary	13.0
Tertiary	26.0
Size and legal status	
Large corporations[a]	31.0
Small corporations	7.0
Large noncorporations	12.0
Small noncorporations	3.0
Location of headquarters	
Local	12.0
International	33.0

[a]*Small* includes firms with twenty-five workers or below. *Large* includes firms with more than twenty-five workers.

Absentees are more likely to be *nonmanual* than manual workers (white-collar workers represented 20 percent of *absent* personnel, as against 16 percent of the working population *present* at the time of the survey). Although absentees have achieved a higher skill level (22 percent of the individuals in the first group were concentrated in skill levels 4 and above, against only 12 percent of the workers in the second), they have both lower aggregate training scores (1.1 versus 3.3) and lower levels of experience in the job actually performed (1.1 versus 6.5 years of seniority on the job). Finally, absentees are less likely to be engaged directly in productive activities (46 versus 65 percent).

[25] In Ghana, Peil notes that absenteeism is high, although there are variations by ownership and nationality of managers. See "Factory Management and Workers in the Accra Capital District," *Economic Bulletin of Ghana* 10(1969):23-35. She notes, however, that neither size nor specialization of the labor force of firms seems to have any impact on this phenomenon. See *The Ghanaian Factory Worker*, p. 99. On the other hand, Guilbot notes that the quality and the nature of work conditions affect absenteeism. See *Absentéisme et mobilité des travailleurs*, p. 45. Finally, although Ingham proposes that absenteeism varies as a reverse function of labor commitment, he suggests that the mechanisms underlying this commitment are not the same between small and large enterprises. See Ingham, *Size of Industrial Organization*, chap. 3.

However, the influence of such patterns is not independent of specific historical factors. Especially in the secondary sector, newer firms tend to adopt personnel policies borrowed from European models and at variance with those pursued by older enterprises. Such differences in personnel policies are associated with contrasted rates of absenteeism, and only 14 percent of secondary enterprises created after independence had some absent workers at the time of the study, as against 27 percent of prewar concerns. In the tertiary sector, a maximal level of bureaucratization characterizes concerns created between the end of the war and the independence period, and it is in such firms that one finds the highest number of units with absentee personnel (29 percent, against 17 percent of their prewar counterparts and 12 percent of the postindependence concerns).

Finally, conversely to my expectations, absenteeism and stability of employment are positively related.[26] Thus absentees have worked for a greater time with the same employer than the individuals present in their job at the time of the survey. Average seniority in the firms is 7.2 years in the first case, but only 5.7 in the second. Individuals working for larger firms are more frequently absent but also more likely to have acquired greater experience in their *current* employment than those working for smaller enterprises.

The average seniority of workers increases with the size of the firms to which they are attached. It exceeds five years in only 24 percent of concerns with fewer than twenty-five workers, but in 36 percent of larger firms. Like absenteeism, commitment to a particular enterprise also varies by branch of activity. The average level of seniority of workers in the largest firms of the secondary sector exceeds five years in only 28 percent of the cases, but the corresponding figure rises to 44 percent in the case of both tertiary and primary enterprises with similar sizes. However, the similarities between primary and tertiary enterprises in this regard are probably misleading: if the stability of personnel working in the first type of business results from the absence of alternative opportunities the stability of the workers attached to tertiary enterprises probably reflects the regularity and importance of the rewards they derive from their employment.

Organizational Complexity and Salary Policies

The activities and the organizational characteristics of Camerounian firms influence not only their hiring and promotion practices but also their salary

---

[26] Ingham, ibid., suggests that empirical findings reveal that the relationship between the characteristics of a firm and those two measures of commitment does not follow the same pattern and does not have the same profile (p. 25). The same is suggested for Africa by J. Guilbot, *Absentéisme et mobilité des travailleurs*, p. 59. Hauser suggests that absenteeism resulting from work accidents is the only form of absenteeism associated with stability. See *Les Ouvriers de Dakar*, p. 65.

policies. Indeed, there are significant contrasts in the proportion of enterprises of differing size and in different sectors that are able to pay an average salary of over 100,000 CFA to their African workers. As expected, this proportion is higher in the tertiary than in other sectors of the economy. Further, within each sector, aggregate pay rates vary with the size of the concern. Thus, only 7 percent of the firms engaged in secondary activities and employing fewer than ten workers pay their African employees an average of 200,000 CFA, as against 28 percent of those with a labor force of over fifty wage earners. The contrasts are even sharper in the tertiary sector: 17 percent of the smallest enterprises have an average annual pay rate of over 200,000 CFA, whereas this level characterizes no less than 71 percent of the largest organizations. In other words, the differentiation of salary policies by size seems to be more marked in the tertiary sector.

Finally, holding other factors constant, the data show wage policies to be related to the location of headquarters of the organizations studied: about 46 percent of the internationally based enterprises pay their personnel an average of over 200,000 CFA, as against only 21 percent of their locally based counterparts. African workers have perhaps been often criticized for their lack of sense of enterprise, but their motivations in this context are realistic and mirror the trends at work in the labor market. Participating in a large-scale internationally based organization in the tertiary sector not only gives a sense of security—it also gives additional chances of obtaining high wages.[27]

The high salary policies practiced by large-scale concerns seem to uniformly apply to manual and nonmanual personnel. Even though premiums and bonuses primarily affect blue-collar earnings, it is possible to show that the proportion of firms rewarding their manual personnel with high premiums is greater in the tertiary than in any other sector. Further, this proportion is larger among public and semistate-owned corporations than among privately run enterprises, and it tends to vary with the size of the firms. Although 89 percent of public corporations employing more than twenty-five workers in the tertiary sector distribute bonuses that exceed an average of 2 CFA per hour, this characterizes only 22 percent of the smallest privately owned businesses in all sectors of activity. In this sense, participation in large-scale organizations enables manual workers to indirectly close the gap that separates them from nonmanual incomes.

As the access of African wage earners to higher skill positions varies negatively with the size of the European labor force, one could infer that the proportion of European workers present in a firm also negatively influences the salaries of African employees. Yet Camerounian enterprises

---

[27] Thus, occupational stability is perceived as the most attractive feature of a particular job both by Ivory Coast students and wage earners. See Clignet and Foster, *The Fortunate Few*, chaps. 7 and 8.

are confronted with a serious dilemma in this regard. They can define the "wages fund" available to them as predetermined and thus share resources between their European and African workers according to a zero-sum game model. Alternatively, to avoid invidious comparisons between these two categories of personnel and a lowering in the morale of their African labor force, firms might be obliged to pay them a salary proportionate to that paid European supervisors and higher technicians.

Table 46 shows that the second assumption is more valid. In all three sectors of activity, firms with more than two Europeans on their staff are more prone to pursue higher salary policies than those without expatriates. Among agricultural, fishing, and forestry concerns, only 6 percent of those without Europeans on their payroll pay an average annual income of over 100,000 CFA, as against 19 percent of those with only one European and less than 35 percent of those with two Europeans or more. In the secondary sector, the proportions increase from 18 to 58 and 87 percent, respectively. Among banks, transport industries, and import/export concerns, the range is narrower: 31 percent of the businesses without Europeans pay their African personnel an annual average salary exceeding 100,000 CFA, against 85 percent of those with one European employee and 99 percent of those with two expatriates or more.

In brief, the presence of a European labor force, although detrimental to the learning by Africans of highly skilled, administrative roles, is still beneficial to local workers in terms of salaries. This suggests a complexity in the issue of Africanization: access to higher skill levels and access to substantial monetary rewards are not necessarily the same, and Africans must therefore choose between the short-term and long-term implications of Africanization. Further, the firms that facilitate access to higher skill levels and those that have high salary policies are not always the same, and this raises the question of identifying the enterprises that are the best targets for a policy of Africanization.

Wage policies, however, are affected not only by the degree and the form of the bureaucratization espoused by a firm but also by its age. Enterprises created a long time ago have been accustomed to adapt themselves to a situation of absolute scarcity. As such a scarcity pertains to material as well as human resources, many employers were not particularly keen to accord high pay to their African workers. They often tended to rationalize their decision by arguing that Africans had basically low consumption aspirations and that high rates of pay induced them to quit their employment and to return to their village of origin in order to reap the social benefits of easily acquired cash. These firms would accordingly adopt lower wage schedules than the large-scale internationally based concerns without experience of African conditions, which would be more likely to follow the general guidelines of their headquarters and to retain the high wage policies that ensured their success elsewhere.

TABLE 46

Distribution of Firms by Sector, Number of European Employees, and Annual Income of Their African Labor Force

Average annual income of African labor force (thousands CFA)	Primary sector			Secondary sector			Tertiary sector		
	Number of Europeans			Number of Europeans			Number of Europeans		
	0	1	2 and over	0	1	2 and over	0	1	2 and over
Less than 29	30.3	6.2	0.0	9.5	3.2	1.5	7.9	0.0	0.0
30 to 49	45.4	37.5	29.0	19.0	0.0	0.0	14.1	0.0	0.0
50 to 69	9.1	18.8	19.3	25.0	7.8	0.0	20.5	0.0	0.0
70 to 99	9.1	18.8	16.3	28.5	31.2	11.5	23.6	15.0	0.9
100 to 199	6.1	18.8	22.5	16.7	50.0	64.9	26.9	55.0	39.2
200 to 299	0.0	0.0	12.9	1.1	7.8	19.8	1.2	10.0	36.1
Over 299	0.0	0.0	0.0	0.0	0.0	1.9	3.8	20.0	23.8
Total	100.0	100.0	100.0	99.8	100.0	100.0	100.0	100.0	100.0
N	(33)	(16)	(31)	(84)	(64)	(131)	(78)	(100)	(130)

However, the greater visibility of older Camerounian organizations exposes them to great suspicion. Under such conditions, some of these firms may be currently more anxious to escape the accusations of "colonialism" than enterprises more recently settled in the country and thus less sensitive to local feelings.

In effect, the influence of historical factors differs across the various sectors of the economy. In the primary sector, only recently have labor costs been defined as problematic. It is hence only recently that tasks have been rationalized and managers have become concerned with individual productivity. There are accordingly marked changes in the wage policies pursued by agricultural concerns created at different points in time. No less than 59 percent of agricultural firms created after independence accord their personnel an average pay that exceeds 100,000 CFA per annum, as against 15 percent of the enterprises created between 1945 and 1960, and only 5 percent of those created before the war. In short, in the primary sector, the relative liberalism of the wage policies followed by employers varies as a reverse function of the length of their experience in the Cameroun.

In the secondary sector, patterns of technological development parallel the amount of time during which individual enterprises have been operating in Africa. More likely to innovate than their long-established counterparts, some of the recently arrived organizations pay higher rates. Thus, at the lower end of the continuum, no less than 10 percent of the oldest firms pay their workers *less* than 69,000 CFA per year, as against 4 percent of those created later. Yet older firms tend also to employ personnel with more seniority, and at the upper end of the continuum no less than 31 percent of the enterprises created before the war pay salaries and wages whose average value exceeds 200,000 CFA, as against only 24 percent of those created between 1945 and 1960 and 12 percent of firms which arrived in the Cameroun after independence. In other words, there seems to be a positive association between the age of secondary organizations and the pay they distribute, but there is also an increased differentiation in their respective wage policies.

Finally, in the tertiary sector, the relationship between the age of individual firms and their wage policies follows a curvilinear pattern. I have shown that the organizational, hiring, and promotion policies of the concerns created between 1945 and independence differ from those of the firms created either before the war or after independence. The same contrast characterizes as well their wage policies: some 51 percent of concerns created between 1945 and 1960 pay their personnel an average of over 200,000 CFA a year, as against only 36 percent of those organizations created after independence and 42 percent of those that began their operations before the war.

To summarize, the meanings to be attached to historical factors are manifold. The date at which employers begin to be attracted by colonial ventures affects the images and stereotypes they hold about African workers. To the obsolescent image of an African labor force unable to adapt to the demands of Westernization and thus deserving minimal pay succeed the more recent stereotypes that have accompanied pressures toward greater Africanization.

A Typology of Camerounian Firms

Having explored the extent and determinants of variations in the organizational profiles of Camerounian firms as well as their distinctive hiring, promotion, and salary policies, one can now see whether these traits cohere. This involves a factorial analysis of the largest businesses (with forty-five employees and more, Table 47).[28]

Four factors account for almost half of the variance in the distribution of the largest Camerounian enterprises. The first factor isolates the tertiary sector from other branches of activity. Enterprises in this sector have the legal status of corporations; employ a large number of European supervisors and high-level technicians; have a relatively progressive personnel policy in the sense that they have large proportions of highly educated African nonmanual workers whom they pay on a monthly basis and whom they recruit for or promote to relatively high positions. Finally, they practice higher salary policies and tend to be located in Douala, the major economic center of the country.

The second factor isolates the most technologically advanced firms in the secondary sector. These firms use the services of qualified wage earners and tend to recruit their personnel from the ranks of those whose first occupational experiences were acquired in the context of large-scale organizations. Located in a variety of cities and towns within the Cameroun, these firms tend to recruit their labor force from specific ethnic groups. Hiring a larger number of Beti-Fang workers than other types of concerns, they also tend to employ a smaller number of Bamileke.

The third factor isolates the older plantations of the hinterland. These plantations seem to be characterized by a certain amount of stagnation, and they require the services of a large number of unskilled laborers who, in view of the few alternative opportunities offered to them, tend to be older and thus to have spent a larger period of time on their current job than the remaining groups in the working population.

Finally, the last factor characterizes what one might term marginal enterprises. As local businesses themselves are ranked according to a definite hierarchy, some of them are obliged for reasons that I have not

---

[28] I have concentrated on such enterprises, because it is inappropriate to compare the aggregate characteristics of firms which differ too much in size. Indeed, the percentages computed on smaller firms are meaningless, for they reflect dimensions that vary randomly.

TABLE 47
Typology of Firms with Forty-five Employees and Over
(183 firms)

	Factors			
Variables	Tertiary sector	Secondary sector	Agriculture	Small scale
1. N of production units	0.649	-0.059	0.150	0.085
2. Location of main branch in Douala	0.583	0.198	-0.118	0.303
3. Public corporation	0.505	0.041	0.059	0.314
4. International headquarters	0.663	0.048	-0.096	0.199
5. Tertiary sector	0.724	-0.287	-0.151	-0.207
6. Average education of Africans	0.746	0.422	-0.081	-0.158
7. Average annual salary	0.767	0.281	0.048	-0.269
8. % Africans with high skills	0.672	0.091	0.017	-0.425
9. % nonmanual workers	0.862	0.082	-0.125	-0.362
10. % in staff positions	0.786	0.017	-0.115	-0.258
11. % Douala workers	0.634	0.229	-0.012	-0.024
12. % monthly paid personnel	0.793	-0.145	-0.063	-0.337
13. % with lateral mobility between first and present job	0.770	0.023	-0.159	-0.269
14. % with lateral mobility between first and present job	0.715	0.221	-0.183	-0.174
15. % of Europeans	0.556	0.271	0.229	0.051
16. % semiskilled, nonmanual positions	0.859	-0.104	-0.146	-0.313
17. Secondary sector	-0.137	0.741	-0.081	0.244
18. % Ewondo	-0.154	-0.525	0.141	0.201
19. % Bamilekes	-0.085	-0.642	-0.193	0.201
20. % daily paid persons	-0486	-0.614	0.021	-0.031
21. % having participated in a formal training program	0.133	0.776	0.155	0.032
22. % highly skilled manuals	-0.192	0.749	-0.013	-0.072
23. % unskilled manuals	-0.444	-0.633	0.240	0.081
24. % without vocational training	-0.428	-0.715	0.276	-0.010
25. Size of African labor force	0.112	0.139	0.723	0.145
26. Average age	0.027	-0.092	0.878	-0.053
27. Number of hours legally worked	-0.183	-0.261	0.755	0.106
28. Average job experience	0.009	-0.060	0.726	-0.256
29. % with top skill levels	0.213	-0.002	-0.039	-0.645

TABLE 47 *(continued)*
Typology of Firms with Forty-five Employees and Over
(183 firms)

Variables	*Tertiary sector*	*Secondary sector*	*Agriculture*	*Small scale*
		Factors		
30. % with technical diploma (BEI and above)	0.362	-0.007	-0.014	*-0.505*
31. % downwardly mobile between past and present job	-0.054	-0.039	0.105	*0.670*
32. % top skilled nonmanual positions	0.429	0.006	-0.063	*-0.599*
Percentage variance explained before rotation	22.13	12.10	8.07	7.90

Note: Only the variables with loadings higher than ±0.500 have been retained as significant.

identified to use the services of "marginal groups" in the local working population. Such firms have fewer skilled African workers than all other enterprises, and this is particularly so in the nonmanual sector. They also tend to employ primarily individuals who have been downwardly mobile between the time of the survey and the time of their entry into the labor force, and this suggests that processes of mobility do not only pertain to changes in *occupation* but to changes in *employment* as well—certain firms have better reputations than others.

In brief, factor analysis confirms the results of the cross-tabulations. Organizational traits are closely interrelated with the types of activity performed by Camerounian enterprises; each type of activity has a specific profile and adopts a distinctive personnel policy.

Conclusions

Camerounian firms differ in their organizational complexity. Engaged in varying activities, they also differ in terms of their legal status, the dispersion of their operations, the location of their headquarters, and the date at which they began to operate in the Cameroun. These differences are associated with contrasts in their patterns of division of labor, the size of their labor force absorbed in coordinative functions, and their use of European personnel.

These structural features affect personnel policies. As their complexity increases, firms are more likely to recruit highly qualified Camerounian personnel and to provide them with easier access to higher level jobs and higher incomes. Such differentials also affect patterns of commitment. Thus, the labor force of complex organizations is not only more stable, but it is also characterized by higher rates of absenteeism.

Two major conclusions can be derived from this analysis. First, the influence of increased complexity on personnel policies is not necessarily consistent. Thus, although complexity often implies the presence of European workers, this presence limits the involvement of Africans in coordinative functions but facilitates the access of local wage earners to top level jobs and higher incomes. The age of a firm has no cumulative effects either. Often newest and oldest firms are more alike than those founded between the end of the war and independence. Further, independence and hence, societal complexity seem to accentuate the differentiation of local enterprises, and this might in turn slow down further modernization.

The second conclusion concerns the influence of technological complexity on the composition and occupational history of the labor force attached to various economic sectors. If there are few variations in the organization of tertiary concerns, there are sharp differences in the equipment and technology used by various industries in the primary and secondary sectors. Correspondingly, an increase in their size or in their patterns of division of labor cannot have the same effects on the work histories of their personnel. Thus, the opportunities enjoyed by various groups of the Camerounian labor force vary with the specific traits of the environment in which they participate.

Chapter 6

INTERACTION BETWEEN WORKERS AND EMPLOYERS: A CONTEXTUAL ANALYSIS

In Chapters 3 and 4, I have demonstrated that there are contrasts in the profile and occupational history of white- and blue-collar workers. In Chapter 5, I have suggested alternatively that there are also sharp differences in the organizational patterns of Camerounian firms and hence in their personnel policies. As the functioning of labor markets corresponds to an interactive process, it is now time to merge the two perspectives of analysis to show that although the segmentation of the Camerounian labor force into two distinct populations results from the differential requirements accompanying the performance of manual and nonmanual tasks, it also reflects the varying positions of employers in the economy and hence the varying demands they can make vis-à-vis their workers.

Thus, it is not sufficient to state with Goldthorpe that "wage earners do not necessarily choose different kinds of employment randomly but rather tend to form labor forces which are in some respect self-selected and in this regard quite homogeneous. . . . The choice of these wage earners is to a significant extent located externally to the industrial enterprise and reflects nonwork aspects of the individual total life situation, for instance, his mobility, his community, and his status position."[1] If wage earners tend to choose employers on such a basis, they also make such choices in terms of the rules of the game which they perceive to be imposed on them by the various enterprises they may contact.

The main purpose of this chapter is to demonstrate that, far from being uniform, the differential determinants of occupational attainment between manual and nonmanual workers depend on the profile of the enterprises to which they are attached. Thus, the activities of clerical workers in the operation of banks and insurance concerns tend to be more rationalized and standardized than those of their counterparts employed in other sectors of the economy.[2] This should enhance the relative *universality* of

---

[1] See J. Goldthorpe, "Orientation to Work and Industrial Behavior: A Contribution to an Action Approach in Industrial Sociology" (unpublished), as quoted by Ingham, *Size of Industrial Organization*, p. 47.

[2] This standardization results from the increased and more uniform use of modern data-processing techniques.

the conditions governing the recruitment of bank and insurance employees, their access to supervisory roles, their participation in daily work routines, and the earnings they may claim. In contrast, the activities of manual workers employed by agricultural concerns and construction or public works firms tend to be less standardized and rationalized than in any other sector. This should enhance the *particularity* of the criteria underlying the recruitment of blue-collar workers in these branches, their access to the top positions of the occupational hierarchy, their modes of participation in daily routines, and their salaries.

In short, to be a nonmanual or manual worker has not necessarily the same implications in firms which (a) are geared toward primary as opposed to secondary or tertiary activities and have variations in the proportion of nonmanual employees, (b) are internationally based large corporations or, alternatively, small privately owned businesses, and (c) have been created at different periods of time.

As nonmanual skills are more easily transferable, the second goal in the chapter is to demonstrate that occupational attainment is less likely to vary with the characteristics of the enterprises by which individuals are employed in the case of nonmanual than of the manual labor force.

Recruitment Patterns of Manual and Nonmanul Workers

The distributions of manual and nonmanual populations across the various sectors of the Camerounian economy have differing profiles. Characterized by a low level of technological development and rationalization, plantations as well as construction companies and public works concerns each absorb approximately one-third of the manual labor force. One-fifth of these manual workers are employed by mechanical and metal industries, and the remainder is relatively evenly spread among other sectors. In contrast, nonmanual wage earners tend to be less significantly concentrated in particular branches of activity. Import/export concerns absorb one-third of the nonmanual labor force; metallurgical and mechanical concerns one-fourth, and construction and public works firms one-fifth.[3]

Educational characteristics of workers attached to distinctive types of firms.

There are sharp variations in the educational and vocational qualifications of nonmanual and manual workers employed by distinctive types of

---

[3] Variations in the relative concentration of manual and nonmanual workers by branch of activity should influence the "reference groups" used by individual workers. To be a manual worker in a firm where few individuals have this classification cannot have the same meaning as where the majority of workers are manual. For example, the comparisons they make between their own situation and that of "significant others" will not be the same when manual wage earners constitute the minority (as in the case of banks) as when they are in the majority (as in the case of garages).

enterprises. White-collar workers with *minimal* educational and vocational qualifications are least numerous in banks and insurance concerns. Only 20 percent of the labor force in this type of activity have an aggregate training score of less than 7.0, as against 54 percent of the individuals employed by the railroad industry or 56 percent of those employed by industries primarily engaged in the processing of raw materials. Symmetrically, if one-third of the workers in banks and insurance concerns have the equivalent of more than seven years of formal schooling, this characterizes only 8 percent of the white-collar labor force in the primary sector and 12 percent of clerical workers in the processing industries.

Among blue-collar workers, the proportion of individuals with less than the equivalent of seven years' formal schooling varies from a maximum of 93 percent among those employed by agricultural and primary concerns to a minimum of 75 percent among those working for mechanical and metallurgical concerns. At the other end of the scale, about 7 percent of the manual workers attached to the latter type of concern have the equivalent of over seven years of formal education, as against less than 1 percent of those employed in the primary sector.

As expected, variations in individual aggregate training scores by branch of activity are more marked among the manual than the nonmanual population. Thus, the proportion of white-collar workers with high educational credentials is only *four and one-half times* greater in the banking industry than in the agricultural concerns. By contrast, the proportion of qualified manual workers with such high credentials is *seven times* greater in the mechanical and in metallurgical industries than in the primary sector.

Further, whereas the proportion of educated manual and nonmanual individuals does not vary between small-size internationally or locally based concerns, the manual and nonmanual employees of internationally based enterprises with one hundred wage earners or more tend to have higher qualifications than those attached to a locally based concern of similar size (Table 48). As expected, the relevant contrasts are proportionately more marked in the blue than the white sector of employment. Yet although the relative number of blue-collar workers with high academic credentials is independent of the size of the enterprises to which they are attached, an increase in the size of internationally based concerns is associated with a parallel rise in the educational qualifications of their individual white-collar employees. Conversely to my initial expectations, the educational credentials of the nonmanual labor force are therefore *more* sensitive to the specific work environment than those of manual workers.

The distinction between international and local concerns does not, however, remain constant over time. As a result of educational development, there is growing differentiation in the expectations that

TABLE 48
Educational Level of Workers by Selected Characteristics of Firms
(size and location of headquarters)

Size	Total population	Skill level 4	Skill levels 5-7
1 to 10			
Manual			
Local	16.3	19.2	46.1
International	15.4	18.2	*
Nonmanual			
Local	51.8	57.1	71.4
International	59.3	65.5	64.7
11 to 25			
Manual			
Local	9.9	11.4	18.5
International	12.7	16.7	*
Nonmanual			
Local	54.9	58.6	28.0
International	61.9	67.8	79.0
25 to 100			
Manual			
Local	61.9	63.9	73.4
International	67.9	74.3	85.8
Over 100			
Manual			
Local	11.3	34.1	39.5
International	21.1	33.3	64.1
Nonmanual			
Local	51.8	58.8	69.4
International	72.9	75.2	87.2

*Figures too small to be translated into percentage terms.

Note: Proportion of manual and nonmanual workers having the equivalent of at least seven years' formal schooling, by skill level and selected characteristics of firms (size and location of headquarters).

international and local concerns entertain about educational qualifications. Although international concerns have always been more prone to attract individuals with higher credentials, the contrasts are more significant in the case of those enterprises settling in the Cameroun *after* independence. Such contrasts are also sharper for blue- than white-collar workers (Table 49).

To summarize, the influence of educational and training background on access to manual and nonmanual jobs varies both as a function of the branch of activity and the location of the headquarters of firms, although

TABLE 49

Educational Level of Workers by Selected Characteristics of Firms
(date of foundation and location of headquarters)

	Total population	Skill level 4	Skill levels 5-7
Postindependence			
Local			
Manual	11.5	19.4	24.3
Nonmanual	51.9	56.4	72.2
International			
Manual	21.1	28.5	61.5
Nonmanual	79.3	78.2	70.2
1945 to 1958			
Local			
Manual	14.7	20.2	33.3
Nonmanual	51.8	52.3	85.9
International			
Manual	17.9	28.9	65.6
Nonmanual	70.2	73.8	88.0
Before 1945			
Local			
Manual	12.1	34.9	64.9
Nonmanual	54.8	57.4	66.7
International			.
Manual	14.7	19.7	55.5
Nonmanual	64.0	69.9	84.9

Note: Proportion of manual and nonmanual workers with the equivalent of at least seven years' formal schooling by skill level and selected characteristics of firms (date of foundation and location of headquarters).

the effects of the last variable are contingent on the size and the age of the concern.

Variations in the economic rewards attached to educational qualifications.
Although the annual income of both manual and nonmanual workers tends to increase with their academic credentials, the extent of this increase varies with the characteristics of their employers. First, the influence of educational qualifications on income is not the same in the context of organizations whose headquarters are not similarly located (Table 50). The white-collar labor force of local concerns tends to earn less than the clerical personnel of internationally based enterprises, but individuals with top level qualifications still tend to be proportionally better paid in the former than the latter case. Local and international firms cannot adopt similar

TABLE 50

Mean Adjusted Annual Income of Workers by Aggregate Training Score, Age of Firm, and Location of Headquarters

(in thousands CFA)

Aggregate training score	Local						International					
	Post-independence				Before World War II		Post-independence				Before World War II	
	Manual	Nonmanual	Manual	Nonmanual	Manual	Nonmanual	Manual	Nonmanual	Manual	Nonmanual	Manual	Nonmanual
0	81.1	--	118.2	--	93.5	--	103.2	--	126.7	--	120.4	--
0.1 to 1.5	110.1	--	120.7	--	105.7	--	122.4	--	148.5	--	137.1	--
1.6 to 6.9	114.0	175.0	130.8	203.8	121.8	258.6	135.4	233.3	184.2	254.3	142.4	275.1
7.0	106.7	181.0	123.4	216.3	115.8	265.4	135.4	229.6	142.1	300.4	133.3	318.0
7.1 to 12.0	146.5	253.1	135.2	261.3	236.1	293.5	154.3	315.2	266.1	370.2	171.3	358.1
Beyond 12.0	*	719.2	*	*	1,427.1	929.6	*	*	*	619.2	*	605.1
Percentage of total population earning more than overall average	11.7	19.2	23.6	26.8	26.8	36.8	41.1	31.8	51.7	41.7	30.2	43.2
N	8,632	1,254	528	4,894	3,211	626	1,417	289	3,315	1,342	1,713	769

*Figures too small to be translated into percentage terms.

strategies toward workers who enjoy the greatest range of choices. The "fortunate few" who have had more than the equivalent of twelve years of formal schooling are able to obtain compensation for the fact that they work for locally based employers with a relatively low reputation.

In addition, the rewards derived from educational qualifications vary both with the age and the headquarters of the firms studied. Thus, it is among the employees of the newest locally based enterprises that the incomes linked to variable amounts of education and training are most differentiated. In such firms, the annual incomes of those nonmanual workers who have reached the top of the educational and vocational ladder are about four times greater than those earned by individuals with minimal aggregate training scores. By contrast, the corresponding ratio is only 3.7 for the white-collar personnel of the oldest locally based firms and drops to 2.2 in the case of individuals employed by international concerns settling in the Cameroun before the war.

The influence of formal educational and vocational qualifications on the annual earnings of manual workers is even more markedly contingent on the relative age and the headquarters location of the enterprises for which they work. Thus, although illiterate blue-collar employees working for long-established, locally based firms earn a median annual income of 93,000 CFA, their counterparts with the equivalent of twelve years' education tend to earn fifteen times as much.

Finally, the influence of formal schooling on earnings varies also with the size of economic organization (Table 51). The income of workers with minimal educational qualifications is perhaps independent of the size of the firms to which they are attached, but the earnings of individuals with top educational credentials are still higher in the case of large rather than small firms. The influence of academic credentials on income is most visible in the context of locally based large-scale enterprises. Thus, the highly educated manual labor force employed by this type or organization earns *fourteen times* as much as illiterate individuals; similarly, the white-collar workers employed by such organizations who have the equivalent of twelve years of formal schooling and training earn four times more than their colleagues who have had less than seven years of formal training. To sum up, employers do not evenly sanction the differential educational experiences of their personnel, but the relevant contrasts are narrower for the white- than the blue-collar labor force.

However, both occupational achievement and earnings do not depend only on educational credentials but also on occupational histories. Thus, an assessment of the differential weight that employers attach to the academic or vocational credentials of their personnel must be accompanied by a complementary examination of the value accorded to occupational background.

In effect, the various branches of the Camerounian economy do not demand similar educational and occupational experiences from their

TABLE 51

Mean Adjusted Annual Income of Workers by Aggregate Training Score, Size of Firm, and Location of Headquarters
(in thousands CFA)

Aggregate training score	1-10		11-25		Local 26-100		Over 100	
	Manual	*Nonmanual*	*Manual*	*Nonmanual*	*Manual*	*Nonmanual*	*Manual*	*Nonmanual*
0	36.5	--	75.8	--	76.7	--	88.2	--
0.1 to 1.5	115.2	--	111.6	--	114.5	--	117.5	--
1.6 to 6.9	105.7	173.5	119.0	204.2	125.4	219.1	121.8	198.1
7.0	87.2	201.3	121.2	205.1	119.6	229.4	113.1	220.5
7.1 to 12.0	125.6	172.8	126.3	245.8	135.7	312.4	207.8	258.8
Above 12.0	*	*	*	*	*	935.4	1,276.2	899.0
Percentage earning more than overall average	15.1	21.0	20.8	24.5	24.7	33.0	22.1	21.4
N	496	276	1,583	466	4,000	608	10,578	1,054

aSize refers here to the production unit rather than to the firm itself.

*Figures too small to be translated into percentage terms.

manual and nonmanual personnel. For example, the relative number of blue-collar workers who have both high seniority in the firm and a high educational attainment is limited in textile and timber-processing industries, in firms processing local raw materials, or in banks and the import/export concerns (Table 52). In these instances, individuals who have high vocational and educational qualifications probably leave their employment before acquiring additional seniority, because seniority is not associated with any substantial increment in monetary rewards. In brief, workers probably have a clear understanding of the differential rewards that employers attach to education and seniority.

Second, the various types of firms do not equally remunerate high formal qualifications and high seniority when these are considered jointly. Among white-collar workers, the rewards derived from the simultaneous presence of these traits are maximal in the case of the railroad but minimal in the case of primary concerns. Railroad clerical employees who have both high qualifications and high seniority earn more than five times as much as newcomers with low aggregate training scores, whereas the corresponding ratio declines to 2.2 in the case of the wage earners in agricultural plantations. The range of variations in the rewards that employers attach to the educational and occupational qualifications of their blue-collar personnel is more limited. The employees of construction firms who have both high seniority and high aggregate training scores earn three times as much as those with minimal educational and occupational experience, but the corresponding ratio is only 2.2 in the primary sectors. In short, the rewards derived from maximal educational and occupational experiences are lower in the manual than in the nonmanual sector, and this contrast corresponds to my general hypothesis. But these rewards are also less uniform in the second of these sectors, in contrast to the terms of the same general assumption.

Differential Work Routines

Contrasts in the nature of manual and nonmanual work and, hence, in the conditions governing access to these two types of employment may mask the internal heterogeneity of the two kinds of activity. Both groups are expected to perform highly different tasks within their own spheres of activity. Thus, nonmanual work involves different jobs such as typing, accounting, and salesmanship which have their own specific requirements. Regardless of these contrasts, white-collar workers may also perform their activities at the "center" or, alternatively, in the "peripheral" services of the organization for which they work.[4] Similarly, although manual work

---

[4] Clearly, this distinction involves different jobs. For example, storekeepers in a garage will be most often in the general staff services, for their job is to maintain the supply of spare parts necessary for the functioning of the garage itself. If the garage sells these parts to the public, some storekeepers will be in external services. Most secretaries will be in the general staff of

TABLE 52

Income Structure of Workers by Aggregate Training Score, Seniority in the Firm, and Branch Activity

	Primary		Processing Industry		Textile and timber		Mechanical and metallurgical	
	Manual	Nonmanual	Manual	Nonmanual	Manual	Nonmanual	Manual	Nonmanual
Minimal aggregate training score and *minimal* seniority (*N*)	(1,573)	(17)	(165)	(13)	(86)	(4)	(1,596)	(59)
Mean annual income (in thousands CFA)	72.6	142.1	121.5	157.2	126.4	*	125.7	158.4
Percentage earning more than overall average	8.4	5.8	21.9	7.7	53.6	*	24.6	3.3
Medium aggregate training score and *medium* seniority (*N*)	(152)	(33)	(9)	(7)	(19)	(10)	(142)	(112)
Mean annual income (in thousands CFA)	81.6	157.2	*	*	220.1	273.2	138.2	196.2
Percentage earning more than overall average	3.3	3.0	*	*	73.7	30.0	48.0	12.6
Maximal aggregate training score and *maximal* seniority (*N*)	(10)	(13)	(3)	(4)	(4)	(11)	(62)	(62)
Mean annual income (in thousands CFA)	157.4	351.2	*	*	*	449.0	430.1	464.2
Percentage earning more than overall average	40.0	46.1	*	*	*	90.9	10.0	64.5

TABLE 52 (continued)

	Construction		Banks		Transport		Import/export	
	Manual	Nonmanual	Manual	Nonmanual	Manual	Nonmanual	Manual	Nonmanual
Minimal aggregate training score and *minimal* seniority (N)	(2,587)	(25)	(48)	(20)	(217)	(32)	(515)	(164)
Mean annual income (in thousands CFA)	123.8	226.5	123.6	193.2	106.8	121.5	115.6	172.7
Percentage earning more than overall average	18.3	28.0	20.8	5.0	12.9	3.1	20.7	14.0
Medium aggregate training score and *medium* seniority (N)	(118)	(60)	(8)	(83)	(19)	(39)	(35)	(171)
Mean annual income (in thousands CFA)	131.4	904.7	*	327.1	185.3	159.2	117.8	254.8
Percentage earning more than overall average	26.2	16.7	*	41.2	47.4	5.8	18.1	26.5
Maximal aggregate training score and *maximal* seniority (N)	(84)	(56)	(1)	(44)	(10)	(15)	(7)	(69)
Mean annual income (in thousands CFA)	458.3	492.6	*	719.8	275.1	638.1	*	406.8
Percentage earning more than overall average	97.1	66.1	*	95.4	100.0	93.3	*	71.1

Note: Minimal refers to aggregate training scores below 7.0 and less than two years of seniority; *medium* refers to aggregate training scores of 7.0 and between 2 and 5 years of seniority; *maximal* represents an aggregate training score of over 7.0 and more than 5 years of seniority.

*Figures too small to be translated into percentage terms.

involves a variety of techniques, it is also performed in the context of different services, and maintenance work, for instance, differs from involvement in direct production processes. Far from being uniform, however, the consequences attached to the internal differentiation of manual and nonmanual tasks vary across sectors of activity.

Differential positions of nonmanual personnel.

To suggest that there are differences in the nature of nonmanual work to be performed at the center as against the periphery of an organization, is to imply that to be a secretary, for example, does not have the same meaning in a variety of contexts. In a university, to be a *departmental* secretary does not involve the same tasks as to be an office worker within one of the "pools" attached to the central administration or to be a secretary for one of the higher officials of the institution. As these secretaries interact with different persons, they do not enjoy comparable forms nor amounts of power in the three settings. Similarly, in the military, to be a field as opposed to a staff officer does not have the same rewards nor demands.[5] As activities located at the hub and the periphery of an economic organization are not similarly defined by the holders of the jobs themselves nor by the persons with whom they interact, these activities do not attract the same individuals. In other words, the differential requirements and rewards of these positions are paralleled by contrasts in the educational and occupational experiences of the wage earners who hold them.

However, differences between the personnel working at the periphery and at the center of an organization vary by branch of activity. Banks and textile firms, for example, do not have the same type of clients.[6] Banks

---

any enterprise, except where external services have their own resources for typing the materials they use in their transactions. For a general discussion of the organizational and socio-psychological effects of the distinction, see A. Stinchcombe, "Social Structure and Organizations," in J. March, ed., *Handbook of Organizations* (Chicago: Rand McNally, 1965), pp. 148-193. See also M. Haire, "Industrial Social Psychology," in G. Lindsey, ed., *Handbook of Social Psychology* Cambridge, Mass.: Addison-Wesley, 1954), pp. 1104-1123, and C. Argyris, "Some Problems in Conceptualizing Organizational Climate: A Case Study," *Administrative Science Quarterly* 2(1958):501-520.

[5] In the military as in the diplomatic service, to be in the general staff is less rewarding monetarily than to be in the field. At the same time, a staff job can be considered an important investment if it is associated with closer contacts with the personnel department of the military or of the diplomatic service and hence with faster promotion.

[6] The significance of contacts with the public is affected by the extent to which a particular enterprise engages in retail operations. The direction and the magnitude of the contrasts between central and peripheral positions vary with (a) the number and specificity of the clients with which the personnel of external services enters into contact, (b) the degree to which these contacts are face-to-face rather than written, and (c) the degree of competition prevailing in the market for the particular product or service. In the case of banks, contacts with the public are important because clients are both numerous and derived from various social groups, because the contacts take a variety of forms, and because there is intense competition among individual enterprises. Banks differ from many local export concerns, for the clientele of the latter is specific and physically distant and the nature of the transaction does not promote competition among firms.

compete with one another to have easier access to a larger number of increasingly differentiated clients. In contrast, the existence of wholesale and retail networks minimizes the importance of the contacts that textile firms establish with the outside world.

As a result, the relative number and the characteristics of nonmanual workers engaged either in coordinative functions at the hub of an organization or in its peripheral services vary markedly by sector of activity. In the case of primary and textile industries, nonmanual workers tend to be concentrated in general services (for example, in personnel and accounting). Alternatively, the importance of contacts with the public leads the population of the peripheral services of banks, insurance, transport, and import/export concerns to be proportionately more numerous than that of the staff. General services absorb 83 percent of nonmanual workers employed by primary concerns and 86 percent of the clerical labor force working for timber-processing and textile firms, but the corresponding percentages drop to 48 in the railroads, 44 among export/import concerns, and 29 among banking and insurance firms.

In addition, no less than 41 percent of individuals in the peripheral services of this latter branch of activity have more than the equivalent of seven years of formal qualifications as against only one-fourth of their colleagues in staff positions. The same pattern tends to obtain in the transport industry, but the trend is reversed among import/export concerns. Both the dependence of local transactions on international markets and the specialized nature of the clientele probably minimize the importance of peripheral roles. As a result, almost 23 percent of nonmanual export/import staff personnel have an aggregate training score of over 7, against only 14 percent of their colleagues working in peripheral services (Table 53).

The employment of nonmanual workers in staff or peripheral positions depends not only on their formal qualifications but also on their level of occupational commitment (as measured by the amount of time spent in the current firm). However, if transfers to positions located at the hub of the organization constitute the rewards sanctioning an effective performance in the context of peripheral services, the importance of contacts with an outside clientele may also require an initial and closely supervised socialization to the tasks to be performed at the center of the organization. Whether centrifugal and centripetal moves within an organization reflect differential socialization processes or differential reward structures, contrasts in the occupational experience of peripheral and staff personnel should parallel the differences that characterize their respective educational attainments.

However, this is not the case. In construction and public works firms, 73 percent of the usually less educated individuals engaged in peripheral activities have more than five years of experience with the same firm, against only 58 percent of those holding staff positions; similarly, in the

TABLE 53
Educational Characteristics of Nonmanual Workers by Work Position and Branch of Activity
(percentage distribution)

Aggregate training score	Primary		Food processing		Wood and textile		Mechanical and metallurgical	
	Staff	Other	Staff	Other	Staff	Other	Staff	Other
Less than 7.0	50.4	55.7	51.8	73.6	20.0	47.3	28.1	45.1
7.0	37.0	34.6	33.9	21.0	41.2	26.3	49.4	39.2
7.1 to 12.0	12.0	9.7	16.3	6.4	34.1	26.3	21.4	14.9
Above 12.0	0.6	0.0	0.0	0.0	4.7	0.0	1.1	0.8
Total	100.0	100.0	100.0	100.0	100.0	99.9	100.0	100.0
Percentage staff	92.3	--	62.4	--	85.6	--	72.5	--
N	843	81	65	39	90	15	746	282

Aggregate training score	Construction		Banks and insurance		Transport		Import/export	
	Staff	Other	Staff	Other	Staff	Other	Staff	Other
Less than 7.0	36.6	44.1	25.4	19.0	48.7	58.1	30.1	49.9
7.0	44.1	40.2	50.0	40.8	39.5	27.4	47.4	35.7
7.1 to 12.0	14.9	14.0	22.5	33.3	9.2	11.1	19.8	12.5
Above 12.0	4.4	1.7	2.1	6.9	2.6	3.4	2.8	1.9
Total	100.0	100.0	100.0	100.0	100.0	100.0	100.1	100.0
Percentage staff	54.4	--	29.2	--	48.3	--	44.2	--
N	503	421	151	400	155	166	675	851

textile and timber-processing industries, 58 percent of the usually less educated peripheral wage earners have been with their current employer for more than five years, against 47 percent of those employed at the hub of the organization. The pattern is reversed among transport and import/export firms, where staff workers have *more* seniority than peripheral personnel. No less than 70 percent of the railroad employees working in general staff services have more than five years' seniority, as against only 39 percent of their less educated "external" colleagues. In import/export enterprises, the corresponding figures are 41 and 32 percent.

The differential seniority and educational attainment of staff and nonstaff personnel by branch of activity suggest that pressures for Africanization vary by type of organization. Certain firms (notably those in the textile and construction sectors) prefer to recruit their staff personnel and hence their cadres and supervisors from the outside. By contrast, more bureaucratic organizations such as the railroad company or export/import concerns will recruit potential supervisors from the inside and from among the ranks of the nonmanual workers who have shown their loyalty toward the organization. This last pattern is not specific to the Camerounian scene. It tends also to characterize metropolitan bureaucratic enterprises, within which seniority is the prime determinant of access to the economic and noneconomic rewards controlled by the organization.[7]

Clearly, this distinction is of importance, as it affects the patterns of social interaction prevailing in the industrial scene. Indeed, promotions from *within* and *without* local personnel entail different types of tensions among rank-and-file workers as well as between them and their supervisors.[8]

The differential allocation of workers into staff as opposed to peripheral jobs is associated with parallel contrasts in the respective incomes of the two subgroups of workers. Staff jobs are more financially rewarding than peripheral positions for individuals who have the equivalent of seven or fewer years of formal schooling and training (Table 54). Alternatively, peripheral roles become more rewarding for those who have had some form of postprimary training. Indeed, the demands attached to these two types of tasks are not homogeneous. Participation in external services is more rewarding for individuals with higher levels of qualification, because of the greater responsibilities that their type of work involves. As the meaning of such participation varies by branch of activity, it is not surprising to note that the peripheral employees of a bank are better paid than their counterparts employed in staff positions but that the relevant differences run in the opposite direction for the labor force of agricultural enterprises (Table 55).

[7] For an illustration, see Crozier, *The Bureaucratic Phenomenon,* and particularly his description of processes of promotion in the tobacco industry.

[8] For a brief review of the literature on this theme, see, for example, R. Corwin, *Militant Professionalism* (New York: Appleton-Century-Crofts, 1971), pp. 274-276.

TABLE 54
Mean Adjusted Annual Income of Manual and Nonmanual Workers by Aggregate Training Score and Function
(in thousands CFA)

Aggregate Training Score	Nonmanual		Manual	
	Staff	Nonstaff	Production	Maintenance
0	--	--	78.2	124.0
0.1 to 1.5	--	--	117.2	130.7
1.6 to 6.9	237.1	209.1	124.0	136.3
7.0	264.2	234.1	123.2	130.1
7.1 to 12.0	313.1	319.2	150.2	218.1
Beyond 12.0	561.5	699.2	*	511.6
Percentage of total population earning more than overall average	34.2	29.7	22.6	39.6
N	(2,592)	(2,365)	(15,449)	(7,651)

*Figure too small to be translated into percentage.

Differential positions of manual workers.

The differentiation of the tasks performed by manual workers is similarly relative and depends on the level of technological complexity achieved in a particular sector.[9] The more routinized and simple the tasks incumbent on individuals attached to production processes, the more numerous these workers are in relation to maintenance activities. Alternatively, the proportion of production workers is minimal in branches of activity which require a large labor force for the handling of input and output materials. In short, contrasts in the relative number of production and maintenance wage earners vary markedly by sector of activity (Table 56).

In addition, variations in the complexity of the tasks to be performed in the context of the production process are also associated with parallel contrasts in the differential educational and occupational profile of production and maintenance workers. Among those industries where production involves the use of few and/or crude machinery, the proportion of workers with a *minimal* aggregate training score is significantly higher in production than in maintenance. In the primary sector, 49 percent of production workers are unable to communicate in French, compared with

---

[9] For example, a painter will be in the production line exclusively in cases where he is employed by a painting firm. In all other cases he will be a maintenance worker. Similarly, a mechanic will be a maintenance worker when he is employed by a textile firm or a plantation.

TABLE 55

Income Structure of Manual and Nonmanual Workers by Branch of Activity and Function

	Primary	Processing Industries	Timber and Textile	Mechanical and Metallurgical	Construction	Banks	Transport	Import Export
Manual								
Maintenance N	(1,912)	(251)	(351)	(1,385)	(1,926)	(147)	(387)	(1,212)
Mean annual income (thousands CFA)	91.6	130.6	225.5	132.6	171.7	129.1	198.5	125.3
Percentage earning more than overall average	15.7	39.5	86.9	35.8	59.0	29.9	78.5	26.4
Production N	(5,303)	(335)	(114)	(3,473)	(4,463)	(0)	(1,418)	(345)
Mean annual income (thousands CFA)	67.4	132.0	218.4	142.5	128.0	*	110.2	138.3
Percentage earning more than overall average	3.6	39.6	78.1	46.8	25.7	*	8.4	54.0
Nonmanual								
Staff N	(260)	(65)	(90)	(746)	(503)	(151)	(155)	(675)
Mean annual income (thousands CFA)	224.8	228.1	351.8	259.5	251.8	295.6	237.2	303.1
Percentage earning more than overall average	10.1	23.1	51.0	34.0	33.2	34.3	21.4	43.8
Nonstaff N	(65)	(41)	(19)	(319)	(437)	(416)	(171)	(897)
Mean annual income (thousands CFA)	148.5	154.2	273.2	258.4	277.2	370.1	166.1	205.2
Percentage earning more than overall average	6.2	0	21.1	33.8	32.7	56.4	12.8	20.7

*Figures too small to be translated into percentages.

by their current type of employment. Thus, whereas the greater seniority of maintenance workers in the construction industry probably results from an absence of alternative opportunities, the greater seniority of their counterparts employed by the railroad company possibly results from the organizational skills of the union leaders attached to repair and maintenance departments. As already suggested, the organization of the Camerounian railroad industry follows the French metropolitan model, and the "overcommitment" of the workers employed in such a context enables them to use seniority as the major criterion for gaining access to the economic and noneconomic rewards of the system.

Contrasts in the educational and occupational experiences of production and nonproduction manual workers are associated with differences in their respective earnings. Minimal at the lower end of the educational continuum, differences in salaries increase as one moves up the educational continuum; the higher the qualifications of a maintenance worker, the more likely he is to be involved in the repair of a complex machine or in the carrying out of sophisticated operations, and the greater will be his earnings. However, these distinctions differ across sectors of activity. Maintenance activities require more qualifications than direct participation in production processes for agricultural concerns, construction firms, and the railroad. Correspondingly, in such contexts the earnings of maintenance workers tend to be greater than those of individuals engaged in production (Table 55).

To sum up, variations in the qualifications and the earnings of individuals performing distinctive tasks are more limited among white-than blue-collar workers. The nature of nonmanual tasks enables both employees and employers to share a same system of values and expectations. This minimizes the number and significance of imperfections prevailing in the corresponding labor market.

Overtime work.

Firms do not demand the same amount of overtime work of their hourly paid labor force (Table 57). This proportion is maximal in construction and public works firms or in the timber industry, which are characterized both by a low level of rationalization in their patterns of work and by seasonal variations in level of activity; it is far lower in the mechanical or metallurgical concerns' production processes, which are generally more rationalized.[11]

In addition, the amount of overtime work performed varies with the location of the enterprise. On the whole, the need for overtime is greater in semiurban and urban environments than in the rural hinterland. The lower

---

[11] For a discussion of the implications of the particular patterns of organization prevailing in construction industries see Stinchcombe, "Social Structure and Organizations," in March, ed., *Handbook of Organizations,* pp. 142-193.

level of economic development of the hinterland minimizes pressure to achieve a certain volume of production within a limited period of time. Further, the labor force of firms located in the hinterland is often less aware of legal requirements governing conditions of employment, and employers are less likely to register the actual number of overtime hours worked. In brief, urban-rural differences hinge on variations in the amount of work which is either performed or recorded.

Finally, variations in the number of manual workers doing overtime depend on the organizational profile of enterprises. Only 5 percent of the workers attached to enterprises with fewer than five employees work more than a hundred hours over the legal period, against 50 percent of those attached to enterprises with more than one hundred wage earners. Further, contrasts in the percentage of workers who work overtime are minimal between local and international concerns which employ fewer than five workers but maximal at the other end of the continuum among enterprises with more than a hundred employees. In this latter case, almost two-thirds of the workers attached to international firms work more than one hundred hours beyond their obligations, against 44 percent of those workers attached to locally based enterprises.

To summarize, organizational size and complexity affect work patterns of individual workers. Although, as noted, I am unable to determine whether the corresponding contrasts reflect real rather than merely recorded conditions, they do affect the salaries earned by various segments of the manual labor force.

Even when Camerounian employers do not always pay their personnel the *minimal* legal income defined by the government, they still use bonuses and hence overtime work to modify the legal hierarchy of salaries. Thus, overtime work may be randomly distributed across all categories of manual workers, in which case it primarily results from the objective requirements of the production process; but it may also be differentially distributed among various categories of wage earners, in which case it reflects a particular economic strategy.

In certain sectors, such as the railroad industry and to a certain extent the concerns involved in the processing of raw materials, employers reward the loyalty of their personnel and allocate a disproportionate share of overtime work to individuals with maximal seniority. In other sectors, conversely, such as banks and mechanical concerns, overtime work primarily facilitates a narrowing of the differences in the earnings of individuals with varying levels of seniority, and individuals working more than one hundred overtime hours per year tend to be more numerous among populations with only two years' seniority in the firm than among those who have spent over ten years with their current employer. Finally, in a last group of activities, the allocation of the extra work seems to be more strongly affected by the demands of the market rather than by the neces-

TABLE 56
Aggregate Training Score of Manual Workers by Type of Work and Branch of Activity
(percentage distribution)

	0	0.1-1.5	1.6-6.9	7.0	Above 7.0	Total	% Production	N
Primary								
Production	48.8	17.5	27.1	6.2	0.4	100.0	73	(5,303)
Other	31.7	22.4	36.1	7.8	2.0	100.0	--	(1,912)
Processing								
Production	28.8	29.1	32.7	8.4	0.9	99.9	57	(333)
Other	19.5	31.9	42.6	3.6	2.4	100.0	--	(251)
Wood and textile								
Production	7.9	27.2	44.7	14.9	5.3	100.0	24	(114)
Other	24.5	20.5	33.6	12.5	8.8	99.9	--	(351)
Mechanical and Metallurgical								
Production	9.1	17.2	48.0	18.2	7.6	100.1	71	(3,473)
Other	19.2	24.5	39.9	10.5	5.9	100.0	--	(1,385)
Construction								
Production	16.8	21.5	47.1	11.3	3.3	100.0	63	(4,463)
Other	28.8	18.2	32.1	8.0	12.9	100.0	--	(1,926)
Transport								
Production	37.1	27.9	29.6	4.7	0.7	100.0	77	(1,418)
Other	25.3	19.4	40.8	8.0	6.5	100.0	--	(387)
Import/export								
Production	22.6	20.5	37.1	13.6	5.1	100.0	21	(345)
Other	24.7	30.9	34.1	8.0	3.1	100.0	--	(1,292)

Note: Banks are excluded from this table because all manual workers in this branch are maintenance workers. Only 18 percent of them have a score of 7 and above.

only 32 percent of those engaged in maintenance activities, and the situation is the same in the railroad industry, where 38 percent of wage earners involved in the handling of rolling stock have this minimal level of qualification, as against only 25 percent of those employed in repair and maintenance services. In contrast, the pattern is reversed in enterprises where production requires the use of relatively complex equipment. Whether in textile, mechanical, or construction firms, the proportion of individuals able to speak French is always higher in production than in nonproduction-oriented departments.

Yet, because the proportion of manual workers with a *maximal* aggregate training score is also uniformly greater in maintenance activities than in production processes, it is clear that the educational level of maintenance workers is highly heterogeneous and reflects the variety of tasks to be performed.[10] Such tasks involve menial jobs (cleaning and painting) as well as highly technical activities dealing with the maintenance and repair of production equipment.

With regard to seniority, branches of activity can be divided into three distinctive subgroups. In primary concerns, production workers have significantly more experience than their counterparts engaged in maintenance activities: no less than 55 percent of the former have been with their present employer for over five years, as against only 41 percent of the latter. This may result from the fact that the needs of primary concerns for maintenance personnel are seasonal and that this category of worker is probably the first to be laid off. Or it may result from the alternative opportunities enjoyed by the maintenance workers of such concerns. In the second group (processing, textile, mechanical, and export/import concerns), the two types of manual worker have spent similar amounts of time with their current employers, and their seniority is irrelevant to their placement in differing departments. Finally, in both construction firms and the railroad industry, maintenance workers tend to have greater seniority: 55 percent of individuals employed in maintenance tasks by construction firms have been with their current employer for more than five years, compared with only 15 percent of those working on the assembly line. In the railroad industry, the corresponding figures are 71 and 54 percent.

Thus, the occupational stability of the manual labor force varies not only by branch of activity but also with the specific tasks to be performed within these branches. This stability reflects both the differential number of alternative opportunities available to production and nonproduction workers and the differential economic and noneconomic rewards offered

---

[10] Obviously, maintenance in public works firms involves both highly skilled mechanical work (the repair and maintenance of heavy equipment) and general unskilled labor (the maintenance of the offices used by the firm, for example). See, for example, G. Friedman, *Le travail en miettes* (Paris: Gallimard; Nouvelle Revue francaise, 1956).

TABLE 57

Annual Overtime for Manual Workers by Activity and Salary Zone

(percentage distribution)

Branch of activity	Overtime hours per year					
	0	1-25	26-100	Over 100	Total	N
Primary						
Rural	58.2	1.1	12.9	27.9	100.1	(6,201)
Semiurban	46.0	2.7	9.8	41.6	100.1	(339)
Urban	48.0	1.5	12.7	37.8	100.0	(675)
Processing						
Rural	96.3	0.0	0.0	3.7	100.0	(54)
Semiurban	78.8	7.6	4.5	9.1	100.0	(66)
Urban	30.8	1.3	6.1	61.9	100.1	(464)
Wood and textile						
Rural	0.0	0.0	0.0	100.0	100.0	(10)
Semiurban	0.0	0.0	0.0	100.0	100.0	(10)
Urban	21.6	0.9	3.1	74.4	100.0	(465)
Mechanical and Metallurgical						
Rural	83.9	0.0	10.7	4.5	100.0	(112)
Semiurban	77.5	4.9	7.7	6.9	100.0	(142)
Urban	48.7	2.7	7.7	40.9	100.0	(4,604)
Construction						
Rural	46.3	0.0	0.0	53.7	100.0	(67)
Semiurban	18.9	0.0	0.0	81.1	100.0	(111)
Urban	31.3	1.4	4.9	62.4	100.0	(6,211)

TABLE 57 *(continued)*

Annual Overtime for Manual Workers by Activity and Salary Zone

(percentage distribution)

Branch of activity	Overtime hours per year					
	0	*1-25*	*26-100*	*Over 100*	*Total*	*N*
Transport						
Rural	0.0	0.0	0.0	0.0	0.0	(0)
Semiurban	0.0	0.0	0.0	0.0	0.0	(0)
Urban	58.0	0.2	1.2	40.7	100.1	(1,805)
Import/export						
Rural	93.5	0.0	0.0	6.5	100.0	(108)
Semiurban	91.7	0.0	4.1	4.1	99.9	(121)
Urban	67.3	2.3	5.6	24.9	100.1	(1,408)

Note: Banks are excluded from this table (1) because their wage earners are all located in the largest cities and (2) because 87 percent of them do not work overtime.

sities of particularistic personnel strategies. Such is the case in the primary sector (Table 58).

As various branches of activity do not similarly reward seniority in their allocation of overtime work, any assessment of the influence of overtime work on overall annual earnings requires the introduction of appropriate controls. Yet an examination of the influence of overtime work on the overall salaries of the most "loyal" wage earners shows that bonuses paid for overtime do not necessarily eradicate contrasts in incomes (Table 59).

An increase in the amount of overtime is often associated with a moderate rise in individual annual average earnings, but this is not the case in the construction or transport industries. In these two instances, individual annual remuneration tends to decline as a direct function of the duration of the work effectively performed.[12]

In brief, employers reward long seniority in the firm in two distinct ways. The "royal reward" involves direct or indirect access to top skill levels, and individuals so rewarded do not need the bonuses that go with overtime work in order to obtain high annual earnings. The "common reward" consists in allowing unskilled individuals with high seniority to work overtime and to obtain higher earnings than those to which their low level of skill entitles them. Clearly, however, the second form of reward is less effective than the first.

Differential Access to Top Skill Levels

In the light of my general propositions, access to supervisory roles should be less affected by the characteristics of the firms in the nonmanual than in the corresponding manual sector. In addition, educational and occupational prerequisites for access to the top rungs of the occupational ladder should be more uniform in the case of the nonmanual population.

The first hypothesis is unwarranted (Table 60), for the percentage of workers employed in higher skill categories varies within relatively narrower limits among blue- than white-collar workers. Thus, only 6 percent of nonmanual employees in primary concerns have reached skill level 4, as against almost one-third of their counterparts employed by mechanical and metallurgical firms. Similarly, the percentage of nonmanual workers who have reached the highest skill levels (5-7) varies from a low of 2 percent in agricultural and primary producers to a high of 21 percent in banks and insurance concerns. In contrast, the proportion of manual workers in skill level 4 only varies from a low of 3 percent in the primary sector to a high of 9 percent in the mechanical and metallurgical industries. For individuals in skill levels 5 to 7, the corresponding figures vary from

---

[12] This apparently paradoxical result suggests that any assessment of the influence of overtime on annual earnings requires the introduction of appropriate controls not only on the seniority of the population examined (as has been done here) but on its skill level as well.

TABLE 58
Percentage of Manual Workers with Over 100 Hours of Overtime Per Year by Branch of Activity and Seniority

Type of industry	Less than 2 years		2-5 Years		Seniority in the firm 5-10 Years		10-15 Years		15 Years	
Primary	29.6	(1,868)	32.7	(1,447)	30.1	(1,660)	21.4	(839)	27.3	(1,401)
Raw material processing	35.5	(200)	62.8	(148)	51.2	(162)	69.5	(69)	*	(5)
Wood and timber	72.6	(117)	71.8	(103)	84.8	(145)	69.5	(92)	*	(8)
Mechanical and metallurgical	40.5	(2,291)	38.0	(1,120)	49.9	(1,049)	33.3	(294)	17.3	(104)
Construction	67.6	(3,314)	84.9	(1,318)	56.0	(603)	68.0	(691)	41.1	(463)
Banks	17.1	(64)	7.8	(51)	*	(4)	*	(8)	*	(0)
Transport	24.2	(284)	31.3	(491)	50.8	(429)	51.0	(434)	42.2	(180)
Import/export	19.3	(636)	23.0	(438)	24.8	(354)	25.3	(106)	18.6	(43)

Note: N in parentheses.
*Figures too small to be translated into percentages.

TABLE 59
Income Structure of Manual and Nonmanual Workers with Ten or More Years' Seniority in the Firm by Activity and Overtime Hours Worked

Overtime hours worked per annum	Primary	Processing	Timber and textile	Mechanics/ metallurgy	Construction	Banks	Transportation	Import/ export
None								
Mean annual income (thousands CFA)	66.5	122.9	221.5	172.5	218.1	148.2	132.1	134.8
Percentage earning more than overall average	3.8	28.1	79.5	50.9	72.1	41.3	27.9	37.0
1 to 50								
Mean annual income (thousands CFA)	67.3	148.3	*	177.4	190.1	*	*	151.4
Percentage earning more than overall average	5.8	61.1	*	53.6	69.0	*	*	42.8
51 to 100								
Mean annual income (thousands CFA)	70.1	218.2	*	17,941	164.2	*	99.0	40.9
Over 100								
Mean annual income (thousands CFA)	81.1	194.2	270.1	235.1	170.2	*	130.3	181.4
Percentage earning more than overall average	8.7	58.7	96.3	85.1	68.5	*	13.6	63.3

*Figures too small to be translated into percentages.

zero percent in banks and insurance concerns to 2 percent in the mechanical and metallurgical industries.

Thus, the hierarchical profiles of manual and nonmanual labor forces are quite distinctive. In the manual sector, the skill mix hardly varies by branch of activity, and the percentage of individuals with high skill levels averages 7 percent for the blue-collar labor force as a whole. Alternatively, there are wide sectoral differences in the skill mix of nonmanual workers (Figure 1). In the case of primary enterprises or of those involved in the processing of raw materials, the proportions of nonmanual wage earners employed in skill levels 4, on the one hand, and 5 to 7, on the other, are uniformly low. Although the top of the hierarchy is much broader in construction and banks or insurance concerns, the hierarchical profile of nonmanual workers is more constricted at the top in export/import concerns and metallurgical industries, where there are roughly three individuals in category 4 for each employee in categories 5 to 7. But do the prerequisites governing access to supervisory manual and nonmanual roles vary differentially with the characteristics of employers?

Educational prerequisites for access to top skill levels.

The proportion of nonmanual workers in skill levels 5 to 7 with the equivalent of more than seven years of formal training and schooling ranges from a high of 65 percent in banks to a low of 35 percent in the construction and mechanical industries. In the blue-collar sector, the percentage of individuals in similarly high positions and with the same educational and vocational background varies from 41 percent in construction and public works enterprises to 8 percent in primary concerns. Thus, employers of a particular industry do not make the same use of educational or vocational credentials for recruiting their most skilled workers. Further, and as generally expected, the corresponding variations have a proportionately greater range in the blue- than the white-collar sector.[13]

However, conclusions do change when one looks at variations in selectivity ratios by economic sector, that is, at intersectorial variations in the relative differences between the formal qualifications attained by highly skilled individuals and those of all other workers.[14] Among nonmanual populations, individuals with more than seven years of formal training are almost eighteen times more numerous in the highest skill levels than in the

[13] The same pattern characterizes as well patterns of access to positions involving the performance of complex tasks with low supervisory functions (skill level 4). As one could anticipate, variations in the importance that distinct industries attach to educational credentials in this respect are even sharper than for access to top skill levels. Indeed, convergences in the definition that employers give of specific jobs should be more marked at the top than at lower rungs of the occupational hierarchy.

[14] Calculation of a selectivity ratio involves the division of the percentage of individuals with selected characteristics in the top echelons of the hierarchy by the percentage of individuals with the same characteristics in the population at large.

TABLE 60

Profile of Manual and Nonmanual Workers by Branch of Activity

	Primary		*Raw material processing*		*Wood and textiles*		*Mechanical and metallurgical*	
	Manual	*Nonmanual*	*Manual*	*Nonmanual*	*Manual*	*Nonmanual*	*Manual*	*Nonmanual*
Percentage in skill level 4	3.0	6.0	4.1	10.5	6.2	14.2	9.2	31.9
Percentage in skill levels 5-7	1.1	2.2	1.7	7.1	0.2	8.5	1.7	9.8
Percentage in skill level 4 with aggregate training score of over 7.0	3.6	11.2	0.0	18.1	37.9	40.0	16.4	27.4
Selectivity ratio[a]	4.5	5.0	0.0	1.4	4.7	3.6	2.3	1.5
Percentage in skill levels 5-7 with aggregate training score of over 7.0	7.7	39.3	0.0	*	*	*	36.6	34.6
Selectivity ratio[a]	9.6	17.9	0.0	*	*	*	5.1	1.7
Percentage in skill level 4 with 11 or more years' seniority	31.0	28.7	25.0	54.5	37.9	26.6	24.6	28.6
Selectivity ratio[a]	1.0	5.1	1.9	1.0	1.7	1.8	3.0	1.3
Percentage in skill levels 5-7 with 11 or more years' seniority	47.4	35.7	50.0	*	*	*	17.0	48.5
Selectivity ratio[a]	1.5	6.3	3.8	*	*	*	2.0	2.3
N₁[b]	(7,215)	(1,317)	(584)	(104)	(465)	(105)	(4,858)	(1,028)
N₂[b]	(219)	(80)	(24)	(11)	(29)	(15)	(450)	(328)
N₃[b]	(63)	(28)	(10)	(8)	(1)	(9)	(82)	(101)

TABLE 60 *(continued)*

	Construction		Banks		Transport		Import/export	
	Manual	Nonmanual	Manual	Nonmanual	Manual	Nonmanual	Manual	Nonmanual
Percentage in skill level 4	8.0	29.8	2.7	24.3	6.0	19.1	4.6	27.3
Percentage in skill level 5-7	1.3	14.0	0.0	20.5	1.1	10.5	0.6	11.4
Percentage in skill level 4 with aggregate training score of over 7.0	26.6	17.3	*	33.5	10.9	14.7	5.2	21.5
Selectivity ratio[a]	4.2	1.1	*	0.9	5.7	1.1	1.4	1.2
Percentage in skill levels 5-7 with aggregate training score of over 7.0	40.6	34.6	*	64.5	20.0	38.2	*	37.1
Selectivity ratio[a]	6.5	2.0	*	1.8	10.5	3.0	*	2.2
Percentage in skill level 4 with 11 or more years' seniority	40.9	59.8	*	20.1	50.5	47.5	28.9	21.2
Selectivity ratio[a]	2.2	1.1	*	1.3	1.3	1.3	2.2	1.4
Percentage in skill levels 5-7 with 11 or more years' seniority	52.1	56.9	*	25.6	65.0	61.7	*	33.7
Selectivity ratio[a]	2.8	1.1	*	1.6	1.9	1.6	*	2.2
N_1[b]	(6,289)	(924)	(147)	(551)	(1,810)	(321)	(1,637)	(1,526)
N_2[b]	(511)	(276)	(4)	(134)	(110)	(61)	(76)	(418)
N_3[b]	(96)	(130)	(0)	(113)	(20)	(34)	(5)	(175)

Branch of Activity

[a]Quotient of the percentage of individuals with selected characteristics in skill level X over the percentage of individuals with the characteristics in the population as a whole.

[b]N_1 refers to the size of the total population; N_2 to the size of the population in skill level 4, and N_3 to the size of the population in skill levels 5-7.

*The number is too small to make percentages significant.

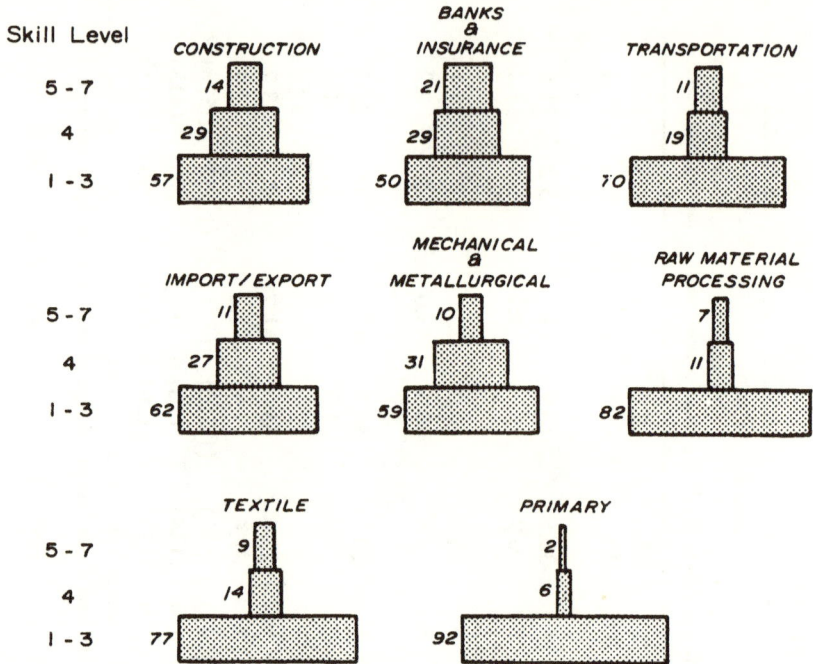

Figure 1. Distribution of nonmanual workers by industry and skill level. *Note:* All pyramids are drawn to the same horizontal scale (2 inches equal 100 percent); actual percentages are indicated by the appropriate bracketed number.

total working population of primary concerns, but the corresponding ratio declines to 1.7 in the mechanical and metallurgical industries. In other words, a high level of formal qualifications is a far more crucial determinant of access to supervisory positions in the former than in the latter instance. Conversely, for manual workers, such selectivity ratios only vary from a low of 5.1 in mechanical and metallurgical industries to a high of 9.6 for those in the primary sector. Thus, in contrast to my initial assumption, the educational and vocational selectivity underlying the recruitment of highly skilled workers is less likely to vary by branch of activity in the case of manual than of nonmanual labor forces.

The relationship between educational credentials and access to top positions also varies with the organizational profile of the firm (see Table 48). Whereas nonmanual selectivity ratios evolve uniformly below 2.0, independently of the size of the firms and of the location of their headquarters, selectivity ratios for the manual population range from over 3.0 in the case of the bureaucratically oriented international organizations with over a hundred employees to less than 2.0 among local enterprises employing between eleven and twenty-five workers. In this sense, the prerequisites for gaining access to the top of the nonmanual hierarchy are more universalistic.

However, the differential importance that international and local concerns attach to vocational and educational qualifications in the recruitment of their skilled manual or nonmanual labor force does not remain constant over time (see Table 49). The proportion of highly skilled white-collar workers with the equivalent of at least seven years of formal schooling differs markedly between local and international organizations created before the war (85 against 67 percent), but such contrasts decline for those enterprises more recently established in the Cameroun (the relevant figures are 70 and 72 percent). In other words, the growth of educational facilities induces perhaps a slight decline in the role formal schooling plays in the recruitment of skilled white-collar workers but this growth is also more significantly associated with a sharp decrease in the differential educational criteria that such enterprises use for recruiting their skilled white-collar personnel. In this sense, the market is becoming more perfect.

In contrast, a reverse pattern characterizes the recruitment of highly skilled blue-collar workers (Table 49). The proportion of skilled individuals with an aggregate training score of 7.0 and above differs more markedly between the newly established local and international concerns than between their counterparts created before the war. In other words, the greater scarcity in the supply of educated adults before the war prevented local and international firms from pursuing distinct policies in their recruitment, whereas current educational development enables internationally based companies to be more demanding in the conditions they impose for access to manual supervisory functions. In this sense, the manual labor market is becoming more differentiated and hence more particularistic.

To sum up, the various rewards that internationally and locally based enterprises accord to the formal schooling of their manual and nonmanual workers do not evolve according to the same dynamics. When these rewards are defined in terms of skills, the manual labor market seems to follow *divergent* principles, whereas there are increased *convergences* in the educational standing of highly skilled nonmanual wage earners employed by distinctive types of firms. When rewards are defined in terms of income, it is clear that the salaries accorded to highly educated nonmanual workers differ most significantly between local and international firms recently settled in the Cameroun, but conversely that there are increased convergences in the rewards that educated blue-collar workers attached to differing types of enterprises derive from their formal schooling. Thus, the processes of segmentation of the labor market correspond to heterogenous functional principles: the logic is not the same in the case of skill and income distributions; nor is it the same for manual and nonmanual populations.

Influence of occupational experience.

As enterprises are characterized by distinctive levels of technological development as well as by differing size, one might expect them to accord differential weight to the seniority of their workers as a condition of entry into supervisory jobs. Indeed, they are not likely to similarly recruit their lower cadres from *within* or *without* the enterprise. The number of highly skilled nonmanual workers with over ten years' seniority in the same firm varies from a minimum of 26 percent among banks and insurance concerns to a maximum of 62 percent in the railroad industry. Among blue-collar wage earners, the corresponding proportions vary from a low of 17 percent for mechanical and metallurical concerns to a high of 65 percent in the railroad industry. Thus, the influence of seniority in the firm on occupational attainment depends in part on the organizational patterns of the industry by which they are employed. For political reasons,all Camerounian railroad workers have obtained the same advantages as their metropolitan counterparts, whereas other "modern" employers have retained a personnel policy more independent of metropolitan models.

Further, as it is still in the least complex sectors (agriculture for nonmanuals and, processing industries for manuals) that a high level of seniority most sharply distinguishes highly skilled workers from the working population at large, one suspects that it is such sectors which are the most particularistic in their employment policies and which are the most likely to reward the loyalty of their employees by giving them access to supervising functions.

Finally, firms also differ in the importance they attach to educational and occupational experiences considered jointly as prerequisites for access into the top positions of the hierarchy. In the manual sector, no less than 21 percent of the construction workers placed in skill levels 5 to 7 have the equivalent of seven years of formal schooling as well as at least ten years of experience within the firm, as against only 2 percent of their counterparts placed in the same skill category but employed by other concerns. Similarly, in the nonmanual sector, 26 percent of the individuals placed in the top jobs of the railroad companies have both a minimum of seven years of formal schooling and of eleven years of experience with the same employer, but these educational and occupational credentials characterize only 10 percent of their peers employed in other branches of activity. Thus, distinct types of concern do not entertain similar expectations toward the personnel they want to employ in supervisory and junior executive positions.

There are also sectorial variations in the relative trade-off between education and seniority. In the nonmanual sector, construction firms are relatively more frequently inclined than mechanical or metallurgical concerns to hire highly skilled individuals with *high* academic credentials but *low* seniority. Almost 12 percent of the individuals employed in skill categories 5 to 7 by the first type of enterprise have an aggregate training score of over 7.0 and less than two years of seniority, as against only 5 percent of those employed in garages, repair stations and other mechanical concerns. Alternatively, no less than 23 percent of the skilled clerical workers employed by construction firms have limited educational credentials but over ten years of experience within the firm, as opposed to less than 8 percent of their counterparts employed by banks and insurance firms. In short, banks do not reward the loyalty of their white-collar labor force to the same extent as other employers.

The situation is the same in the blue-collar market. Although high credentials uniformly fail to compensate for limited seniority as a prerequisite for gaining access to the top jobs of the manual hierarchy, there are significant variations in the proportions of highly skilled individuals with *low* academic credentials but high seniority. Thus, three-quarters of the railroad's top manual workers have at least ten years with the firm but less than seven years of overall formal training, as against 32 percent of their counterparts employed by construction firms and 26 percent of their peers working in garage and mechanical concerns. In brief, variations both in the technological development of Camerounian enterprises and in the organizational abilities of their respective workers are paralleled by contrasts in the degree to which seniority overrides formal schooling as a determinant of individual access to the top of the manual hierarchy.

Occupational Attainment: A Composite Image

Determinants of individual skill levels.

Up to now, I have examined the influence of selected determinants of occupational attainment considered independently of one another. Because of the transferable character of the relevant skills, access to the top of the nonmanual hierarchy is more frequently based on universalistic criteria and, hence, on achievement-based traits of individual workers, whereas access to the top rungs of the manual hierarchy tends to be more dependent on environmental factors.

Indeed, the combined influence of specific environmental factors on individual careers is greater in the case of manual than of nonmanual workers.[15] The characteristics of enterprises (branch of activity, size, location of headquarters, and so forth) account for only 4 percent of the variance in the distribution of skill levels among nonmanual workers but for 11 percent of the variance in the corresponding distribution among manual workers. When one allows each independent variable to enter in the equation according to its level of statistical significance, the

---

[15] This refers to the fact that I introduced exclusively environmental variables into the equation.

characteristics of firms play still a greater role in explaining the skill level attained by blue-collar individuals (Table 61). The rank ordering of the corresponding variables is higher in this latter case.

In addition, the structure of the skill distribution of the nonmanual population is simpler: only five independent variables are sufficient to explain 35 percent of the variance in the nonmanual distribution. By contrast, seven variables are required to explain this variance in the case of the manual distribution. This confirms my hypothesis about the differential nature of manual and nonmanual work; occupational attainment in the second sector is explained by fewer variables more directly related to the background characteristics of individual wage earners.

The images so obtained, however, are composite. In earlier sections of the present chapter, I demonstrated that variations in the organization and technology of Camerounian firms exert divergent influences on the careers of the manual and nonmanual labor forces. By considering only one particular branch of activity, one might reduce random fluctuations in the skill distribution of manual and nonmanual populations and explain accordingly a larger part of the newly reduced variance.

As my concern is to highlight the role of exposure to modern educational and occupational factors, I concentrated on the nonmanual labor force of banks and insurance concerns and on the manual workers of mechanical and metallurgical concerns. Indeed, it is in these two sectors that the work patterns of the two types of wage earner are most rationalized and bureaucratized; the tasks imposed on the manual labor force of the mechanical and metallurgical industries are relatively sophisticated, and they correspond to a certain extent to the complexity of the nonmanual tasks performed in the context of banks and insurance concerns.

The variance in the distribution of manual and nonmanual skills is explained to a greater extent within one particular economic sector rather than within the labor market as a whole (Table 62). Yet the corresponding increases are not alike in the two populations, and although one can account for 59 percent of the variance in the distribution of skills among the white-collar personnel of banks and insurance concerns, one can explain only 45 percent of the variance of the distribution of skills in the blue-collar labor force of the mechanical and metallurgical industries. Further, environmental variables play an increasing role as determinants of occupational attainment among the clerical workers of banks and insurance concerns. In contrast, the variance in the distribution of occupational attainment among the blue-collar workers of mechanical and metallurgic industries is more closely related to the various facets of the individual history of each worker.

TABLE 61

Multiple Regression Analysis of Skill Level Distributions among Manual and Nonmanual Populations

Manual Workers			
N	23210		
Mean	1.707		
Standard deviation	1.01		
R_2	0.383		
Intercept	0.654		

Variables	Beta	t	R^2
1. *Joint* aggregate training and seniority scores (interaction)	0.002	43.20	0.176
2. Upward mobility between second job learned or performed and present job[a]	5.568	52.90	0.233
3. *Joint* number of jobs learned or performed and aggregate training scores	0.049	45.16	0.298
4. Participation in agricultural activities[a]	-4.249	36.80	0.340
5. Age	0.141	23.74	0.359
6. Participation in maintenance functions[a]	2.380	20.82	0.372
7. Douala[a]	4.433	20.43	0.383

Nonmanual Workers			
N	4915		
Mean	3.079		
Standard deviation	1.309		
R^2	0.349		
Intercept	0.845		

Variables	Beta	t	R^2
1. *Joint* aggregate training and seniority scores (interaction)	0.008	17.99	0.188
2. Aggregate training score	0.009	23.96	0.255
3. Age	0.372	17.21	0.302
4. Number of jobs learned or performed	1.969	12.70	0.330
5. Participation in peripheral services (maintenance)[a]	-6.501	11.79	0.349

[a] All these variables have been treated as dummy variables.

TABLE 62
Multiple Regression Analysis of Skill Levels for the Manual Population
of Mechanical Industries and for the Nonmanual Population
of Banks and Insurance Firms

	Manual workers in mechanical industries		
N	13158		
Mean	1.91		
Standard deviation	1.06		
R^2	0.456		
Intercept	0.727		

Variables	Beta	t	R^2
1. *Joint* aggregate training and seniority scores (interaction)	0.013	37.52	0.225
2. Upward mobility between second job learned or performance and present occupation[a]	4.956	33.83	0.306
3. Number of jobs learned or performed	3.923	48.42	0.383
4. Downward mobility between past and present jobs[a]	-4.902	22.49	0.415
5. Seniority on the job	0.358	46.25	0.437
6. Aggregate training score^2	0.007	21.34	0.456

	Nonmanual workers in banks and insurance firms		
N	567		
Mean	3.308		
Standard deviation	1.368		
R^2	0.594		
Intercept	0.659		

Variables	Beta	t	R^2
1. *Joint* number of jobs learned or performed and aggregate training scores (interaction)	0.002	4.09	0.218
2. Seniority in the firm (log)	0.343	9.69	0.377
3. Participation in peripheral services[a]	-1.198	8.42	0.483
4. Aggregate training score^2	0.008	7.65	0.528
5. Age	0.037	6.48	0.561
6. Participation in peripheral services (sales)[a]	0.463	5.30	0.579
7. Age of the firm (log)	-0.231	4.53	0.594

[a]All these variables are treated as dummy variables.

To summarize, contrasts between the relative determinants of manual and nonmanual attainment are greater when one considers the most modernized sectors of activity than when one analyzes simultaneously *all* branches of the Camerounian economy. This confirms what could be derived from a more impressionistic observation of the work processes in these two contexts. The definition of occupational performance is perhaps more standardized and structured in one specific branch of activity than in the market as a whole. But this degree of standardization is still greater in the case of nonmanual work.

In addition, the standardization of individual performance in banks and insurance concerns is associated with a relative decline in the influence of individual background on achievement. Correspondingly, this achievement is more dependent on variations in the organizational profile of individual enterprises. In contrast, variations in the technological complexity of the mechanical and metallurgical industries imply greater variability in the patterns of successful individual adaptation to the demands of employers. In this sense, the dynamics underlying the occupational histories of manual and nonmanual workers in *specific* industrial contexts are quite distinct.

Determinants of income.

The final task in this chapter is to synthesize the observations concerning the influence exerted by individual characteristics of Camerounian workers and by the profile of their work environment on their annual earnings.

The initial step of the analysis consists in assessing the relative weight of "individual" as opposed to "environmental" factors. One of the major themes of this study has been to underline the greater universality of nonmanual markets, and this leads one to expect the annual incomes of nonmanual workers to be more independent of the profile of the enterprises which employ them. Indeed, although environmental variables, considered *in toto,* account for only 8 percent of the distribution in nonmanual yearly income, such variables account for no less than 19 percent of variance in the corresponding distribution among blue-collar wage earners (Table 63). Further, only import/export firms stand aside in their nonmanual salary policies, and the incomes of clerical workers in that particular branch are lower than in the remaining part of the market. Blue-collar annual earnings follow a more complex pattern. No less than three branches of activity (agricultural, food-processing, and mechanical industries) appear to adopt distinctive policies and strategies with regard to the remuneration of their blue-collar labor force.

Thus far, I did not allow individual characteristics to enter into the equation. The second step of the analysis involves, therefore, the introduction of *all* individual and environmental variables in the sequential order defined by the level of significance of their contribution. Obviously, I still have eliminated skill levels from such an analysis for, as already

TABLE 63
Multiple Regression Analysis of Manual and Nonmanual Income
(environmental variables only)

	Nonmanual population		
N	4915		
Mean	305.00		
Standard deviation	249.58		
R^2	0.082		
Intercept	193.32		

Variables	Beta	t	R^2
1. Monthly payments[a]	17.851	20.33	0.057
2. Employment in import/export activities[a]	- 8.955	11.49	0.082

	Manual population		
N	23.210		
Mean	140.50		
Standard deviation	107.23		
R^2	0.188		
Intercept	108.23		

Variables	Beta	t	R^2
1. Participation in agricultural enterprises[a]	- 3.399	20.91	0.067
2. Interaction of size and age of firm	0.005	35.10	0.134
3. Monthly payment[a]	5.258	28.89	0.150
4. Participation in processing industries[a]	8.796	19.00	0.163
5. Participation in mechanical industries[a]	3.498	21.33	0.177
6. Overtime work	0.049	17.42	0.188

[a]All these variables are treated as dummy variables.

indicated, this particular variable acts as a powerful filter for all other environmental and individual variables and as such is likely to mask the latter's relative contribution. In Tables 64 and 65, I examine the variance in the annual earnings of manual and nonmanual workers, considering successively the totality of and certain privileged sectors in the labor market.

A comparative inspection of these two tables suggests the three following conclusions: (1) the amount of variance accounted for is analogous for both the manual and nonmanual distributions. In this sense, I have failed to demonstrate that the nonmanual labor market is more perfect and more rational than the blue-collar one. (2) As already suggested by the results in

TABLE 64
Multiple Regression Analysis of Manual Income in the Total Labor Force and in Mechanical or Metallurgical Industries

	Total labor force		
N	23210		
Mean	140.50		
Standard deviation	107.23		
R^2	0.323		
Intercept	100.22		

Variables	Beta	t	R^2
1. Interaction of seniority in the firm and aggregate training score	0.002	72.17	0.227
2. Participation in agricultural enterprises	-5.020	39.36	0.275
3. Interaction of size and age of firm	0.001	30.06	0.300
4. Participation in an internationally based firm[a]	2.668	20.34	0.311
5. On-the-job training with a large firm[a]	2.259	19.28	0.322

	Mechanical and metallurgical industries		
N	13158		
Mean	154.78		
Standard deviation	133.73		
R^2	0.422		
Intercept	64.91		

Variables	Beta	t	R^2
1. Interaction of seniority in the firm and aggregate training score	0.003	63.50	0.332
2. Interaction of age and size of firm	0.001	19.40	0.362
3. Seniority on the job	0.027	20.97	0.379
4. Participation in an internationally based firm[a]	3.325	19.15	0.400
5. Number of jobs learned or performed	1.312	16.76	0.412
6. Monthly payment[a]	3.148	14.30	0.422

[a] All these variables are treated as dummy variables.

the first step of the analysis, the role played by environmental factors on the determination of annual income is more significant in the case of the manual than of the nonmanual distribution. The number of variables reflecting the different characteristics of employers is greater in the first instance, and these variables are more likely to enter early in the multiple

TABLE 65
Nonmanual Income in the Total Labor Force and in Banks

Total labor force

N	4915
Mean	305.00
Standard deviation	249.57
R^2	0.349
Intercept	127.31

Variables	Beta	t	R^2
1. Interaction of seniority in the firm and aggregate training score	0.002	23.47	0.211
2. Aggregate training score^2	0.002	20.76	0.282
3. Age	0.640	15.63	0.313
4. Monthly payment[a]	7.740	10.74	0.334
5. Participation in banks[a]	9.651	10.25	0.349

Banks and insurance firms

N	567
Mean	419.12
Standard deviation	349.75
R^2	0.321
Intercept	213.34

Variables	Beta	t	R^2
1. Interaction of seniority in the firm and aggregate training score	0.003	62.02	0.133
2. Aggregate training score^2	0.002	72.18	0.220
3. Age	1.072	56.00	0.266
4. Age of firm (log)	0.008	16.86	0.286
5. Firm size (log)	0.396	52.23	0.296
6. Interaction of age and size of firm	-0.015	44.51	0.320

[a]All these variables are treated as dummy variables.

regression equation. (3) When the analysis is limited to the most advanced branches of activity, I explain an additional variance in the distribution of manual incomes but fail to do so in the case of white-collar earnings. Further, as was the case for skill levels, the role played by work environmental factors seems to decline in the first instance but to increase in the second. In other words, as the definition of a manual task becomes more specific, educational and vocational qualifications explain a proportionately larger amount of the variance in distribution of earnings. In contrast, as the definition of nonmanual tasks becomes narrower, contextual variables make a more significant contribution than they did in the case of the working population at large. Differences in the relative role played by environmental factors in the determination of annual earnings among manual and nonmanual populations suggest that the meaning and the implications of job specificity are not the same in the two sectors of employment.

To sum up, the dynamics at work in the two labor markets are not comparable. Nor, indeed, are the meanings and implications attached to the notion of job specificity in the two sectors of employment. Because of the universalistic structure of the nonmanual labor market considered as a whole, restrictions in the scope of the analysis accentuate the influence of particularistic factors in accounting for the differential incomes of individual wage earners. By contrast, because of the more particularistic nature of the manual labor market, any restriction in the scope of the analysis lowers the significance of these particularistic variables and correspondingly enhances the influence of educational and occupational antecedents as predictors of the differential income and attainment of blue-collar workers.

Employers, employees, and collective bargaining strategies.

Earnings do not result from free negotiations. A man's income does not depend solely on his educational and occupational attainments nor on the weight that employers are willing to accord such factors. As already noted, pay rates are institutionalized through the variety of collective-bargaining agreements operating in the Cameroun, and workers as well as employers develop their strategies within the legal framework imposed on them by political authorities. In other words, earnings do not reflect individual choices but the characteristics of entire groups.

Under such conditions, it is important to determine how each individual income stands in relation to the legal scale laid down by collective bargaining agreements. As I want to assess the relative bargaining power of various groups of workers, I must first enter individual pay on an artificial universal scale which is meaningful both in terms of the different salary zones in the country and of the variety of collective-bargaining agreements. Thus, any estimate of the relative bargaining power of employers and employees initially requires elimination of institutionalized differences in the salaries offered or obtained. Indeed, to note that an agricultural wage earner in the rural hinterland obtains a lower salary than his counterpart employed in a bank based in Douala is meaningless, for a large part of the difference reflects only distinct legal prescriptions. Therefore, I eliminated those components of income associated with legal prescriptions and standardized wages in terms of both region and type of activity.

In addition, the variety of collective-bargaining agreements operating in the

Cameroun defines in clear terms both the conditions of access to the various rungs of the official skill hierarchy and the bases of remuneration at each rung. In other words, an individual placed in the institutionalized top skill categories does not necessarily have to meet the same requirements when he is hired by a construction firm as when he is hired by a garage or an industrial concern. Nor is he entitled to receive the same pay. Although it is impossible to artificially standardize the conditions of access to the distinctive rungs of each occupational hierarchy, it remains possible to harmonize the types of remuneration linked to the same skill level across branches of activity. In other words, it is possible to compute for each skill level an indicator that takes into account both the mean and the standard deviation of the distribution of salaries that the thirty-three collective-bargaining agreements specify for such a qualification. This being done, one is in a position to standardize the incomes attached to a particular skill level across branches of activity or collective-bargaining agreements and to assess the relative bargaining strength that employers and employees have in the labor market considered in its totality. This involves then a direct comparison between the *actual* earnings of Camerounian workers and the *theoretical* sums to which they are entitled in view of their skills and qualifications.

The relative bargaining power of local workers may be artificial when it results from their placement in a skill category lower than that they are in fact entitled to claim. This situation obtains in agricultural concerns whose workers enjoy higher bargaining strength than that of secondary and tertiary enterprises (Table 66). Although the former enterprises pay less than the latter, they pay their personnel at a higher rate than the legal minimum. The bargaining power of African workers is similarly greater in long-established than in newly arrived concerns and in smaller than larger businesses. The same principle seems to operate in these three context: smaller and long-established firms, particularly in the primary sector, do not want to jeopardize their economic future. Instead of following the rules governing the placement of their workers in the skill categories defined by collective-bargaining agreements, they prefer to accord their workers a lower level of qualification *and then pay them more than they are supposed to*.

The picture changes somewhat when one concentrates on the largest firms, that is, those with forty-five employees and more. Even in this context employers tend to compress the theoretical range of salaries they are supposed to offer. Indeed, the zero-order correlation coefficient between the indicator of collective-bargaining power and the average theoretical salary to which workers are entitled is -0.509. In other words, the higher the theoretical average salary that the firms with forty-five employees or more *should* allocate to its workers, the lower will be the average actual remuneration that it *will* offer. In short, the *actual* range of salaries

TABLE 66
Percentage of Firms whose Labor Force Enjoys Maximal Bargaining Power
(over 1 CFA difference between real and theoretical standardized hourly rates)

Branch of activity	Fewer than 25 employees	25 employees or more
Primary	92	40
Raw material processing	70	67
Textiles and timber	69	2
Mechanical and metallurgical	60	6
Construction	39	6
Banks and Insurance	21	22
Import/export	49	10
Date of foundation		
After independence	40	11
1945-1958	31	8
Before 1945	45	28

adopted by Camerounian large-scale enterprises is more limited than the *theoretical* scale defined by the government.

Yet the corresponding practices are not evenly distributed among all types of firms. Thus, the bargaining power of the local labor force is negatively associated with the size of local enterprises (the zero-order correlation between these two variables is -0.271). At the same time, the aggregate bargaining power of the personnel of internationally based concerns is greater than that of workers for local concerns (the relevant zero-order correlation is 0.314). It is similarly greater in nonagricultural concerns (the relevant correlation is 0.325) and among enterprises with a large number of production units (the correlation is 0.136). In brief, the bargaining power of workers depends first on the characteristics of local economic organizations.

Obviously, aggregate bargaining power also depends on the characteristics of the labor force itself. It is positively related to its aggregate educational level (the relevant correlation is 0.202); it increases with the proportion of nonmanual workers in the firm (the correlation is 0.360) and with the proportion of employees engaged in coordinative and staff functions (the correlation is 0.344). Finally, it is associated with the aggregate patterns of mobility undergone by individual workers: the greater the proportion of individuals who have moved down the ladder between their current job and their previous job or the position they occupied at the time of their entry into the labor market, the lower their overall average bargaining power (the relevant correlations are -0.161 and -0.191).

A multiple regression analysis enables one to summarize the factors influencing the relative aggregate bargaining power that African workers hold vis-à-vis their employers. Ten variables account for almost three-quarters of the variance in the distribution of this power across the various types of enterprises. These variables can be divided into three subgroups. The first and most important reflects the degree to which workers are underclassified in terms of skill level and obtain an income lower than that to which they are entitled in terms of the rubrics of collective-bargaining agreements. As their theoretical salaries increase, wage earners lose bargaining power. The second group reflects variations in the function and the organizational size of firms: international concerns engaged in nonagricultural activities and with a large number of dispersed production units are more willing than other employers to yield to the demands of their African workers. Finally, the last group of factors reflects the degree to which workers are able to take advantage of the conditions of the market and to play the appropriate game in the most efficient manner. Indeed, with an increase in the proportion of manual and nonmanual workers at top skill levels, individual wage earners tend to obtain more than their "fair" salary.

To sum up, it is evident that employers tend to adopt patterns of behavior that are at variance with the regulations adopted by the government. As an example, workers in the hinterland do not obtain the annual salary to which they are legally entitled: depending on their own characteristics as well as on the characteristics of their employees, employers do not enjoy the same negotiation power vis-a-vis their personnel and do not reward their workers according to a similar set of principles. An evaluation of individual incomes is therefore insufficient: one must also, as I did, identify the *mechanisms* used by workers and employers to extract from each other the maximal amount of concessions.

Conclusions

The main purpose of the present chapter has been to show that the occupational history of individual workers is not independent of the characteristics of the environment in which they participate. Thus, I have suggested that the social definition of the differential productivity achieved by manual and nonmanual workers does not remain constant in the various parts of the labor market. More specifically, variations in the complexity of local enterprises as well as in their activities are associated with parallel contrasts in the rewards that employers seem to attach to educational and occupational credentials. Indeed, employers do not give the same definition of staff as opposed to peripheral positions with regard to nonmanual work, or to production as opposed to maintenance manual tasks for blue-collar workers. Finally, differences between manual and nonmanual or among manual yearly incomes vary with the duration of the work performed. Employers do not make a same use of overtime work and have different strategies for allocating resources among their workers. Thus, in some cases, opportunities for overtime seem to be monopolized by senior workers, whereas in others these opportunities are provided preferentially to more junior personnel.

In brief, gross comparisons between the manual and nonmanual working populations tend to mask very substantial variations *within* the two groups. All workers are employed in distinct types of job performed in varying locales and types of organization which make their own very specific demands and generate correspondingly different kinds of rewards. Thus, to analyze income distribution in terms of the sole characteristics of wage earners may be misleading. The labor market is segmented in too many ways, and employers do not share similar technologies, similar modes of finance, or similar personnel philosophies. In addition, it is insufficient to only examine the take-home pay of wage earners. An analysis of the mechanisms by which employers allocate resources reveals the strength and the stability of the bargaining power acquired by both labor and management.

At the same time, the rapid rate of educational development in the Cameroun affects differentially the skill level of manual and nonmanual wage earners. There seems to be a growing *uniformity* in the importance that various types of firms attach to the educational and vocational qualifications of their clerical labor force, but a growing *differentiation* in the demands that various types of economic organizations impose on their manual workers. Alternatively, however, there also seems to be convergences in the salary policies that these organizations adopt toward blue-collar labor forces but divergences in the strategies they retain toward their nonmanual employees. Thus, the dynamics underlying changes in the determinants of the two facets of occupational attainment are not alike.

Chapter 7

CONCLUSIONS

A cursory inspection of the literature concerned with social change in Africa reveals strange disparities in the concerns of Western social scientists. Between the end of World War II and the independence of African nations, there has been a plethora of studies examining the extent and determinants of similarities and contrasts between urban and rural life styles but few and tardy research dealing with the income of populations living in urban centers.[1] Similarly, there have been an increasing number of books describing both the patterns of access to educational institutions and the occupational aspirations or expectations of the student population but few articles analyzing the actual occupational destination of school graduates.[2] In the same vein, there have been a few studies dealing with the attitudes of African workers and their patterns of association both within and without their firms, but a dearth of studies investigating contrasts in their work conditions and more specifically in the economic behavior that employers adopt toward them. In brief, it looks as if the study of many aspects of industrialization has been treated as a taboo.[3]

As noted in the introduction, planners and political leaders have often asserted without supporting evidence that the relationship between growth and redistribution is not problematic: in their perspective, the growth of educational institutions harmoniously enhances the productivity of both the entire economy and of the individual, and there is an automatic consensus as to the methods to be used to allocate the ensuing profits. Such a stance rests on the proposition that interindividual differences in the amount of schooling acquired, in educational achievement, or in both are legitimately accompanied by parallel interindividual differences in occupational placement and attainment. Yet such a proposition raises three problems which will be summarized in this conclusion.

---

[1] For a general view of this literature, see Hanna and Hanna, *Urban Dynamics in Black Africa.*

[2] The book of M. Peil often quoted in this study as well as her articles offer an interesting exception.

[3] From a sociology of knowledge perspective, one cannot but wonder whether the absence of such studies reflect the ideological stances of the researchers, the lack of financial support which would have been accorded to such research, or more simply the particular disciplines most heavily represented in the field of African studies.

Problems Raised by Educational Differentiation

At face value, the proposition seems to indicate that as the range of possible educational experiences gets wider, an increase in educational attainment is automatically accompanied by a commensurate increase in occupational attainment. Thus, empirical studies conducted in twenty-seven countries show that on the average individuals with more schooling earn higher incomes than those with less schooling.[4] Yet it is clear that an increment in the number of years spent at school is not uniformly associated with a corresponding rise in individual earnings. In the Cameroun, differences in the salaries earned by individuals with four and those with seven years of postprimary training are greater than the contrasts between the incomes of the former and of the population who left school after having completed their primary cycle of study. Such results are not unique and confirm those obtained by Lambert in India.[5] Similarly, in this country, the incremental return to a year of schooling in which a degree is granted is much greater than for intermediate years.[6] Thus, some years of schooling count more than others.

Second, the rewards derived from a same amount of formal schooling are not alike for all social groups. In the present study, I have shown that individuals from different ethnic groups but with similar aggregate training scores do not necessarily earn the same amount of money. Such observations confirm those made by Lambert in India.[7] Similarly, in 1969 it was observed in the United States that white males earned about 33 to 40 percent more than nonwhite males with a same amount of academic experience and that the particularistic effects of ethnicity in this regard are especially visible among populations with lower levels of schooling.[8] Particularistic variations in the rewards accruing to a same educational experience are not surprising if one assumes that the function of schooling is not necessarily to enhance objective individual contribution to production but to legitimize the current hierarchy of social and ethnic groups and, hence, to perpetuate current patterns of social and ethnic stratification.

Third, the rewards derived from formal schooling are probably not independent of the organizational patterns of the educational institutions where the corresponding educational experiences are acquired. In the case of the Cameroun, one may ask whether the relationship between educa-

---

[4] See G. Psacharopoulos, "Rates of Return to Investment in Education around the World," *Comparative Education Review* 16(1972):54-67.

[5] *Workers, Factories, and Social Change in India,* p. 163.

[6] *Work in America* (U. S. Department of Health, Education, and Welfare. Cambridge, Mass.: MIT Press, 1973), p. 135.

[7] *Workers, Factories, and Social Change in India,* pp. 162 and 164.

[8] M. Carnoy and D. Marenbach, *The Return to Schooling in the United States, 1939-1969* (Stanford: Stanford University Press, 1972).

tend to dominate individual occupational attainment, whereas among white-collar wage earners this attainment is more a function of the achievement-oriented characteristics of the individual himself.

Differences in the rules of the game applied to manual as opposed to nonmanual labor markets concern both modes of entry into the labor market and modes of moving within and across its various subsegments. Thus, higher levels of education facilitate access to the jobs deemed to have the highest scalar properties and, hence, to white-collar occupations. As mobility between manual and nonmanual sectors is limited and asymmetric, the influence of education on initial modes of participation in the labor force has enduring consequences.[16]

In general, white-collar workers have then a relatively easier access to the top rungs of the hierarchy.[17] Educational and vocational attainment is a more important determinant of their career or chances for promotion than of the successive experiences undergone in the market by their manual counterparts. In addition, the role of occupational antecedents differs between the two sectors. In effect, overall occupational experience and seniority in the firm tend to be more crucial determinants of individual access into top level jobs in the nonmanual sector. Similarly a nonmanual worker who changes activities has more chance of being upwardly mobile than his manual counterpart. Finally, as one might expect, the financial rewards derived from participation in the higher levels of the nonmanual hierarchy are not only greater but also uniformly more frequently based on achievement. In short, the outcome of a nonmanual career is more predictable, and this predictability is particularly attractive in the context of developing countries, because of the scarce as well as unstable opportunities that local economies offer to the working population. After all, security of employment is one of the most crucial factors that Africans take into consideration when they join the labor force.[18]

In brief, both the system of values operating in the Western world and the organizational abilities of white-collar workers enable them to obtain greater rewards from their educational as well as from their successive occupational experiences. In contrast, the attainment of blue-collar workers is more strongly influenced by the varying stereotypes adopted by employers. The influence of these sterotypes on managerial policies explains why workers with less education may attain the same or a higher productivity than their counterparts with higher educational attainment,

---

[16] Because of the hierarchy between the two types of jobs, there is more mobility from manual to nonmanual activities. This asymmetry is not specific to the Cameroun, having been observed in other African countries as well as in the United States. In this latter instance, see G. Palmer, *Labor Mobility in Six Cities* (New York: Social Science Research Council, 1954).

[17] The same is true of Mexico. See *ibid.*, p. 213, and for Peru, see Chapin, *The Peruvian Labor Force.*

[18] For a discussion of the importance attached to stability of employment, see Clignet and Foster, *The Fortunate Few,* chap. 6.

and why in India, for instance, rural-born workers with a given amount of schooling have a higher productivity than their urban-born counterparts.[19]

However, the relationship between education or experience and attainment varies not only between but also *within* such groups. Both within manual and nonmanual roles, there are contrasts in the nature and, hence, in the economic significance of the tasks assigned to individuals. In the white-collar categories, peripheral and staff roles have differing requirements and rewards which also vary significantly by branch of activity. The nature of the market served by each firm as well as the prevailing modes of relation between labor and management affect the relative preeminence of peripheral over staff functions. Variations in such a preeminence are in turn associated with parallel differences in the educational and occupational experience of the two types of nonmanual population and, hence, in their income. Similarly, in the manual sector there are contrasts between maintenance and production work. Whereas the preeminence of maintenance work varies with the level of technology prevailing in a particular branch of activity, the corresponding variations are accompanied by parallel differences in the educational or occupational background of the two types of manual population as well as in their respective earnings.

Yet to explain the differential attainment of manual and nonmanual workers in terms of their contrasted backgrounds or in terms of the rules of the game set up by employers is insufficient. These rules of the game and the segmentation processes of the Camerounian labor market also pertain to the behavior adopted by employers. Correspondingly, differences in the attainment of white- and blue-collar workers and in the determinants of the skill level or the earnings of these occupational categories are not constant but vary with (a) the organizational complexity of Camerounian firms, (b) their overseas experience, (c) their legal status, and (d) the location of their headquarters.

The personnel of large-scale bureaucratic organizations tend to obtain more substantial monetary rewards than the labor force of small-scale locally based enterprises, even though the corresponding differences vary both by sector of activity and with the amount of time during which entrepreneurs have operated in the Cameroun. Further, there are also significant contrasts in the strategies that both employers and employees use to determine a particular pay rate. Such contrasts are not specific to the Camerounian scene. In India, Lambert has shown that the job histories of individual workers vary with the age of the firms he examined and with their patterns of division of labor.[20] Similarly, Bàlan has contrasted the

[19] See I Berg, *Education and Jobs: The Great Training Robbery* (New York: Praeger, 1970), and W. Fuller, "Education, Training, and Productivity: A Study of Skilled Workers in Two Factories in South India" (Stanford University, SIDEC, 1970), mimeo.

[20] Thus, Lambert notes the importance of distinguishing between work situations where individuals tend machines in gangs, where they are individual operators clustered on the factory

occupational profile of the Mexican labor force of a large-scale concern operating in the Monterrey area with that of the wage earners employed by small-scale local concerns; and, finally, in Peru, Chaplin has shown that contrasts in the organizational pattern of various textile firms are accompanied by parallel variations in the rewards they give their workers.[21]

Stability of the Relationship between Educational and Occupational Differentiation

Although the analysis deals with a picture of the Camerounian labor force at a single point in time, it is still necessary to ask whether the processes of segmentation observed here are likely to become more evident and whether the dynamics underlying such processes are the same as those observed elsewhere.

Initially, it is clear that the segmentation of the local market, far from remaining stable, depends both on educational development and the disparities between school enrollment and job opportunities. Among the youngest cohorts of wage earners, for example, differences in the educational qualifications of manual and nonmanual workers are less marked than they used to be, and there is a correspondingly declining relationship between levels of schooling and occupational placement as well as attainment. Correspondingly, there is a decline in the rates to return to levels of schooling, and this decline hits first populations with the most limited educational experience.[22] However, such declines seem to have two major implications. On the one hand, they seem to be accompanied by an erosion of the boundaries between modern and murky enterprises. On the other, they seem also to be accompanied by a redistribution of job seekers with varying levels of education throughout the various types of enterprises. Whereas there is a growing uniformity in the nonmanual Camerounian labor force, there is an increased differentiation in the manual characteristics of the population that various entrepreneurs are able to attract.

But the segmentation of the Camerounian labor market depends not only on internal forces but also on the conflicting pressures exerted by divergent European interests. On the one hand, the functioning of labor markets in developing nations is certainly influenced by the peripheral position that local economies occupy vis-a-vis industrial centers.[23] On the

---

floor by the type of machine they serve and the nature of the product, and where the individual worker both feeds and directs the machine (pp. 12 and 13).

[21] See *Men in Developing Societies*, p. 304.

[22] Carnoy, in "Schooling, Income," (OECD paper, Dec. 1973), shows both differences and similarities in the relationship between age, education, and income in the United States (1969), India (1961), and Kenya (1968). One wonders, however, whether this relationship does not differ between countries where educational policy follows industrialization and those where the development of educational institutions results from economic growth.

[23] Arrighi, in "International Corporations," p. 252, takes this view.

other hand, the relationships that the oligarchies of the industrialized metropoles are anxious to impose on African or Asian societies are certainly more differentiated than certain Marxian analysts would like to believe. The models used by such oligarchies depend on their own history, and the managerial personnel of multinational concerns such as United Fruit Company, Société Commerciale de l'Ouest Africain, or Renault do not necessarily follow the same policies when they enter a new market. Because these firms owe their very growth to differing types of "colonial" situations, their leaders are unlikely to respond uniformly to the demands and expectations of local workers.

To summarize, it is not sufficient to examine, as I have done here, whether the segmentation of a particular labor market reflects the differing scalar properties of job families and types of employment. It may very well be that the differential relationships established between classes of employers and employees are not constant but evolve with the scalar properties of the society at large under study. In brief, it is necessary to examine whether processes of segmentation differ between societies with varying levels or rates of industrialization and whether such processes reflect primarily *current* patterns of tension between countries and social systems or, alternatively, the *enduring* models that actors use to justify and develop their behavior in the economic context.

The Dilemma of Policies of Africanization

Correspondingly, governments and planners are still confronted with dilemmas not necessarily solved by reference to the experiences of other countries which have passed earlier through the same processes of industrialization and modernization. My observations concerning the problems raised by an Africanization of the Camerounian economy offers a case in point. Thus, the presence of European staff in a firm has divergent effects on the occupational attainment of African workers. It restricts the access of local wage earners to supervisory functions and, hence, prevents them from exerting any major degree of control over their own economic, technical, and social future. But the presence of European cadres also seems to lead to the adoption of a higher wage policy. Thus, the meaning of the concept of Africanization is double: it corresponds to an increased individual occupational mobility regardless of earnings, and, as such, hinges on a redistribution of "political" power, but it also implies a more equitable allocation of the rewards derived from work and thus focuses mostly on a redistribution of economic power.

Clearly, the differential stress placed on a redistribution of "economic" as opposed to "political" power has distinct implications. A first view of Africanization stresses the need to develop African-owned business and, more specifically, the need to stimulate an intermediate type of enterprise designed to erode the tensions arising from the coexistence of large-scale European-run organizations and traditionally oriented, artisanal, commercial and agricultural activities. As against this first view of Africanization, a second model recognizes implicitly the positive influence of bureaucratic organizations on national integration and economic development and, correspondingly, aims merely at increasing the number of African workers engaged in managerial and high-level technical activities within such organizations.

Although these two models are not mutually exclusive, they rely on distinctive theoretical orientations. In the first perspective, one assumes similarities not only between the current situation of African countries and the position of European nations during the nineteenth century, but also between their respective developmental patterns. Thus, development is seen as following a "push" model, resulting mainly from forces operating within the system itself. Conversely, in the second perspective, one emphasizes the implications attached to the diffusion of the organizational forms currently prevailing in more industrialized societies. Development is thus seen as following a "pull" pattern and, hence, as primarily dependent on forces operating outside the local system.

However, the dilemmas that African governments confront with regard to the definition and implementation of policies of Africanization are not only theoretical but political as well. First, these governments must determine the extent to which industrialization may modify the current distribution of political and economic power. The development of various types of modern enterprises in differing parts of the country affects not only the distribution of the active population between urban and rural areas but also the level of resources of their respective inhabitants. As these changes are associated with the development of tensions among regions and their inhabitants, African governments may be tempted to favor the development of small-scale African-owned enterprises.[24] But if such a strategy prevents the negative effects of social and ethnic differentiation, it may also slow down overall economic development and limit interaction between the local economy and international markets.

Second, governments that advocate the industrialization of their countries must choose among the variety of strategies attached to the notion of Africanization. In one perspective, what counts is a mere change in the system of allocation of the profits accruing to modern activities. Governments are anxious to facilitate the emergence of technically developed enterprises in order to enhance the size of the "pie" to be shared. In brief, this particular perspective asserts that development comes first and that Africanization, that is, an increase in income per capita, is the offspring of development and industrialization. But an increase in the size of the pie is

---

[24] Tanzania has moved recently in that direction.

not necessarily associated with an equal increase in each one of the shares assigned to various social categories.

In a second perspective, governments feel that a mere redistribution of profits is insufficient and that for both economic and political reasons an increasing number of Africans must gain access to top positions and managerial roles within modern European enterprises. Although this strategy is likely to decrease invidious comparisons between Europeans and Africans, it is likely to accentuate social differentiation among African workers and, hence, to enhance the possibility of conflict among them.

There is some evidence to suggest that most governments tend primarily to hover between the first and the second strategy. This study has shown, however, that the Camerounian government tends to mix three strategies: it intervenes quite directly in the functioning of the labor market by imposing minimal incomes (standards), even though such standards may be lower than the basic needs of the wage-earning population. At the same time, it has shown its commitment to the second facet of Africanization by supporting a massive program of Africanization of governmental services (through replacing European by African personnel at the administrative level) and by giving preferential fiscal treatment to the foreign investors who are willing to train their African personnel to perform managerial and highly technical functions. Finally, since independence, the government has facilitated a differentiation of employers, and there are an increasing number of small-scale African-owned enterprises. This differentiation, however, is not always functional, for it accentuates contrasts in the rewards attached to given levels of formal qualifications or occupational experiences. Thus, in certain cases, small-scale employers may offer better pay to highly skilled individuals who want to compensate for their relative lack of security by obtaining higher immediate income. Does the corresponding segmentation of the rewards attached to similar qualifications impede or accentuate further development and national integration?

This brief analysis of the dilemma confronting governments with regard to the whole issue of Africanization is yet incomplete, for governments are also concerned with the problem of identifying the strategies most likely to enable them to achieve any one of the three aspects of Africanization discussed in the preceding paragraph. This dilemma raises the question of the relationship between formal schooling and economic development. Although, as noted earlier, many African countries have seen educational planning as the cornerstone of their policies for economic development and modernization, they are currently confronted with the necessity of redefining their educational policies.

Educational and Labor Policies

In the present study, I have shown that the consequences of formal schooling vary over time. As educational development proceeds, there is a rise in the availability of educated job seekers, and the ensuing greater supply of educated manpower transforms the functioning of the labor market. More specifically, it enhances the size of unemployed populations and limits the chances that the individual has of gaining access to modern as opposed to traditional forms of employment or, alternatively, to non-manual as opposed to manual work. As an increase in the size of the primary school population has already been associated with a relative decline in the social returns derived from primary schooling, and as the development of secondary schools has already similar, albeit less visible consequences, governments might be inclined to limit and even lower the diffusion of formal schooling. Yet with a decline in the social rates of return to a particular level of schooling, families are likely to push their children toward higher rungs of the educational ladder and to enhance the overall demand for education. Correspondingly, the strategies that governments may use to limit enrollment pose a number of problems. To be sure, this goal may be achieved whenever governments cease to subsidize educational enterprises. To cease to do so may, however, entail a considerable political cost, particularly in former colonial countries whose populations have been accustomed to pay a minimal price for the educational benefits that their children are acquiring. In addition, insofar as investors are likely to increase their physical capital only when they are sure to find the appropriate trained labor force they need, they are also prone to maintain a high level of pressure to make sure that governmental bureaucracies continue to participate in the expenses related to the screening and training of skilled workers. Finally, as patterns of access into the educational institutions of many developing nations have remained relatively open thus far, a transfer of educational expenditures from public bureaucracies to individual families is likely to accelerate social stratification. In such a case the benefits of transferring educational investment are likely to be canceled by the costs resulting from an accentuation of existing social and ethnic cleavages.[25]

A second strategy rests on the assumption that the problems raised by the interaction between education and the labor market is not quantitative but qualitative and that individuals do not find a suitable niche in the occupational structure because they have not been exposed to an appropriate curriculum. In this perspective, educators and planners alike have been induced to reevaluate the ideal complementarity between general education and more specific vocational programs.

But is it possible to identify the ideal contribution of schools to the growth of developing economies? I have argued that the low degree of

[25] As noted by Carnoy in "Schooling, Income," there is thus a relationship between social inequalities in the patterns of access to schooling and inequalities in the distribution of income. It is not sure, furthermore, that declines in educational inequalities are associated with corresponding decreases in income inequalities.

division of labor prevailing in such a context makes the definition of individual tasks both diffuse and changing. This definition varies not only between the manual and nonmanual sectors of employment but also among branches of activity and types of industry. As a result, the potential functions of formal school training are highly variable. Regardless of these variations, African governments may aim at enhancing the range of individual occupational choices and, thus, give students a general form of training which enables them to move freely from one activity to another. This strategy, of course, is often viewed as costly, and it is further asserted that to maximize the potential mobility of individual workers leads them to entertain too high a level of economic aspirations. This is deemed likely to discourage potential investors who are attracted to African markets only as a result of the low labor costs of local economies. Additionally, some planners claim that the development of educational structures geared toward general education accentuates conflicts between the orientations and attitudes of the fortunate few who have had access to schooling and, hence, to modern occupational activities and of those who have not been exposed to modernizing influences and are still engaged in traditional economic activities. In other words, this argument suggests that the monolithic structure that goes along with general education accentuates tensions between traditional and modern subpopulations and ultimately slows down nation-building.

Accordingly, many planners prefer an educational strategy that aims at fitting potential job seekers to the very specific needs of each subsegment of the labor market. They justify their choice by arguing that this less costly strategy is also less liable to have negative effects on the more general processes of nation-building. Yet, as the data show, the demands of each segment of the labor market are highly differentiated, and as they change over time, the costs of this strategy may turn out to be higher than those attached to a policy providing more general education. For there is always a time-lag between technological changes occurring in industry and corresponding changes in the curriculum of educational institutions. Further, a maximal differentiation of educational programs does not necessarily lead to a decline in the potential conflicts between the most modernized and the most traditional subgroups in the nation; such tensions result at least in part from the differing economic rewards gained by the two populations, and it is unfortunately quite clear that changes in educational structures have no effect on the perceived hierarchy of occupations.[26] Finally, the returns to a strategy advocating narrow programs of vocational training remain problematic, for many employers believe that the productivity of their labor force is maximized when specific vocational training programs

[26] For a general discussion of this theme in an entirely different context, see Jencks, *Inequality: A Reassessment of the Effect of Family and Schooling in America* (New York: Basic Books, 1972), particularly chaps. 6 and 7.

tional and occupational attainment is similar in the case of public and private schools. Communications between these institutions and the differing types of economic organization are certainly not alike, and therefore one can infer that public and private students probably take different routes to join the labor market and use different strategies to negotiate their formal qualifications.[9]

Fourth, the number of years spent in school is not necessarily the most adequate indicator of adaptability to the industrial scene. Thus, individuals with the same level of formal schooling but differing scholastic abilities may also have differing incomes. In Kenya, for example, Thias and Carnoy have shown that among the graduates of primary schools between twenty-five and twenty-nine years of age, success in the local primary examination is a significant determinant of interindividual differences in earnings.[10] In another context, J. Simmons has shown that within the modern shoe industry of Tunisia certain psychological attitudes account for 22 percent of the variance in the distribution of daily earnings.[11] The problem is then to determine not only what parts of the formal and informal curriculum make a real difference on the behavior that students adopt when they join the labor force, but also whether such parts play a similar role across the various types of local enterprises.

Problems Raised by Occupational Differentiation

Against the views of classical and neoclassical labor economists who treat work as a homogeneous commodity, an increasing number of authors submit that labor markets are repeatedly subjected to processes of segmentation.

In the introduction, I have summarized the typologies that have been proposed to account for such processes. Thus, I have referred to the distinction between primary and secondary jobs but also indicated its possible factual as well as theoretical inadequacies. To stress the variability

---

[9] This point is indirectly suggested by Blaug, in *Education and the Employment Problem,* in his analysis of the Philippines, where there are a large number of public and private institutions of higher learning. In the case of the Cameroun, it would be particularly relevant to follow the occupational trajectories of graduates from public, Catholic, Protestant, and nonsectarian private secondary institutions.

[10] See H. Thias and M. Carnoy, *Cost-Benefit Analysis in Education: A Case Study in Kenya* (Baltimore: John Hopkins University Press, 1972). The two same authors have also found that in Tunisia rank obtained in secondary institutions accounts for a significant part of the differential income earned by the youngest age cohorts of workers in the local labor market. See M. Carnoy, "Schooling, Income, the Distribution of Income, and Employment: A Critical Reappraisal" (paper presented to the OECD Development Center, Paris, Dec. 1973).

[11] See "The Determinants of Earnings: Toward an Improved Model" (Washington, D.C.: IBRD, 1973), mimeo.

of employers' expectations about the emotional motivation of their labor force is perhaps valid in the context of highly industrialized countries, where there is a homogeneous educational level and where patterns of division of labor run in the same way across occupational categories; but the distinction is more problematic in the case of developing nations, for there are sharp cognitive contrasts in the definition of the tasks incumbent on various categories of worker. Further, regardless of the complexity of the economies examined, the components entering the distinction between primary and secondary jobs tend to preclude mobility across occupational categories, a preclusion which should be an empirical problem rather than an a priori postulate.

I have also referred to Arrighi's proposition, which states that the African working class is highly heterogeneous and may be subdivided among four categories of skill level (unskilled, semiskilled, skilled, and high level supervisory), but I have also suggested that to distinguish such categories is to a large extent placing the cart before the ox, for this distinction cuts across the two major occupational categories of developing nations and minimizes the competing importance of achievement and ascription in the process underlying occupational placement.[12]

In contrast, I have suggested that the proposed distinction between white- and blue-collar roles is more appropriate from both a theoretical and empirical viewpoint. First, this distinction is recognized and acted on by employers as well as by employees.[13] In addition, there are ethnic and educational differences between the two populations. Third, in spite of variations in the profile of the specific activities entered in these two broad occupational categories, nonmanual workers have a higher skill level and earn a higher income than their manual counterparts. Fourth and most important, skill level and income distributions within these two segments of the labor force follow distinctive patterns.[14] In short, the rules of the game are not the same in the two cases.[15] For manuals, "group characteristics"

---

[12] Arrighi, "International Corporations," in Rhodes, ed., *Imperialism and Underdevelopment,* pp. 232-233.

[13] There is no reason to believe that Camerounian students (and, hence, future wage earners) or workers differ from their Ivory Coast or Ghanaian counterparts in their evaluation of white- and blue-collar jobs. For an analysis of the homogeneity of such evaluations in these latter cases, see P. Foster, *Education and Social Change in Ghana* (Chicago: University of Chicago Press, 1965), Clignet and Foster, *The Fortunate Few,* and Peil *The Ghanaian Factory Worker.*

[14] T. Vietorisz and B. Harrison, "Labor Market Segmentation: Positive Feedback and Divergent Development," *Economic Review* 61(1973):366-375.

[15] See, for instance, Lambert, *Workers, Factories, and Social Change in India,* p. 237, who shows that in India manual workers have a monthly per capita income of 29.1 rupees, as against 41.1 for their clerical counterparts. Similarly, in Senegal, Hauser suggests strongly that disparities between the incomes of manual and nonmanual workers subjected to the same collective-bargaining agreements have kept increasing. See "Les Problèmes du Travail" in L. Thomas et al, *Dakar en devenir* (Paris: Présence africaine, 1970), pp. 382-383.

are regarded as complementary to general education acquired at school and when industrial workers are able to use their general educational background in order to adapt more rapidly to the specific demands of a particular work environment.[27]

Although the data do not provide any clear answer to the dilemmas confronting African governments with regard to both labor and educational policies, they enable one to assess some of the dimensions of the underlying problems. As educational development proceeds, and as disparities between educational and occupational opportunities increase, there are corresponding changes in the contrasts between manual and non-manual employment, between participation in modern as opposed to traditional activities, and between participation in bureaucratic as opposed to small-scale organizations. With such changes, the process of modernization probably ceases to be cumulative: there are both divergences and convergences in the factors governing individual participation in educational, occupational, and other social institutions. Whereas the study suggests both directly and indirectly the need to know more about the distribution of formal schooling among the various segments of a population, to know more about the traits that employers demand for various jobs, and about how students and teachers view the labor market and play the appropriate game, the brief analysis sketched in the preceding pages also suggests strongly the need to know more about the decision-making processes underlying the use of particular technologies. Correspondingly, planners should be cautious in the use of simple linear models to account for the options available to African governments. In sum, if planners hope to formulate successful strategies for developing a modern work force, they must not only be aware of the kind of complexities discussed here, but they should also accept the idea that social and economic change generates major discontinuities.

[27] See also P. Foster, "The Vocational School Fallacy in Development Planning" in M. J. Bowman and C. A. Anderson, eds., *Education and Economic Development* (Chicago: Aldine, 1963).

AUTHORS INDEX

SUBJECT INDEX